DINNER WITH MUGABE

DINNER WITH MUGABE

The untold story of a freedom fighter who
became a tyrant

Heidi Holland

PENGUIN BOOKS

PENGUIN BOOKS

Published by the Penguin Group
Penguin Books (South Africa) (Pty) Ltd, 24 Sturdee Avenue, Rosebank,
Johannesburg 2196, South Africa
Penguin Group (USA) Inc, 375 Hudson Street, New York, New York 10014, USA
Penguin Group (Canada), 90 Eglinton Avenue East, Suite 700, Toronto, Ontario,
Canada M4P 2Y3 (a division of Pearson Penguin Canada Inc)
Penguin Books Ltd, 80 Strand, London WC2R 0RL, England
Penguin Ireland, 25 St Stephen's Green, Dublin 2, Ireland (a division of Penguin
Books Ltd)
Penguin Group (Australia), 250 Camberwell Road, Camberwell, Victoria 3124,
Australia (a division of Pearson Australia Group Pty Ltd)
Penguin Books India Pvt Ltd, 11 Community Centre, Panchsheel Park, New Delhi
– 110 017, India
Penguin Group (NZ), 67 Apollo Drive, Mairangi Bay, Auckland 1310, New
Zealand (a division of Pearson New Zealand Ltd)

Penguin Books (South Africa) (Pty) Ltd, Registered Offices:
24 Sturdee Avenue, Rosebank, Johannesburg 2196, South Africa

www.penguinbooks.co.za

First published by Penguin Books (South Africa) (Pty) Ltd 2008
Reprinted 2008

Text copyright © Heidi Holland 2008

ISBN 978 0 143 02557 3

Typeset by CJH Design in 10.5/14 pt Charter
Cover image: JP Laffont/Sygma/Corbis/Great Stock

For
Shayleen

CONTENTS

Acknowledgements

I would like to thank a number of knowledgeable guides in Zimbabwe who helped me research this book. Naming them in the country's current political conditions might put them at risk, however.

Several accomplished journalists with wide experience of African politics read the manuscript and contributed their expertise: Author Adam Roberts of *The Economist*, Mugabe biographer David Blair of the *Daily Telegraph*, Rory Carroll of the *Guardian* and Peter Biles of the BBC in London, and US freelancer/author Nicole Itano. In addition, Chris Maroleng of the Institute for Security Studies in Pretoria and Rishon Chimboza of Africa Practice in Johannesburg, both Zimbabweans, kindly reviewed the script.

My sons Jonah Hull and Niko Patrikios were encouraging as always; Adele Lucas was her usual enthusiastic self; Adam Roberts gave me great ideas; Nonie Ward, a former white Rhodesian with a long memory of Zimbabwe's history, proved an invaluable sounding board; Alison Lowry, Claire Heckrath and Gemma Harries of Penguin Books, and Pam Thornley, were supportive and challenging.

I am especially grateful to the people who knew Mugabe personally and agreed to talk about him, most of whom are named in the text. Without their perspectives, I could not have accumulated the fresh information and insights on which the book's analysis of significant external events in Robert Mugabe's life is based. Father Fidelis Mukonori graciously fielded countless calls from me while arranging my interview with Robert Mugabe. Above all, I thank the psychologists who made possible an examination of Mugabe's internal responses to the circumstances that shaped his career: Shayleen Peeke, Eva Hurley and Ben Manyika.

Preface

The identity of my dinner guest was to remain a secret until we met. A friend – a constitutional expert and fellow activist – had asked if he could hold a secret meeting at my house. My job was simply to provide a safe, private place and dinner. So I gave the nanny who helped take care of my toddler the day off and busied myself in the kitchen, preparing a chicken for the oven.

After dark, a taxi drew up outside my ranch-style home. I heard my friend's voice as he stepped out of the vehicle with another man, who was wearing a hat pulled down over his forehead. It wasn't until he stood under the veranda light and looked up as we greeted each other that I recognised him. It was Robert Mugabe.

He was swaggering awkwardly, as he does still. His shoulders were stooped a bit and he looked lean and agile, as if ready and able to sprint. It was 1975, a momentous year for Mugabe. I did not know it then, but he was about to escape into neighbouring Mozambique, having been released from 11 years of political imprisonment but knowing he might be rearrested at any time. Across the border, he was to begin building his guerrilla power base just a few weeks after coming to dinner at my house.

I was more concerned about cooking than politics that night. Knowing too many of the details that might interest the security police was a dangerous burden so I asked no questions. Mugabe had arrived later than expected, announcing that he would soon be fetched to catch a 9pm train at Salisbury's Park Station. I fled to the kitchen to speed up the meal. A connecting door to the dining room remained open as the two men sat down with the glasses of water they had requested, but I didn't have time to eavesdrop.

Mugabe began questioning my friend, the constitutional expert Dr Ahrn Palley, in a quiet, urgent tone. I could hear that he was asking about the economy rather than legal matters. I could also feel the force of Mugabe's subdued but driven personality, particularly in Ahrn's deferential response. As a man whose advice was sought at one time or other by all the country's nationalist leaders, Ahrn was surprisingly in awe of Mugabe. Like me, he openly despised Rhodesian premier Ian Smith and privately pitied the pretenders who tried to cut moderate deals with the whites.

I had first met Ahrn Palley in 1965 when interviewing him for a story about the night he kept Parliament sitting until dawn while MPs were debating Ian Smith's upcoming unilateral declaration of independence from Britain. He was much admired by black Rhodesians for having finally left the House waving the Union Jack in support of Britain after the record-long debate. He was a contemporary of Mugabe's; I was 20-odd years younger. The reason I hung out with him was because none of the other white groups or individuals who were politically active in Salisbury – as Harare, the capital, was then known – quite reflected my own conviction that majority rule meant just that, given our terrible history, and not some wishful compromise between black and white aspirations.

Ahrn had met other nationalist politicians at my house, although it was only on occasions when my conservative husband was out of town on business that I could offer the refuge. I had never had a black man to dinner before.

Unlike most white Rhodesians, I already knew what Mugabe looked like before he came to my house because I had a picture of him tucked away in my desk at the offices of the magazine I edited. It had arrived unexpectedly in a pile of political profiles from a syndication agency in London. Although it was impossible to publish the picture legally in Rhodesia in those repressive days, I often put it on the light box to examine the fine-boned face. One of my conservative colleagues sarcastically suggested I seek psychological help for what he claimed was my obsessive interest in a monster.

I was magnetised by Mugabe's look of pure steel; such a forbidding image for a man who wanted to win votes and influence people. What particularly interested me was the colour of his eyes, which seemed on the transparency as if, in defiance of genetics, they might have been blue rather than brown. Everything about him spelt defiance in that mid-Cold War period. From his upstanding Maoist collar to the cold glint of certainty in his stare, he sent shivers up multiple spines. Ahrn once described him as the black Robespierre, an uncompromising, distilled man with no obvious charisma.

I was delighted to have his picture in my drawer, not only because it was a risky possession and I was young and radical, but because I had decided to publish it as soon as I got the chance. Intrigued by Robert Mugabe, I imagined in his detached gaze a vision of the country's future that nobody else could see. I felt I understood him in a way that few others outside the black community did, although I had never seen him in the flesh. Five years later, again with Ahrn Palley, I watched him from 50 paces, the sole whites standing with an English priest in a large crowd that had gathered at a Catholic-run leadership training academy, Silveira House, to welcome Mugabe home from the bush war shortly before the elections that brought independence.

It was at Silveira House that I met and befriended Mugabe's sister Sabina. She taught dressmaking to aspiring entrepreneurs from the townships around Salisbury. She showed me a photograph of Robert and Sally Mugabe's wedding and allowed me to make a copy of it. He was wearing a dark suit and white gloves, while Sally was covered in lace in the frothy middle-class style of the Christian nuptials of the 50s. He had an appropriately soft look in his eyes on that occasion. The picture provided a laughable contrast to his revolutionary image. I gave it to the London agency that had sent me the head shot of him, thinking it might help to portray Mugabe as human rather than the demon that many Westerners and virtually all white Africans saw.

Later, I ran the original photo of Mugabe's face life-size on the front cover of *Illustrated Life Rhodesia*, much to my boss's fury. Apart from almost costing me my job, it resulted in the magazine being served with a banning order by a uniformed policeman. He strode into my office one morning after the offending issue had been on sale for a day or two. Explaining curtly that publication of Mugabe's image was in breach of censorship laws, he demanded that the magazine be withdrawn forthwith. When the distributors went to retrieve it, though, few copies remained unsold on the news-stands. It was our fastest-selling issue ever.

The dinner was barely served when Mugabe, having rearranged

roast chicken and green beans on his plate but hardly eaten any of it, glanced for the third time at the carriage clock on the mantelpiece. His lift had not arrived. Seeing it was close to 9pm and that Ahrn could not drive, I realised Mugabe would miss his train if I did not take him downtown immediately. With my toddler son asleep in his cot and no time to bundle him into the car, I drove the 20-minute journey frantically fast. Mugabe sat beside me in my battered, beige Renault 4, clasping the dashboard as he continued his conversation with Ahrn in the back seat and I careered around corners, explaining that I was in a rush because I had left my child at home alone.

The next afternoon, to my surprise, a man calling from a public phone rang me at home to thank me for dinner and enquire after my baby. It was Robert Mugabe.

After the night he came for dinner, I had no further personal contact with the tense man whose audacious ideas were to become synonymous with Zimbabwe. Over the next five years, Robert Mugabe waged a bitter war between blacks seeking liberation and white Rhodesians who believed they were combating terrorism.

Peace came unexpectedly. With the greatest reluctance and in their view generosity, Rhodesians conceded power to Zimbabwe in 1980 in the hope that black rule would be moderate and deferential to white interests. Ian Smith had been warning for years that they would lose everything to a Marxist state if the terrorists took control so some whites headed straight for the South African border on Tuesday, 4 March 1980, on hearing that Robert Mugabe had won an absolute majority in the British-supervised elections. Some talked recklessly of reprisals and sabotage. Others wandered around their immaculate suburbs in bewilderment, blaming intimidation at the polls and British treachery for the uncertain future they faced.

I went into my office unusually early that morning. The streets outside were jammed with Africans singing, dancing, ululating and waving branches or in some cases their fists. Expectations were ludicrously high. I surprised our office messenger, who was sitting at the secretary's desk practising the boss's signature. I guessed aloud that he was hoping to take over the company before long. He begged me not to tell and rushed away to make me a cup of coffee.

In the evening, Comrade Robert Mugabe strolled into white living rooms countrywide. Promising reconciliation rather than revenge, he told television viewers that he would honour the British-brokered Lancaster House agreement, thus guaranteeing white pensions and property rights. He also revealed that he had invited the existing commander of the security forces to head a new integrated army. The monster of the morning had begun to morph into a responsible leader by the third beer that night.

Everyone wanted to believe in Robert Mugabe. White Rhodesians longed to retain the agreeable lifestyle to which black Zimbabweans aspired. Britain saw democratic Zimbabwe as a Foreign Office trophy. Conflicting hopes survived for 15 years after independence despite the slaughter by Mugabe's personal militia of thousands of people loyal to the opposition leader Joshua Nkomo in the early 80s. Virtually everyone who should have cried foul looked the other way; whites because they were grateful to be out of the range of fire; the British government because it had to stand by its man up north while trying to bring majority rule to apartheid South Africa; and the international media because it had backed Mugabe to the hilt and could not contemplate its flawed judgement.

As a freelance journalist by then, I went along with the prevailing line, even when my family was forced to flee the country ahead of Mugabe's security police. My husband, a surgeon, had enraged the new government by going behind prison walls in 1982 to obtain medical evidence of the torture of white airmen whom Mugabe had accused of attempting to blow up Zimbabwe Air Force planes, a capital offence. Nobody knew for sure if the airmen had indeed plotted against the state, certainly a possibility in those days. So Mugabe was given the benefit of the doubt, despite the airmen's pledges of innocence.

Looking back ever since, I realise that I and many other well-intentioned individuals may have helped Robert Mugabe to become the man he is today. If we had reacted differently to the early signs of his paranoia, could Zimbabwe have been saved from its current abyss? If whites in the country had been more realistic and acknowledged the impossibility of shifting smoothly from a police state of their creation to the democracy of their self-serving dreams, would they have been more respectful, less provocative? Or is Robert Mugabe simply an example of how power corrupts?

The questions are endless. What, if anything, could the former colonial power and the international community have done to curtail

Mugabe's economic mismanagement before its effects spiralled into disaster? Can we legitimately heap all the blame for Zimbabwe's demise on Mugabe, or did he have some respectable accomplices? Were we who supported Robert Mugabe wrong about him all along?

In my case, the recurring question is a personal one: What happened to the man who was kind enough to phone a young mother and enquire about her child after a brief dinner in 1975? How on earth did he become the cruel dictator who rules Zimbabwe by decree and corrupt patronage more than 30 years later?

They are questions that might never be answered adequately, although the people who have known Mugabe personally and participated in his life may be able to shed some light on his mindset and motives. Many crucial witnesses, like Robert Mugabe himself, are nearing the end of their lives. It is important to speak to them because it is possible that the one-dimensional, demonised character of 'Mad Bob' Mugabe is concealing significant secrets and lessons for history.

Humanising the monster, finding the three-dimensional Mugabe instead of a cartoon villain, is a process of understanding rather than exoneration. According to British actor Sir Ian McKellen, who over a career spanning 40 years has brought to life monsters of every epoch from Iago to Rasputin: 'One of the few lessons I have learnt from studying people who do terrible things is that they are all too human. And that we are all capable of doing almost anything.' Discovering that Robert Mugabe is a real person making hideous decisions is not to let him off the hook but is to observe how and why he lost his way. It might alert us to similarly dangerous propensities in other leaders.

What happened to the gifted scholar who used his time in Rhodesian jails to acquire a long list of degrees; whose only frivolity was a passion for Elvis Presley? Is the story of Robert Mugabe a tragedy – greatness brought low – or is the tragedy entirely Zimbabwe's?

How can Robert Mugabe be framed in terms of other despots? He is certainly no buffoon like Uganda's Idi Amin. And he is far too detached to have blood on his own hands like Jean-Claude Duvalier of Haiti or Mobutu Sese Seko of the then Zaire. Accumulating personal wealth, like Ferdinand and Imelda Marcos of the Philippines, is not Mugabe's motive for tyranny either.

The story of Robert Mugabe is a microcosm of what bedevils African democracy and economic recovery at the beginning of the 21st century.

It is a classic case of a genuine hero – the guerrilla idol who conquered the country's former leader and his white supremacist regime – turning into a peevish autocrat whose standard response to those suggesting he steps down is to tell them to get lost. It is also the story of activists who try to make a better society but bear the indelible scars of the old system. Mugabe's political education came from the autocrat Ian Smith, who had learnt his formative lessons from imperious British colonisers.

Above all, it is the story of one man who lost his moral compass, with dire consequences for many others. Robert Mugabe had the world at his feet in 1980. Slowly but inexorably, he squandered his life's work, betraying the people who trusted him. Why? What drove his self-destruction?

I put these and many other questions to dozens of people. Some are British and some are Zimbabwean refugees now living in Britain or South Africa. Others have had no choice but to hang on anxiously in bankrupt Zimbabwe, waiting for better days. A cast of historically relevant characters – all of whom have known Mugabe personally and influenced him significantly – they offer a range of insights into how power corrupts. Through first-hand observation of Mugabe's descent into tyranny, they illuminate some of the overarching constraints to progress on a continent noted for chaos. Their collective opinion gives the first nuanced and complex biography of a man whose decline and fall from grace has been witnessed by the world.

My mission is to tell the story of 84-year-old Robert Mugabe's life in order to understand how a man who once favoured simplicity became a greedy potentate with a wife half his age and a weakness for luxury. If today he is too cynical to notice that his countrymen are starving because of his failings and excesses, where did his pessimism originate? Was he always a ruthless person or did he gradually become power-crazed?

Most of the research in this book is original; now recorded for posterity. But what is truly unique about *Dinner with Mugabe* is the analysis it brings to his state of mind. I enlisted the help of Shayleen Peeke, a psychologist with 15 years' clinical experience, in exploring the psychology of Robert Mugabe. Familiar with the southern African political perspectives that shaped Zimbabwe's president, Shayleen has worked over the years with a number of civil society human rights initiatives in the region.

Shayleen listened to the tapes of my interviews with people who had dealt personally with Robert Mugabe. Some of them had a profound influence on him before and during his presidency. She and I then discussed what those who had known Mugabe said about him. We talked at length about his world view – judging by what others thought of him and what he said about himself – reflecting on him as a man rather than a monster.

London-based psychologist Ben Manyika, who is Zimbabwean, read and adjusted the manuscript. Eva Hurley, an Irish-trained emotional intelligence consultant living in Dubai but contracted to corporate clients internationally, reviewed all the chapters. The result is a psycho-biography of one of the world's most puzzling and destructive leaders.

In trying to understand a career like Mugabe's, we were careful not to explain away the behaviour of a murderer. By locating some of the causes of his tyranny in society, we were wary of making violence implicitly more acceptable. While some of our explanations invite empathy for the tyrant, partly because we know that someone like Mugabe is a human being like us, we remain acutely aware that recent efforts to understand Hitler, for example, have been described by French philosopher and film-maker Claude Lanzmann as 'the obscenity of understanding'. Can we not counter his argument, though, by asking how we will ever learn from the cruellest chapters of history if attempts to understand tyrants are not allowed?

Timeline: A chronology of key events in Robert Mugabe's life

1924   Robert Gabriel Mugabe born in Kutama, Zimbabwe (then Southern Rhodesia).

1945   Leaves St Francis Xavier College, Kutama, having qualified as a teacher.

1949   Obtains scholarship to University College of Fort Hare, South Africa, achieving first of seven degrees.

1957   Moves to Ghana; meets Sally Hayfron.

1960   Gives first political speech while home on holiday. Joins National Democratic Party (NDP) under Joshua Nkomo, becoming publicity secretary.

1961   Marries Sally Hayfron. Zimbabwe African People's Union (Zapu) formed to replace banned NDP.

1962   Zapu banned; leaders restricted.

1963   Zimbabwe African National Union (Zanu) formed as rival to Zapu.

1964   Mugabe and others detained.

1966   Three-year-old Nhamo Mugabe dies in Ghana; imprisoned Mugabe is denied permission to attend his son's funeral.

1974   Detainees released from prison for settlement talks.

1975   Herbert Chitepo, head of Zanu in exile, is assassinated in Zambia. Mugabe and Edgar Tekere leave Rhodesia to join guerrillas in Mozambique but are initially placed under restriction there.

1977   Mugabe gains control of Zanu and its army.

1978   Zanu military leader Rex Nhongo (aka Solomon Mujuru) crushes internal revolt aimed at toppling Mugabe.

1979   Lancaster House conference takes place in London. Zanu's military leader Josiah Tongogara dies.

1980   Mugabe becomes prime minister of independent Zimbabwe.

1981   Apartheid South Africa embarks on campaign to destabilise Mugabe.

1982   Nkomo sacked from government following discovery of arms caches in Matabeleland. Trial in Harare of white airmen tortured on suspicion of sabotaging air force planes. North Korean-trained Fifth Brigade is unleashed by Mugabe in brutal campaign against dissidents.

1987   Mugabe and Nkomo sign Unity Accord, merging to form Zanu-PF (Zimbabwe African National Union-Patriotic Front). Mugabe changes constitution, becoming executive president.

1988   War veterans launch campaign for recognition of role in liberating Zimbabwe. Edgar Tekere expelled from Zanu-PF for campaigning against one-party state. Willowgate corruption scandal exposed. Mugabe begins affair with his secretary Grace Marufu.

1990   Nelson Mandela released from prison in South Africa. World Bank's Economic Structural Adjustment Programme (Esap) begins in Zimbabwe.

1992   Sally Mugabe dies of kidney failure.

1995   Street riots in Harare against rising prices and unemployment.

1996   Mugabe marries Grace Marufu in lavish ceremony at Kutama.

1997   New Labour government under Tony Blair wins UK election.

1998   Mugabe sends troops to the Democratic Republic of Congo to intervene in civil war and plunder riches.

1999   Repressive action against Zimbabwe's media and judiciary increases. Mugabe is accosted by a gay rights activist in London. Movement for Democratic Change (MDC) is formed in Harare. Relations with Britain deteriorate.

2000   Constitutional reforms rejected by electorate. Squatters seize white-owned farms. Zanu-PF wins narrow victory against MDC in parliamentary elections.

2002   Parliament passes law limiting press freedom. European Union imposes limited sanctions. Mugabe re-elected in presidential polls condemned as flawed by MDC and foreign observers.

2004   Leader of the MDC Morgan Tsvangirai acquitted of treason charges.

2005   US labels Zimbabwe among world's six 'outposts of tyranny'. Zanu-PF wins two-thirds of votes in parliamentary election. Shanty dwellers and illegal street stalls destroyed in urban 'clean up' programme that leaves thousands homeless.

2007   Badly beaten MDC leaders hospitalised after rally arrests. Power cuts for up to 20 hours a day throughout Zimbabwe. Inflation soars. Five men charged with coup plot. Zanu-PF and MDC hold talks in South Africa.

Introduction

Robert Mugabe came to power in Zimbabwe in 1980 after waging a 15-year-long guerrilla war against the white supremacist government of what was then Rhodesia. During his first 10 years in office, despite a pattern of repression and the creation of a de facto one-party state, he was widely hailed as one of post-colonial Africa's most progressive leaders.

His administration guaranteed educational opportunities for Zimbabwe's black population where few had existed before. High school enrolment, which had been about two per cent at the time of independence, grew to 70 per cent by 1990, and Zimbabwe's literacy rate rose from 45 per cent to nearly 80 per cent in the same period.

Mugabe also developed public health facilities to the point where rural dwellers were able to receive medical attention within walking distance of their villages. He did his best to persuade the country's 200 000 whites, including its 4 500 commercial farmers, to remain in Zimbabwe.

Things began to go awry in 2000 when Mugabe was defeated in a national referendum on a new constitution. Exploiting his vulnerability, the National Liberation War Veterans' Association, a group of self-proclaimed ex-guerrillas, pressured Mugabe into giving its members cash, free medical care and education – then land. Suddenly, the government began forcibly redistributing commercial farms and ranches owned by whites. Armed thugs terrorised, assaulted and in some cases murdered the farmers. Telling his supporters that he regretted his earlier policy of reconciliation with whites, Mugabe said, 'When you show mercy to your former enemy ... you think you are being noble. But, if you ask me now how I feel about it, I think we made a mistake.'

Mugabe's cronies and war veterans seized the farms, neglecting them ruinously in most cases. The destruction of the country's agriculture industry, which had provided half of Zimbabwe's foreign exchange, precipitated the collapse of the economy.

Over the next seven years, the situation declined steadily. Thousands of offices, shops and factories closed. The inflation rate soared. At least 80 per cent of Zimbabweans were unemployed. A quarter of the population fled the country in search of a better life in Europe or South Africa. One third of children dropped out of school because their parents could no longer afford the fees. One fifth of Mugabe's citizens were infected with HIV, about 400 of them dying each day of Aids-related infections. The life expectancy of a Zimbabwean woman dropped from 61 years in 1991 to 34 in 2006, the lowest anywhere, according to the World Health Organisation.

Early in 2007, Robert Mugabe celebrated his 83rd birthday with a lavish feast for the ruling elite, while ordinary Zimbabweans faced empty shelves and in some cases starvation. The hunger of his people, some of whom had walked for miles simply to gaze at his enormous, thickly iced birthday cake, did not seem to put a damper on festivities costing around US$ one million. Photographed with his glamorous wife, Mugabe beamed like a four-year-old waiting to blow out his candles. Blaming his country's economic crisis on the European Union and Britain at a subsequent Zanu-PF conference, he complained of 'vicious, ambitious people' in the top echelons of his party who were manoeuvring to get him out of power. 'There are no vacancies,' he said. 'The door is closed.'

One

Brother in the background

Donato Mugabe, Robert Mugabe's only surviving brother, is sitting on an upturned plastic milk crate on the veranda of his home at Kutama, the village where he and his siblings were born and where Donato has remained all his life. Wearing a loose-fitting pyjama-like suit cut from red-patterned cotton featuring Mugabe's smiling face, he is nursing a bandaged foot. His flip-flops are lying in front of him. He is a large, white-haired man with a lot of laughter lines on his face, but he looks decidedly wary on this occasion.

He and his wife Evelyn, who is standing in the doorway to the sitting-cum-dining room while I am being introduced to Donato, invite me indoors reluctantly. Having stifled the urge to dash after the priest from the nearby school who brokered the meeting and dropped me off, I take the proffered seat opposite them. Huddled together on the sofa, they are silent and unblinking. I am acutely aware that few, if any, journalists have been to talk to Donato before me, possibly because we were collectively not interested enough to uncover Mugabe's ancestry in earlier years when the going was good, but later on because it is dangerous to ask leading questions in Zimbabwe, let alone to walk into the midst of the terrorised country's first family.

Their coldness towards me is understandable for other reasons, too. Not only have I arrived out of the blue, albeit once Donato had agreed in principle to meet a writer from South Africa, but I am inevitably a reminder of the former oppressor in a rural village like Kutama. Few whites apart from Catholic clergy have ventured this way before and the couple watching me intently is expecting my demeanour to reveal superiority; they're waiting for judgemental responses to betray the stranger's apparent sincerity.

Our exchange of pleasantries goes on longer than would be necessary in an urban Zimbabwe setting, but not nearly long enough. Understanding Robert Mugabe's early life fully would take months or even years to build a relationship with the couple and their relatives in the area, winning their confidence bit by bit to get, finally, beneath the thin layer of information initially imparted. Such deep immersion in village life is, however, too risky in today's Zimbabwe, where a single question can have frightening consequences.

Donato begins by telling me that for some years during his schooling at Kutama, Robert lived with his maternal grandparents, 'so that he could be watched carefully by them', he says, staring fixedly ahead. 'He was a good boy and he loved to play tennis at school. That was what he did besides reading. He passed teacher training in 1942 but he did not show off. He was quiet and never harsh to anyone. He was always determined. Whatever he wants to do, he can do. He never recognised the word no: it was not in his language. He went to Ghana for teacher training and sent letters to our mother.'

His wife says something to Donato in Shona and he suddenly bellows: 'Sally came from Ghana!' Looking delighted at the thought of his late sister-in-law, his eyes stare into space again for a while. 'She was a lovely person. It was a happy marriage,' he remembers. 'It was a happy time in Zimbabwe.' When I mention Grace, Mugabe's second wife, Donato nods sagely, offering no comment at first. 'She gave him children,' he says on reflection, nodding slowly again.

Kutama, about 100km from Harare, is a village of brick as well as grass-roofed traditional houses. The road linking the president's alma mater to Donato's house is a rough track used mainly by pedestrians and cyclists. Chickens scurry for cover when cars approach and cocks are crowing incessantly outside as I talk to the Mugabes.

Behind the sofa where Donato and Evelyn are sitting is the large official portrait of Robert Mugabe which hangs in government offices and in most public spaces in Zimbabwe. Alongside the couple on a table is a framed, unsmiling photograph of Bona, the president's late mother, her unusually elongated head wrapped in a scarf that typifies the attire of local rural women.

Robert adored his mother. He attended Mass with her every day and twice on Sundays in the years following the deaths of two of his older siblings. Both of the dead children were boys. One of them, Michael, was the acknowledged family favourite, a teenager who was loved by everyone in the village, not only the Mugabes. Donato's description of Michael's cause of death as 'something he ate' is typical of the bare details on offer, not only because the man sitting in front of me does not entirely trust me with his story but because, in the 20s, life at Kutama was austere. People endured, they fell ill, and they died. Donato, who was christened Dhonandho and called Donald at school, does not remember how or why Raphael, the second son of the family, died.

Their father Gabriel left home after Michael's death, says Donato. 'He went to live in Bulawayo, where he could get work, and he remarried there. He was a very good carpenter. Robert remained cross with him because he would never help us with our schooling. He came back later with three children, and died at Kutama.'

That was a lot of loss for Bona to bear. After her husband left, she became depressed by all accounts. She could not cope alone. Robert, although only 10 at the time, stepped into the breach. Suddenly the oldest child, he became his mother's favourite. It was he who set about trying to restore the light in her eyes; to be what she wanted him to be. He could not forgive his father the hurt he had inflicted because Robert's life was so difficult in Gabriel's absence.

Bona's unhappiness, except when teaching the village girls their catechism, may have been because she had arrived at Kutama as a teenager longing to become a nun but her hopes, and those of her devoutly Catholic parents, were thwarted when she met the dashing Gabriel and became pregnant. Having prayed fervently that Michael would become a priest, her expectations fell on Robert after his two older brothers' deaths. It was a lot for a shy, sensitive child like Robert to live up to and the responsibility for his mother's well-being as well as her ambitions for him weighed heavily on the troubled schoolboy.

Kutama was a centre of worship and opportunity but a demanding challenge for those children fortunate enough to win a place at St Francis Xavier College, the top boys' school in the country. Robert took his schoolwork very seriously indeed. He also became an exemplary Catholic: once Bona started taking him with her to Mass in Michael's place, he became almost as pious as she was.

The founder of the mission station at Kutama was a French priest called Jean-Baptiste Loubiere, who had arrived in Rhodesia soon after the turn of the century, reportedly to rehabilitate himself after falling in love with a local girl at his previous posting in Portuguese East Africa. He and his African assistant ruled with a religious zeal described by a contemporary of Mugabe's at Kutama, the distinguished writer Lawrence Vambe, as 'an almost monastic rigidity'. Dispensing with tribal customs and religion, Father Loubiere made no secret of his distaste for African traditional beliefs. In pursuit of his own salvation, he taught Kutama's illiterate tribespeople to regard the entire outside world as an evil place that would engulf them unless they sought guidance through constant prayer. The sons of the villagers at St Francis Xavier were exhorted to save the heathens beyond the borders of their tight-knit community by becoming teachers. Lawrence Vambe says the atmosphere at Kutama in the early days was like Lourdes during a pilgrimage; the name of the village's patron saint, Thérèse of Lisieux, the Little Flower, was sometimes even substituted for the Virgin Mary in prayers.

Bona, who was made to wear high-necked, ankle-length dresses under Father Loubiere's regime, took all the church's teachings to heart. Donato says he did not pray hard enough by his mother's standards and often failed to do his homework because he was more interested in playing with his friends. Left to his own devices by Bona when she tired of trying to mould him, Donato remembers her having a very different approach to Robert. 'If his mother smacked him, Robert must thank her for correcting him; that's what she believed. She did not like to do it. She smacked him maybe thrice and he thanked her every time. The other children used to tease him and he became lonely. He didn't seem to care, but maybe he did,' muses Donato. 'Our mother protected Robert from everyone, especially me, but he himself did not fight. Our (half) sister Bridget was the one who fought with me. She was the strongest one – never Robert. She had the courage of a man, not like him.'

The new Catholic head at Kutama was an Irish priest, Father Jerome O'Hea, a gifted teacher and an exceptional man. He broke down the rigid taboos introduced by his predecessor, encouraging a modern, realistic view of the world. And he devoted his substantial private means to developing the school, first with a new teacher training unit, then a technical wing and finally a hospital, which still bears his name. Father O'Hea soon noticed the solemn, talented Robert Mugabe and began to nurture him as a scholar and a credit to St Francis Xavier. Donato remembers Robert 'hanging around' outside the priest's classroom, ever eager to help the man (who had probably become a father substitute) by carrying his books or cleaning the blackboard.

It seems that Bona may have been depressed even before suffering the loss of her sons and husband. A former teacher at Kutama who did not want to be named said Bona was known in the village as a person who could never be disturbed because she prayed a lot. He claims, however, that Father O'Hea knew Bona was ill much of the time, which was why he kept a close eye on Robert and his siblings.

Unlike the happy-go-lucky Donato, Robert's childhood had effectively ended when his brothers died and his father left home. He found solace from the pressures of Bona's disappointment and expectations in books, not in other children. An introspective child who may have been neglected in babyhood by a burdened mother and therefore failed to develop confidence in himself, Robert began to adopt a lofty attitude towards his siblings and fellow students. As Bona's special one in the family and an increasing favourite among teachers in the classroom, he focused all his energy on being 'a good boy'.

Robert was always a loner, recalls Donato.

He was a person who was not interested in having many friends. His books were his only friends. I was the opposite, talking to everybody and even fighting with some of them. I could run fast but Robert could not: he was lazy, just reading all the time. When he went to herd cattle because our grandfather told him to go out into the fields, he would take his book. He held the book in one hand and the whip in the other. It was a strange thing for all of us to see. When the cattle were settled, he would sometimes sit in the shade under the trees. Sometimes, if our grandfather asked him to get something for supper, he would catch many birds, especially doves. He would cut sticks, tie them with grass and put some soft leaves inside with some few seeds. This nest he would put near the river and wait quietly, reading his book. When the birds came to drink water, he could catch them. He was the only one who could get the birds because he could sit very quietly and that's why grandfather said it was his job.

Robert was different from his siblings in other ways too. He loved to be at school even when his brothers and sisters were home playing. Their house was so close to St Francis Xavier College that he could come and go as he pleased. 'He used to be very serious and not always happy,' recalls Donato. 'He seemed to have matters to think about.'

Then came the prestigious endorsement of Robert's scholarly efforts that was to have profound implications not only for his life but for the future of the country he would lead to disaster six decades later. 'Our mother explained to us that Father O'Hea had told her that Robert was going to be an important somebody, a leader,' recalls Donato. 'Our mother believed Father O'Hea had brought this message from God; she took it very seriously. When the food was short she would say, "Give it to Robert". But he would refuse and say he didn't want to eat. A doctor (academic) from Salisbury came to talk to Robert about his lessons. We laughed at him because he was so serious, until he became cross. Then our mother told us to leave him alone. She believed he was a holy child and she wanted him to become a priest.'

Father O'Hea went out of his way to help the shy Mugabe child he described as having 'unusual gravitas'. With 'an exceptional mind and an exceptional heart', he believed the boy merited extraordinary attention. Promoted to the next class as soon as he could hold his own, Robert was always younger and physically smaller than his contemporaries. His greatest desire was to please his mother and to earn praise from Father O'Hea. However, the favouritism of two such important adults in a tight community made him increasingly the butt of jokes among his peers, including his brothers and sisters. As the children teased him mercilessly, Robert became defiant and presumably angry. With his reputation for cowardice well established, the village children who had not scored highly enough for ongoing study mocked him for constantly having his nose in a book. 'Those who did not value learning tormented him,' says Lawrence Vambe, who was at school with Mugabe. 'And even we who appreciated his diligence felt he was trying to prove too much. The mother and the school, as much as they tried to be good for him, pushed him harder and harder.'

I recall another Kutama schoolboy and relative of Robert Mugabe's, former sociology professor George Kahari, telling me a few months earlier during an interview in Harare how 'impossibly without blemish' Bona was in her piety and how heroically supportive she was to her children – except Donato, who thwarted her constantly. Bona was 'a saintly woman, but it was all so unnaturally good, an aberration', Kahari says. It was partly from his mother that Mugabe learnt the rigidity that characterised his leadership style in later years, he believes. 'Once he's taken a position, that's it – you can't influence him. Robert developed a pathological hatred of his father, for example, and never revised it.' George Kahari believes that by making him 'too good to be true' among his childhood peers, Bona inadvertently created an outcast and gave Robert 'a terrible inferiority complex, which he hides behind his eloquence to this day'. Kahari also believes that the young Mugabe's dependence on his mother helps to explain the homophobia he exhibited in later years.

As he grew up, Robert got his sense of who he was from Bona, a cold, stern nun of a mother. She left him in no doubt that he was to be the achiever who rose above everyone else; the leader chosen by God himself. She may also have viewed him as a substitute for her own failure to serve the church as she and her parents had intended. Aloneness and the inability to cooperate are the dominant features in all the descriptions of Mugabe's childhood. His relative, the late James Chikerema, who grew up at Kutama with Robert, once described the boy's stubbornness: if anyone argued with him while herding, Chikerema remembered Robert simply detaching himself from the group, selecting his own beasts from the herd and driving them into the hills far away from the other boys. He never sought reconciliation or compromise in an effort to fit in with those around him. His standard response to criticism was to warn that he would get even some day, according to Chikerema.

Considering all the available evidence, Mugabe seems to have been driven from very early on by a determination to show those who scorned him and his books, who called him a mummy's boy and a coward, that he was, nevertheless, the king of the castle – and that they would all have to acknowledge it sooner or later. Instead of seeing their taunts accurately as sibling rivalry and jealousy from less accomplished classmates, Robert seems to have felt persecuted, bitterly resenting the failure of everyone around him to appreciate his difficult role in a fatherless family. 'He said he did not have time to play and we always laughed when he said big stuff about himself,' admits Donato.

What the young Robert Mugabe achieved by single-mindedly

pursuing his studies at school, and for years after he left Kutama, was truly remarkable. To become one of the most erudite Africans in the country from the humblest of beginnings – with no electric light to switch on at home and read by, seldom enough food to eat, and little support except from those whose ambitions robbed him of childish things – was a triumph of discipline over adversity in the classic Jesuit style. Against the odds, the angry little boy with no friends did become the king of the castle. But Robert's diligence was also his way of coping with a universe he believed to be against him. Despite periods of contentment, he was to be consumed by distrust for the rest of his life.

According to Donato, who did not complete his secondary schooling, Robert always cared for his extended family as diligently as he looked after Bona. A retired small-scale farmer like Donato lives in one of the biggest houses at Kutama only because Robert gave the property to him and subsidises his day-to-day living. It is a comfortably furnished home containing a conspicuously large television set and hi-fi. The couple receives supplies of fresh vegetables, chickens, eggs and milk from the farm Mugabe owns nearby. While we are talking, an ambulance draws into the driveway to ferry Donato to the local outpatients clinic at the Father O'Hea Hospital to have his leg wound dressed, a service not available to ordinary Zimbabweans. 'He still looks after us,' says Donato. 'I suffer from diabetes and he has always paid for all my treatment. On Saturday he was here with his family for the graduation of my son Albert.'

Mugabe's nephew Albert is named after their half-brother, Donato explains. He inadvertently goes on to give an example of how suspicion tends to be contagious once it is an established part of a political culture, as it was in Zimbabwe under Ian Smith's rule, as well as among Zimbabwe African National Union (Zanu) guerrillas in exile and throughout Mugabe's long presidency. 'Our brother Albert drowned in a swimming pool after independence,' recalls Donato. 'His death was a mystery. I waited with Robert to see the doctor who performed the post-mortem. He told us that Albert did not die from the water he inhaled by drowning and there was nothing else wrong with him before he drowned. That's why some people said he had been murdered, and others who did not like Robert said Albert was killed by his own brother. We never found out what had happened. But Robert was heartsore; he could not hurt Albert.'

The memory of waiting with Robert to hear the pathologist's verdict on Albert's death reminds Donato of other occasions when he helped his brother shoulder family tragedies. After Robert and Sally's only child died in Ghana while Robert was imprisoned for disseminating his political beliefs in Rhodesia, Donato travelled to Ghana on his brother's behalf. 'I went to see the grave and tell Robert about the place he was buried. Our mother was very much interested in nature, the sky and the stars and trees and flowers, and Robert also liked to hear about those things. I went to tell him in prison about the son's resting place. And when his wife died, I was the one who went on a plane to Ghana to tell Sally's family that she had passed away.'

Didn't Robert phone to tell them the news?

'No,' he shakes his head vigorously and stares at me open-mouthed, his yellow teeth full of gaps. 'Some in Sally's family were old people and Robert said we must go there and speak to them, and also to ask them about the funeral for her. He could not go himself so he sent me. I visited his son's grave again.'

Donato's wife has become agitated since the arrival of the ambulance. She nudges her husband and asks in English if she can go with him to the hospital. He nods and smiles as she gets up quickly, excitedly, to change for the occasion. She wants to visit her friend, he explains. I remark that Evelyn is much younger than Donato and he replies, 'Yes, that's how it must be. She must be young enough to look after me in old age.'

Like Grace and Robert?

Evelyn has come back into the room wearing a silvery dress with her hair tucked into a woollen cap. She laughs uproariously at the thought of Grace taking care of Robert. Donato frowns and replies soberly, 'Yes, it's the same with him.' Then they glance at each other, laughing and shaking their heads.

'We used to stay at Robert's house next door to the school,' he says, explaining that it is a big property, with the original cottage Robert shared with Sally standing behind the mansion he built for Grace. 'We used to look after it when he wasn't there but it didn't work out.'

'One man, one house,' adds Evelyn drily.

'He wanted Grace to use the same house as Sally lived in because he loved that one but she refused,' says Donato, shaking his head. 'One woman, one house,' offers Evelyn, laughing hoarsely while Donato eases himself slowly off the sofa and picks up a white floppy hat from the dining room table. Evelyn goes out again, returns with a Coca-Cola bottle full of milk and two eggs in her hands, glances at me dismissively and walks on to the veranda.

I ask Donato if I should return to the school and wait there with our mutual friend the priest until later in the afternoon, when we can perhaps resume the interview. 'No,' he replies firmly. 'It is finished now. You must not come back.'

Two

Mummy and Uncle Bob

Robert Mugabe left Kutama in 1945 with great expectations of himself despite his traumatic youth. Determined to be a teacher at that stage, he set his sights on amassing as many academic qualifications as possible. Over the next decade, he went from a number of teaching posts in Rhodesia to a scholarship at Fort Hare University in South Africa and then to a generous expatriate teacher-training package in Ghana, where revered premier Kwame Nkrumah was setting the African liberation agenda.

Like other accomplished Africans from all over the continent, Mugabe had been invited to Ghana by Nkrumah in the late 50s, a momentous era for activists worldwide. At the time, Fidel Castro was leading his rebel army across the island nation to take control in Cuba, for example; a host of African states were on the verge of being given independence by their European colonisers; and civil rights campaigner Martin Luther King was strutting his provocative stuff in the United States shortly before John F Kennedy assumed office. Southern Africa's white leaders, however, were bolstering their resistance to majority rule.

It was in the heady atmosphere of West Africa's liberation that Robert Mugabe fell for a woman who was completely different from any he had encountered back home in Rhodesia. She was Ghanaian teacher Sally Hayfron, who idolised him, though not in the unquestioning way of the traditional, subservient Shona-speaking wife of the period. She was his equal and he spotted her strength on their first date.

Being a political creature in her own right, Sally shared Nkrumah's dreams of equality. As a member of several of his socialist movements, she hoped to hasten freedom in Africa personally. When she heard there was a newcomer from southern Africa giving lectures at the teaching academy where she was studying, Sally went to listen to him. Afterwards, having missed his introduction, she walked up to the podium in her colourful kaftan and turban, introduced herself and asked who he was. 'I am Robert Mugabe of Rhodesia,' he replied.

The two talked the night away. 'She didn't know much about his country except that the whites there were bad to the blacks. So he started educating her,' explains Sally's niece, Patricia Bekele, who shared a bed with Sally as a child, becoming so close to her aunt that she called her Mummy. As the first girl of six born to Sally's elder sister, who for various reasons couldn't cope with all her children, Sally had informally adopted Patricia. Later, when her aunt moved to Rhodesia, married Robert and he became president, Patricia lived for long periods with the Mugabes at State House.

> Uncle Bob saw Mummy's genuine interest right from the start even though he didn't know in the beginning that she was a politician herself. He told me once how excited she used to get as he spoke about the struggle in Rhodesia; she'd be shouting, 'You people must stand up for your rights! Yes! Fight for your rights!' Mummy was ebullient and theatrical, and Uncle Bob just loved that because he was exactly the opposite – quiet and restrained.

Their courtship began in 1960, when Patricia Bekele was a four-year-old living in her grandmother's double-storey house with Sally and their extended family in Sekondi, an industrial city, the third largest in Ghana. 'Uncle Bob has often said on anniversaries that I was the one who opened the door when he came to see her. He'd say, "I don't know if it was the chocolates I was bringing or if she really wanted me to marry her mother."'

Robert was warmly welcomed into Sally's family. Patricia remembers him being especially pleased to meet her uncle, an attorney known in the neighbourhood as Lawyer Williams, who had an impressive library of law books and family archives. 'Uncle Bob's own origins were humble and I think he was stimulated by the more advanced social environment Mummy inhabited. He was such a gentleman, you know; they all said so. Wonderfully polite and gentle, that's what my grandmother said.'

While on a visit to Kutama to see his mother in July that year, Mugabe was invited to join a march in a Salisbury township to protest against the arrest of two National Democratic Party (NDP) leaders. He was standing with 7000 demonstrators as they confronted 500 white-helmeted policemen in full riot gear, with tear gas and pistols at the ready, when he was hoisted on to a makeshift podium alongside other Joshua Nkomo-led NDP leaders. There, he gave his first political speech. Beginning as a halting description of Ghana as the model for Rhodesian Africans to follow, his talk drew applause when he told the crowd, 'The nationalist movement will only succeed if it is based on a blending of all classes of men. It will be necessary for graduates, lawyers, doctors and others to accept the chosen leadership even if they (the leaders) are not university men.'

Bombarded afterwards by the arguments of those trying to persuade him to join the NDP, Zimbabwe's first nationalist party with mass appeal, Mugabe made it clear that he intended to return to Ghana to resume his career there and marry Sally. The activists were adamant that he should come back to Rhodesia. They also believed he should rather marry someone at home who was suited to the high political office for which they wanted to groom him. When Sally heard that her position at Mugabe's side was being challenged, she undertook an urgent charm offensive to secure a marriage proposal from her beloved Bob. They married in Salisbury a few months later.

Before going to Zimbabwe for her wedding, Sally was asked by Bob to bring with her the little blue Triumph he had bought with a loan from his employers while working in Ghana. 'It was a difficult task but she did anything he asked,' recalls Patricia, explaining that he was sentimental about his first car and wanted it in Rhodesia. To this day, the ancient Triumph remains in Kutama at the site of Bona's house.

Unpopular with some of Mugabe's relatives, Sally fell out badly with his sister Sabina, after leaving her wedding dress in Sabina's care and discovering that her sister-in-law had rented it out to raise extra cash for her own needs. But she got along well with Mugabe's mother Bona, who was much in evidence whipping up the crowds at the major functions and ceremonies her son attended, and who appreciated the lengths to which Sally went to protect and assist Robert.

Because Mugabe was often operating underground and far from home, Sally lived both in Rhodesia and in Ghana after her marriage. Patricia recalls his brief visit to Sekondi for his son's naming ceremony shortly after the child was born. The couple agreed to call him Nhamodzenyika, much to Sally's mother's dismay. 'That's too much of a burden for a little boy to carry around,' wailed the grandmother when she heard that the name meant 'suffering country'. Mugabe replied that the child's parents were virtually separated by the burden of liberating Zimbabwe, which was an inescapable fact of Nhamo's life, so that was going to be his name.

Tragedy struck after Robert Mugabe's arrest and imprisonment by the Rhodesian regime when three-year-old Nhamo died suddenly in Ghana in 1966. Patricia was eight at the time and recalls his death vividly:

> I remember when he got sick. His temperature rose, he was hot and then shivering, feverish. We took him to the hospital but it was too late and he died. When Mummy got the news that Nhamo had gone, she just screamed and screamed. Then she was sad for a long time, so sad. I think she was particularly disturbed knowing she could not even replace this child without a husband, seeing that Uncle Bob was in prison. She was also very sad that Uncle Bob had not been able to see more of Nhamo.
>
> I don't remember how she sent word to Uncle Bob that Nhamo had died but I remember how much she cried again when she heard that they wouldn't release him (from prison) for the funeral. She became quite bitter against the white regime after that. She'd go over and over her disbelief that the Rhodesians didn't realise that Uncle Bob would never, ever, run away from his country. He held his convictions so strongly that he was compelled to meet his goals: the struggle was his destiny, and his wife agreed with it. Did they imagine he would let all his commitment and suffering go just to get out of jail? In later years, she'd often make reference to the fact that Smith had been allowed to stay in Zimbabwe after independence as a free man, saying all sorts of things against Uncle Bob, even after what he had done to hurt Uncle Bob.

Patricia is a good-looking, buxom woman wearing a flamboyant red scarf and gold earrings in a bold Ghanaian design with a matching pendant around her neck. Her manicured fingers display a lot of rings, which I comment on. 'Well, I come from the Gold Coast,' she says, laughing. Her dress shop in Mazoe Street, Harare, is called Sankofa. It is quite busy for the times, when few in Mugabe's bankrupt country have the money to buy the glamorous silk and fine cotton Ghanaian costumes she sells for special occasions. As she introduces me to the women popping in and out of the shop to finger the fabrics or try on her dresses, I realise they are the political elite who alone enjoy what is left of the once-wealthy city destroyed by Robert Mugabe's policies.

A banquet to celebrate 26 years of independence is in the offing and they all need new garments, Patricia explains. I join the oohing and aahing as a large lady in a shiny sky-blue suit with the exaggeratedly puffed sleeves you see all over Ghana steps out of the fitting room. Then a drunken man staggers in. Spotting him, Patricia sweeps a pile of bank notes on top of her desk into the drawer beneath. She sends her assistant out to buy two loaves of bread and greets the staggering visitor effusively, introducing him to me as the son of a deceased political foe of Mugabe's, Ruth Chinamano, who I knew years ago.

After the drunk has been shown the door, rather sooner than he would have liked, clutching the loaves thrust into his arms by Patricia and complaining that he cannot possibly eat both, she tells me that Sally lived with Ruth Chinamano when she first returned from London and never forgot the hospitality. Although Ruth was openly hostile to Mugabe in later years, she explains, often calling him a liar from the opposite bench in Parliament, Sally remained unfailingly polite and kind to Mrs Chinamano. It is an example of her aunt's magnanimity, according to Patricia, but there are many who would disagree. Mugabe dealt a dastardly blow to Ruth Chinamano's political organisation, the Zimbabwe African People's Union (Zapu) and Mugabe's main rivals, when his specially trained militia massacred thousands of its supporters in Matabeleland during the 80s, so Sally's attempt to put a good face on their relationship looks more like hypocrisy to me.

Once the rush in the shop is over, we resume our interview. Patricia opens a photo album she has brought to show me and I am struck by two photos in particular. One is of Nhamo taken the year before he died. He is wearing matching white shorts and a shirt, tucked in and belted at the waist, white socks, lace-up shoes and a tie. 'He looks like a little man, doesn't he?' says Patricia fondly. 'When I look at him in these pictures, I see Uncle Bob in this small somebody with a lot of things on his mind. He was an unusually reflective child, who seemed to have a lot of thinking to do.' The sweet innocence of Nhamo's solemn gaze all those lost years ago brings a tear to Patricia's eye, which she wipes away with her ornamented fingers.

The other memorable photograph is of Sally and Robert standing together in Lusaka, Zambia, in 1975. He looks exquisitely shy, his head turned slightly away from the camera as if seeking refuge on her shoulder. Dressed in an African print shirt and black pants, he is wearing a half-smile. Sally is beaming from beneath an elaborate headdress that matches a two-piece Ghanaian costume like the ones Patricia sells in her shop. What is noticeable is their closeness: the two bodies are pressed together as if joined at the hip.

Sally lived mainly in the United Kingdom after Nhamo died, says Patricia. 'I visited her in London when I was about 15. I adored her because she had been my mother as a little girl. She was very stylish, wearing strapless dresses and high, high heels. She lived in Ealing Broadway, where she'd sometimes leave me alone with enough food so that I didn't have to go outside because she had to go for several days to Sweden or somewhere. We couldn't talk about it for security reasons but I remember one of her visits being to organise uniforms for Uncle Bob's guerrilla forces. We had a special code for knocking on the door so that I would know it was her and I could open up.'

Knowing the university courses Mugabe was studying in prison and which books he was allowed to have in his cell, Sally would copy sections from the banned ones in tiny handwriting on very thin paper:

> She would paste this into a toothpaste box in the hope that the warders would not spot it. She was always doing that with various toiletry packs or biscuit boxes. The time she spent copying these notes to him in the library was incredible. It was clearly for love; sheer love.
>
> She was a really attractive woman. How many like her, educated and sophisticated, would have waited more than 10 years for him to come out of prison? And she never even knew when he was going to be released. When he was eventually released, she fainted on seeing him very briefly in Mozambique and had to be revived just in order to greet him before he was whisked away again. They were man and wife in name only for years,

but Mummy waited for him, serving his interests on a daily basis. She was forever going to church to pray for him, soliciting funds, collecting old clothes and selling them for money to power the struggle. She didn't go out with other young people. I remember her lying in her room every weekend, watching English soccer, which she loved.

There were monkeys pasted all over her bedroom wall in London, and also in their bedroom at State House later on. She loved monkeys, gorillas, baboons and chimps, which she'd cut out of magazines and books and stick all over the wall. She would always watch the animal channels on TV, looking for her monkeys. Once she told me she'd had a dream in which all of them started chasing her.

After being in London for three months, Patricia was told by Sally, who had to move house constantly for security reasons, that it was not safe for the schoolgirl to live with her any longer. 'I used to write to her all the time from Ghana after that. I used to write to Uncle Bob too, by the way. Mummy used to tell me to keep his letters because she knew, even then, that he would be famous. Uncle Bob and I were joking about that recently actually, when one of the university vice chancellors in Harare asked me if I had any material for an archival collection on him and his life. I mentioned not having kept the letters and Uncle Bob laughed and said, "Tell her what we used to write about." So I explained that he was teaching me Shona and I was trying to teach him to speak the Ghanaian language Fanti. The interesting thing is that he had the time and care to reply to the letters from a child at a time when he was either studying in prison or organising the struggle.'

The relationship between Bob and Sally was 'just beautiful', according to Patricia. 'She was exactly the right person for him. I witnessed some wonderful things when I lived with them in Zimbabwe, and it became the model relationship I tried to copy myself. When I first came to stay at State House in 1983, one of the things I noticed was how Uncle Bob slammed the doors each evening when he arrived home. You'd hear him slamming one door after another in this huge house of many rooms in his eagerness to find her – that's what he told me when I asked why he slammed the doors every day. He said, "As soon as I arrive, I start to run through the house, slamming each door so that she will know I am there and come quickly to me."'

At 5.30pm each day, Robert and Sally would sit on the wide veranda or in one of the residence's drawing rooms for what they called their teatime:

> She'd eat custard while he drank his tea. Mummy would always be perched on the arm of his chair, and he'd usually have his arm around her. He'd sometimes be reading a Graham Greene novel. That's how I remember them every evening as the sun went down over the gardens at State House. Sometimes they'd be giving each other little pecks and kisses and I'd cover my eyes because it was a bit embarrassing to be the outsider when they were so close. He'd say, 'What are you fussing about? Did you marry my wife for me? Did you pay the lobola (bride price), or can I do what I like with her?'
>
> You'd hear them laughing, laughing so heartily from their bedroom that you'd wonder what was going on. Mummy would never eat until her husband came home. She'd have breakfast, lunch and dinner with him. I often had meals on my own. She'd rush off from meetings early, saying she had to join her husband for lunch, not because he insisted or it was an obligation, but because it was a pleasure. You could see the spark of love between them: it was unmistakable.
>
> He would wait for her outside her dressing room when they were going somewhere. His idea was to be the first one to see her when she came out, all dolled up. He'd exclaim, 'You look beautiful, my wife. That turban is so different, so stately,' he'd say. Or while he was waiting for her, he'd ask loudly so that we could hear inside, 'What are you girls doing in the dressing room for so long? I want to see my wife.' She brought out the soft, loving side of Uncle Bob.
>
> He could be so playful sometimes. He'd like to tease Mummy and me about our Ghanaian accents. When we'd say 'mirra' instead of 'mirror', he would start imitating us. He'd clown around making a parting in the middle of his hair like the smart men in West Africa used to do, imitating the way we said mirror and comb. When I'd carry on pronouncing the words in the Ghanaian way, he'd ask why I was copying him.

Sally Mugabe was twice imprisoned in Rhodesia while organising Zanu's Women's League. 'She had the guts to stand up to men or the police or whites or whoever. She wasn't afraid of anyone,' says Patricia. 'She used to write slogans in lipstick, I remember, against Ian Smith, the Queen, anybody who oppressed black people. One of her arrests was for denouncing the Queen.'

When Patricia came from Ghana to live at State House, with its many empty guest rooms, shortly after her aunt had been diagnosed with incurable kidney disease, Sally insisted on finding a flat for her niece. 'When she found the flat, it wasn't really expensive and I could have paid the rent myself from the pocket money she gave me while I was at university but she said, "No, you have to share". She wanted to teach me a lesson because she thought I was superior in my outlook. So she brought this girl from her office.' Patricia grimaces and her voice drops to a whisper so that I can barely hear what she is saying about her flatmate except that it is clearly a derogatory description of a person she considered well beneath her own status. 'I protested, but Mummy told me I had to share the kitchen and the bathroom with her because she was a human being and therefore just the same as me. That changed my perception of things very quickly, just as Mummy intended.'

Not many of the women in Zimbabwe were middle class during the 60s, Patricia confides, so Sally had 'to come down to their level' if she was to relate to her husband's people. 'She sat on the floor with them, as was their custom, and ate what they ate, however basic it was. She had just arrived in the country and she wanted them to love her so she knew she had to identify with them. Uncle Bob really admired her for that. It was done for the good of the party and the country, but mainly for him. She was extremely sophisticated, like my grandma, who brought us all up to be ladies, admired for our clothes and our manners. But Mummy never had her nose turned up. She didn't want any distance from the people of Zimbabwe. She played the role of their mother and that's why they called her *Amayi* Sally.'

Patricia says she has been struck over the years at the number of Zimbabweans she has met who have claimed they knew Sally well but who, for various giveaway reasons, could not have known her in the intimate way they claimed. 'For instance, there are those who recall having breakfast with her at State House, or lunch or dinner. It is not true, I know, because nobody came to visit them at State House as those stories claim. It was always just the three of us.' The only other person to stay with them at State House was Uncle Bob's mother Bona, who kept to herself most of the time, says Patricia. She remembers Bona mainly for the odd requests the elderly woman sometimes made while in residence. Once, when Patricia was offering Mugabe's mother sugar in her tea, Bona said '*bitshana*', meaning a little bit. Bob laughed and told Patricia, 'She means eight spoons', which were then piled into her teacup. On another occasion, Patricia remembers Bona asking for a 'blue drink', a request that nobody on the household staff could decipher until Bona went to the fridge and pointed to a bottle of beverage known as Creme Soda, which was green.

Patricia says she enjoys reminiscing with Zimbabweans about the old days at State House, regardless of whether the anecdotes she hears of Sally are true or not. 'I just nod when they tell me those stories because it shows how much they adore her now that she is dead, and want to relate to her. It's a tribute to her. Everyone can own a share of her memory. She would have liked that because she particularly believed in sharing, as well as fairness.'

Robert Mugabe liked fairness, too, says Patricia, pausing to consider whether fairness in politics is defined differently from the personal variety. He was always fair to the staff, she recalls. And if he gave his nieces and nephews Z$40 to buy themselves something at Christmas, he'd always give Patricia Z$40 too, even though she was not one of his own. He brought some 18-inch TVs on one of his trips abroad, she recalls, and gave one to everybody in his family, including her.

He would encourage everybody and anybody to go to school and university. Patricia remembers hearing him talking outside her window to a gardener at State House, encouraging him to take up a correspondence course in order to qualify for university:

And afterwards, Uncle Bob actually gave that gardener some tuition because he was himself a teacher. At one time, he set aside a few hours on a regular basis to give lessons to all the staff at State House. One of the gardeners is now the controller of the residence: he has a degree, thanks to Uncle Bob. Zimbabwe's current transport minister attended lessons given by Uncle Bob at State House too.

What I particularly like about Uncle Bob is his listening ear. He can just keep quiet and listen, which has taught me to be more attentive to what's being said around me. If you listen, you learn more; you learn and pick up a lot and you have time to organise your thoughts: he taught me that. I think it's such a strength, and it is *his* strength. He is very disciplined. A friend of mine, who was one of Uncle Bob's guerrilla fighters, said he taught his army to observe both internal and external discipline.

Internal discipline is what he's mastered. What to do with anger, for instance: he is able to control it and not show it. He can sit face to face with his opponents and detractors, smiling and talking and listening, even if he's boiling inside. That's where he keeps his anger – inside. Mummy wasn't like that; she'd tell you straight what she thought and felt. They were complementary in that way, although he taught her over the years not always to retort and reveal. Sometimes it's better to keep it to yourself so that they don't know what you feel or what you think, he used to tell her. That way you don't betray yourself. But you'd always know from Mummy's body language or the expression on her face what she was really thinking, even if she picked the passive approach. With Uncle Bob, he could be so placid that you would never be able to pick up what he was thinking.

Sally was one of the few people who could challenge Mugabe's ideas without offending him, and she sometimes stimulated debate in his political circles. A number of his ministers and advisers told me how they remember him listening to the prevailing arguments but then, undecided himself, declaring that he was going home to consult Sally. Patricia confirms this:

The only person Uncle Bob really trusted with his feelings and even his political problems was Mummy. Whenever he reshuffled the Cabinet they would talk about it for hours, going over and over the details; what was needed, what was wrong. His style is to play everything close to his chest and nobody knew what was coming up except him and Mummy. She supported him by doing all the research for him. She'd even go to the grassroots to find out who was suitable for a particular ministry and who wasn't. If she gave him information, he knew it was valid. The Cabinet reshuffle was a serious event at home and he listened to everything she had to say.

They were mates, they had a common background as teachers and politicians, they both wanted everyone to have their legitimate rights as well as their responsibilities. She gave him her strength, loyalty and reliability, and he gave her a mission in life. She always had potential but she needed something to ignite it, and that something was him, Robert Mugabe of Zimbabwe. If she hadn't met him she would still have been in politics in Ghana because she wanted fairness and equality long before she met him. That was her, and she would definitely have worked in some avenue of social justice.

He respected her and she respected him. Mummy knew how to honour her husband, which is maybe an old-fashioned thing to say but Uncle Bob is of an older generation – she was too. I'm sure they had quarrels but she would never expose him to a third person as anything but perfect. She had really arrived as a lady of the old school and it was her mission lifelong to honour and support him. Even when he took up with that young woman (his current wife) before Mummy died. Of course, she didn't like it but she did what she used to tell me to do: 'Talk to your pillow if you have problems in your marriage. Never, ever, humiliate your husband.' Her motto was to carry on in gracious style.

She was his right hand, best friend, mentor, political partner. He was extremely lucky to have her. She covered her husband so beautifully and made him feel so good about himself. She played her chosen role brilliantly, not as a submissive woman. No, she wasn't that and he didn't want that. She had her own ambition, which was to get people to understand what her husband's goal was – what he wanted for them.

Suddenly, Patricia screams, '*pamberi*', meaning 'long live', and thrusts her fist in the air in imitation of Sally's fervour. 'Mummy was always there alongside him, supporting him,' she declares proudly. 'Not for a moment did she falter, even when she was dying at the young age of 60.'

As she got sicker, Mummy was in and out of hospital. She finally died at Parirenyatwa Hospital after being there for a week. I was beside her constantly and so was Uncle Bob. But on the Sunday night before she passed away, she insisted we both leave. She was sitting in a white nightgown, wearing a little blue sleeping cap, and I commented on how beautiful she looked. She joked that sick people always looked better just before they died and I begged her not to say things like that. She insisted, 'Oh, Bob, go home. You're tired, you must rest', and eventually he went. I stayed a bit longer and she said, 'Pray for me', which I did. Then I left at about 2am. It was the last time we saw her alive.

The doctors were called at about 5.30am and by 5.45am she was gone. They didn't call us, which is very sad. Uncle Bob said he hadn't been able to sleep. At 4am he was wide awake, just sitting in their bedroom. And I couldn't sleep the whole night after my husband and my first-born had counselled me, telling me that death is part of life, that sort of thing.

After Sally's death, Mugabe was 'extremely depressed', explains Patricia, who used to go to State House from her own home every day after breakfast to be with him.

We planned the funeral and the long period of mourning together. And we cried a lot together. He was suffering so much, and so was I. He referred to Mummy all the time, and he still does whenever I see him. He misses her still: I know because he never fails to tell me. Mummy did not have a lot of friends and he has none so they were especially important to each other. It is always difficult to detect changes in his moods because he's so disciplined and gives nothing away. But over that period he was so sad and devastated: you could see it and hear it.

At the last memorial service for Mummy at Heroes Acre he thanked people for coming and said everyone there knew only too well what the anniversary meant to Sally's family. 'So you can imagine what it means to her husband,' he said. He has had to move on of course, but whenever he can remember Mummy's deeds publicly and pay tribute to her, he does. He says to me sometimes, 'Where do you get all the tears?' but he cries too at those ceremonies.

Interestingly, Patricia says she does not know Mugabe's children by his second wife because she has never been invited into his new family. 'But I know he relates closely to me. I was his favourite little girl back then. He is able to be himself with me and to remember Mummy freely and how it was once, all happiness, in his life.'

Acknowledging the fallacy that Sally was loved by everyone, Patricia regrets that Zimbabweans did not support Sally when she was alive. Zimbabweans criticised her constantly, many resented the fact that their president had chosen a foreigner when he could have had his pick in Zimbabwe, according to Patricia, who notes that Zimbabweans speak equally unkindly about Mugabe's second wife, who is Zimbabwean. 'It didn't bother Mummy. She had her vision for him and the country, not for herself, and she kept focusing on that. Uncle Bob appreciated what she did and that's all she really cared about.'

During the last years of her life, Sally founded and presided over the Zimbabwe Child Survival Movement. Apart from charities supporting children, she was particularly drawn to the care of social outcasts. She headed the Zimbabwe Leper Society, 'comprising people from every background, including Asian doctors, Jewish benefactors, rich and poor, young and old. Mummy never having been a racist, ageist, or sexist because all she saw was injustice,' according to Patricia.

Sally regularly adopted lost causes, like the growing ranks of prostitutes who were threatening to dominate the small town of Marondera near Harare during the late 80s. Under her patronage, the young women were given sewing machines in the hope that they would become seamstresses rather than commercial sex workers. Sally presided over a housing scheme so that they could live decently without having to sell their bodies, much to the dismay of local families who had been waiting a long time for decent accommodation. Once, when asked in Parliament during a regular session known as the Prime Minister's Question Time about the hookers of Marondera, Mugabe referred the questioner to his wife: 'They're Sally's prostitutes,' he replied matter-of-factly.

Not surprisingly, Patricia's idealised account of life with Sally and Uncle Bob leaves out some telling details. While Sally adored children, according to Patricia, I recall one of Mugabe's former Cabinet colleagues describing an occasion when she adopted a young orphan very publicly but never returned to collect the child from the orphanage. Widely thought to be corrupt, Sally was involved in a motor vehicle scam dubbed Willowgate that brought down some important political figures in the late 80s. One of the exposed Willowgate crooks was so ashamed that he committed suicide, yet the first lady sailed on innocently. Patricia flatly denies that Sally ever embezzled money, citing the paltry sum left in her Zimbabwean will as evidence when, in fact, her aunt's fortune was stashed offshore. Like Sally, Patricia is a firm believer in spin: life at State House was wonderful all the time.

Mugabe may not have been overtly corrupt at a personal level in those days but he turned a blind eye to his wife's dishonesty. When she died and he discovered that she had left all her money to her twin sister in Ghana, he was so angry that he hurled a chair through a plate glass window at State House, according to the handyman who repaired the damage.

Sally loved Robert and supported him wholeheartedly. As his confidante and only real friend, she boosted his self-esteem to heights no one had seen before. But like Bona, she had her own reasons for promoting his career. Sally was looking for a platform for her own ambitions when she first met him, and she saw herself as the queen of Utopia from then on. In the years before Mugabe went to prison, it was Sally's lofty influence that encouraged the sense of omnipotence bestowed on him by Bona via Father O'Hea in earlier years.

What also comes through Patricia's recollections is the emptiness of their lives despite Sally's attempts to master the common touch. The Mugabes had no friends; nobody ever came to State House for the sheer pleasure of being with them. As a child, Patricia felt left out of their insulated world, eating alone because Sally was always waiting to attend to her famous husband. Sally made much of teaching her niece a lesson in humility, something she knew nothing about.

Had Sally been genuinely warm and giving, rather than the imperious first lady Zimbabweans distrusted, Robert Mugabe might have had to adjust his own grandiose delusions. I remember going with a media contingent to their home in Quorn Avenue, Mount Pleasant, in Salisbury, shortly after Mugabe returned from Mozambique for the country's decisive election in 1980. We were taken to the back of the house where Sally, decked out in her customary Ghanaian regalia, elegant headdress and all, was squatting beside an outside tap washing a bowl of prawns. An incongruous image, her immaculate attire being at odds with the chosen domestic activity, it was so obviously designed to portray her as humble when she was nothing of the kind.

Three

The prisoner's friend

The few years he shared with Sally before being arrested and detained by the Rhodesian government put Robert Mugabe in touch with his long-buried emotions. Once incarcerated on an indefinite basis, however, he returned to his old bookish ways to escape the pain and uncertainty of prison life. 'We were at the mercy of people we could never trust and from whom we had little or no information as to what was in store for us,' he later explained to journalists.

Moved constantly from one ill-equipped jail to another during the first three years of his detention, Mugabe shared a dark, cold cell and a single toilet bucket with six other political prisoners for 23 hours a day at a detention centre near the small Midlands province town of Gwelo. The food, always scarce and unappetising, was sometimes rotten. Rats darted among the bodies sleeping on the cement floor at night and lice crawled everywhere.

Then he was held without trial in a makeshift prison camp at Sikombela in bush lands surrounding a mining town called Kwe Kwe, previously known as Que Que. Feeling revived with more physical space in the isolated detention centre, he began to emerge as an inspiring teacher among the demoralised men. Not only were they receiving disappointing reports in prison that the two successors of the original NDP, Zanu and Zapu, were fighting among themselves for supremacy in the country's townships, but their own ranks in detention were continually swelling as police cracked down on the nationalists' self-defeating political activity. Mugabe bolstered morale by urging his fellow detainees to use their time behind bars to prepare for the liberation that must eventually come: 'These months, these years, however long it takes, must not be wasted,' he urged.

He began to organise lessons at all levels of education. Detainees with qualifications, however modest, would teach the illiterate ones during morning classes, using books and materials provided by organisations such as Christian Care. In the afternoons, the 'teachers' would do their own studying. Mugabe was immediately elected headmaster. Already enrolled with the law faculty at the University of London, he went on to obtain a total of six degrees, in addition to the Bachelor of Arts he had been awarded in South Africa while in prison. A fellow detainee remembered Mugabe 'turning the nights into days' as he read and typed long after the others were asleep so that he would have time to supervise their classes during the day.

The greatest personal tragedy of Robert Mugabe's life, the sudden death of his toddler son Nhamo, occurred soon after he had been moved from the Midlands to Salisbury Remand Prison. He was given the news one morning in December 1966 by his sister Sabina. Summoned to the visitors' section, he emerged from the dark corridor that led to his cell to find her on the other side of the thick plated glass through which prisoners spoke to their relatives and friends. She was one of his few visitors as Sally was in Ghana and he had told his impoverished family to come only when there were pressing matters to discuss. He smiled when he greeted Sabina, not seeing her tears at first.

She immediately told him of the child's death from encephalitis. The little boy, aged three years and three months, had passed away a few days before in a fever, assumed to be malaria, at the Ghanaian home of his maternal grandparents. Mugabe broke down, his shoulders crumpled and heaving. Watching helplessly as he sobbed, Sabina called his name over and over again through a microphone in the glass partition that separated them until a warder came and escorted him back to his cell.

The Special Branch policeman who was present during the visit, Tony Bradshaw, remembered Mugabe being inconsolable for days. Friends at Christian Care and the chaplain general of the prison service, Reverend Bill Clark, helped the distraught prisoner petition the government to release him briefly from jail on compassionate grounds. Pleading to be allowed to bury his son and mourn the loss of his only child with his wife, Mugabe was aghast when the authorities – allegedly at the insistence of premier Ian Smith – refused.

Edgar Tekere, a Zanu colleague in the same prison, wrote to the justice minister asking for clemency. He explained that Mugabe was so committed to his cause that he would undoubtedly return to his prison cell, seeing that it was an honour among struggle credentials to be imprisoned. But to no avail.

In one of his routine reports, Reverend Clark noted Mugabe's response. 'He shook his head in disbelief, repeatedly confirming with us that even Tony Bradshaw, with whom he had had bitter arguments in the past, had supported his petition by confirming that the prisoner could be trusted to return.'

The experience haunted the Mugabes for years afterwards, according to Reverend Clark, who was one of Mugabe's closest confidants in prison. Sally particularly regretted how little Mugabe had seen of his child, though she understood the sacrifice because she had always encouraged her husband's political commitment. 'All in all, my husband saw the baby as a tiny tot in Dar es Salaam, and then only for a few days when he visited Ghana for a meeting,' she told a journalist in 1983. 'He never had the chance to get to know his child, let alone play with him. I was better off. I knew our little boy for three and a quarter years. His death is something we can never forget.'

Alone in his cell for 11 hours a day until he felt able to resume his usual busy schedule teaching English and mathematics to classes of fellow detainees, Mugabe was left to contemplate a grim irony. Having deeply resented being abandoned by his father Gabriel at the tender age of 10, Mugabe struggled to come to terms with the fact that he had barely known his own small son at the still more pitiful age of three. It was a battle for Mugabe to hold on to his sense of self and purpose, according to Reverend Clark. Deprived of loving relationships in prison and confused by the life choice he had made as a family man, it was only by clinging to the intellectual way he had learnt to manage emotional turmoil in his childhood that he survived the crisis and returned to his books.

If he was bitter in the wake of a tragedy made worse by the decision to deny him the solace of attending his son's funeral, Robert Mugabe did not reveal it to the man who describes himself as the Zimbabwe president's friend, former Rhodesian policeman Mac McGuiness.

McGuiness is a towering figure; well over six-foot tall, weather-beaten but clearly built for endurance even in his seventh decade. Having risen to the highest rank of Ian Smith's secret service, McGuiness retired as the intelligence head of the country's feared counter-insurgency unit, the Selous Scouts, early in 1980 when Mugabe's Zanu-PF gained power.

He and Mugabe first met during the mid-60s when Detective Inspector McGuiness was in charge of the state's political prisoners. 'My earliest recollection of Robert Mugabe was in Gwelo Prison, sitting in a group in the courtyard at my feet while I was censoring their mail,' he tells me during an interview in a hotel near Pretoria in December 2005. 'I used to go there every Monday and Friday to clear the mail coming in and censor the letters going out. The detainees would fetch me a chair and bring me a cup of tea while I put my black pen through the lines they were not allowed to read. It was usually quite pleasant between us, believe it or not, because I used to send my truck out to Kwe Kwe, where there were large fruit farms in those days, and bring mangos, oranges and other fresh produce back for the detainees. They knew I didn't have to do that for them; they recognised it as a human gesture on my part, even though it also enabled me to do my job because it meant I could more readily recruit informers once they liked me.'

Mugabe was solemn and uncommunicative in those days, recalls McGuiness:

He was not the kingpin among the nationalists in detention. The big names then were Joshua Nkomo on the Ndebele-speaking side and among the Shona it was Ndabaningi Sithole, or 'Rubber Dinghy' as we called him, who I eventually sent to jail as a convicted prisoner for three years for trying to assassinate Ian Smith. Sithole had a young woman visiting him in the detainees section who was actually a plant of mine. He would give her instructions about arms and ammunition for use in the plot and she would bring his plans straight to me. I had everybody who was anybody in the nationalist movement locked up under my watchful eye at some time or other. It was my job to know exactly what they were doing and thinking, and there wasn't much that escaped our informers.

Although I had met Mugabe before, I only got to know him when I drove him once from Gwelo to Salisbury. It would have been sometime in the late 60s. I remember it was almost lunchtime when we were leaving

Gwelo in my car. I knew he wasn't going to get food in Salisbury Prison so I stopped at the Golden Mile Hotel. We walked into the dining room, sat down at a table and had a look at the menu. I was asking Robert what he wanted to eat when up came the manager, the co-owner, who had been sitting in the bar having a beer with some locals as we walked in. He bent down and spoke to me, saying, 'Sorry, we don't serve blacks here.'

McGuiness says he shoved back his chair and, looming over the hotelier, told him in crude language that if he refused to serve the two of them, he would never take another order. His kitchen would be locked and the whole establishment closed down, the policeman warned.

He got a bit chirpy, saying, 'You can't do that.' And I replied, 'Oh yes I can, just watch me. There isn't a hotel kitchen in this country that I can't close down for lack of hygiene or on some or other technicality.' When I told him who I was – the Special Branch was highly respected – he rushed off to get our steak, egg and chips. At the end of the meal, when I asked for the bill, he even tried to give it to us free of charge. I insisted on paying and thanked him courteously. He was hanging around in the foyer with a bunch of farmers and miners from the bar when we left – probably making sure that nothing blew up. Mugabe thanked him very politely too, I remember. He said, 'A very nice lunch. I enjoyed it,' and gave a little bow as he walked out.

McGuiness' account of the hotel incident is mainly about him having his power challenged but it also shows the prisoner and the jailer being thrown into a brief alliance. No doubt having McGuiness stand up for him as a black prisoner made Mugabe feel momentarily humanised after years in jail, yet he would not for a second have forgotten that he was at the other man's mercy. In the terrifying world of imprisonment where everyone had two faces, a man might buy you lunch but you knew there was an ulterior motive because his job as jailer was to forfeit, not foster, human values.

Did Mugabe join in and fuel the fracas at the Golden Mile Hotel?

Oh no, not at all. He was always a gentleman. He looked shattered. He told me in the car afterwards that he was afraid there was going to be a punch-up, which wouldn't have bothered me a bit. I think he would have preferred to leave at the first sign of trouble. He definitely didn't want a scene. But there was a scene until the manager realised that I meant business. I always hated that sort of petty discrimination, you know. I always believed in being fair at a personal level. I brought my garden boy with me to South Africa when I left Zimbabwe immediately after Mugabe came to power. The chap had been with me for nearly 15 years by then and I couldn't just leave him behind when I went to live down south. He was part of the family. Politics was something else. I did my job by being pleasant to people but I wouldn't have hesitated to shoot someone or extract information by any means from someone I considered dangerous, if necessary.

He pauses, sinking back into the leather sofa and watching me as he sips his coffee. He has brought his tall, muscular son Gavin with him to the interview, presumably as a witness to what he is telling me, but also perhaps to boast of what he considers his accomplishments to the burly young man who was a boy in the days we are discussing. 'You shouldn't be hearing all this,' he tells Gavin in a stage whisper as we talk. There appears to have been no questioning by McGuiness of his role in the oppression of Rhodesia's black population while he was a key member of the country's security apparatus. His failure to acknowledge what he did to men like Robert Mugabe while the prisoners sat at the feet of the jailer, entirely at his mercy, is scary. To talk so casually about his own dark duplicity and indeed torture in front of his son, with a reasonableness that the younger man evidently condones, is chilling.

During their long drive together, the prisoner and the policeman discussed many things, McGuiness says.

We chatted about the state of the country mainly; about things that concerned us both. He insisted that Zimbabwe should be run by blacks and he argued his case calmly. I found him completely genuine. I wanted to know if he felt there were sufficient people with sufficient knowledge and experience on his side to run the country. He admitted that there weren't but insisted on their right to run their own affairs. He said there could be as many whites as you liked to help run things initially. He claimed he didn't want to see anyone leave Rhodesia. There was absolutely no animosity towards the European as far as I could see. We talked about his time in the Catholic mission school in Kutama, where he was educated, and he made it clear that he was grateful for all that the holy fathers had given him there. He had no hard feelings, no rancour at all.

Surely Mugabe resented being imprisoned?

McGuiness shakes his head and replies swiftly, 'He regarded it as a battleground for power, which it was. We talked about that. He saw it as a battle of wits and strategy, he said. And believe you me, Mugabe had a first-class brain for the job.' McGuiness sounds as if he believes Mugabe was speaking from the heart. What he apparently fails to take into account is that no prisoner is going to reveal himself fully to the jailer who controls the game. The prisoner may talk and laugh but his reactions are obviously going to be measured.

I ask McGuiness if he was trying to recruit Mugabe as an informer. 'Oh no, I didn't need him,' he responds with a dismissive snort. 'My sources were already very well established, both internally and externally. And he was too dignified to approach, somehow.'

McGuiness recalls that he and Mugabe talked a lot about the need to restore land, as well as the sacred ancestral spirits of Shona traditional beliefs, to Zimbabweans.

He believed profoundly in his people, the living as well as the dead. You can say of some Africans that there is a thin veneer of civilisation as we know it in the West. But Mugabe, who was undoubtedly civilised and much better educated than most of us, still held African beliefs very dearly in his heart. I think this is one of the reasons he pushed the white farmers off the land. He was always acutely aware that African beliefs reside in the soil: their ancestors are in the soil. He always believed very, very strongly that nobody had the right to give or take away the land of the people because that meant giving away the ancestors who held the whole nation together. We discussed it thoroughly on that trip. Uppermost in his mind was to take back the land. That is why we feared him more than some of the others. He was saying all the same things then that he says now; about the land having been stolen by the British and the settlers and therefore his government not needing to pay compensation to get it back.

After he had dropped Mugabe off at Salisbury Prison on that occasion, McGuiness seldom saw the quietly spoken nationalist in person during the course of his intelligence duties. They exchanged little more than a cursory greeting or two until 1974 – the year Mugabe was released from detention – when Superintendent McGuiness was appointed joint commander with Lieutenant Colonel Ron Reid Daly of the top secret Selous Scouts. While he and Mugabe did not meet at all after that, Mugabe's every move was studied by McGuiness, whose mission had become the clandestine elimination of infiltrating guerrilla fighters, or terrorists as they were known to the Rhodesians.

It wasn't until the beginning of June 1980, shortly after Robert Mugabe had been installed as prime minister of the newly independent state of Zimbabwe, that Mac McGuiness was suddenly summoned to the premier's office. At the time he was making preparations with his family and many former members of the Rhodesian security forces to leave Zimbabwe for South Africa. Although he would have preferred to stay, he says his wife feared that the new country might become too risky a place to bring up their two school-going children.

> Mugabe was sitting in his office in a suit. He got up when I walked in, came quickly around the desk and clasped my hand. He was sort of patting me on the shoulder, I remember. He ordered tea and spoke a little bit about Gwelo Prison, saying it had been quite pleasant there, all things considered. He had no hard feelings at all. I think he talked about his prison years being an opportunity politically, giving him and his colleagues time to formulate, to plan – you know how he speaks, repeating everything in slightly different words. I joked about things having turned out all right for him, not too bad, quite well really, and he laughed.

A long conversation followed about the epic defeats and triumphs of the bloody 15-year-long armed struggle:

> We agreed that we had had an unnecessary war in which a lot of good young people had died. We had quite a discussion about what had gone on at various stages of the war; a detailed post-mortem, if you like. Eventually, he told me that we had done some terrible things and they had done some terrible things. 'It was war,' I said. And he replied, 'You are right; it was war. But now,' he told me, 'the war is over. Now we can sit and talk as friends.'

Accompanying McGuiness to the meeting was a young Special Branch officer, Dan Stannard, the policeman who had been credited with saving Mugabe's life a few months earlier and who was subsequently decorated for bravery.[1] McGuiness concedes, when prodded to explain why he had brought Stannard, a relatively junior officer, with him to meet the president, that it was he who had tipped Stannard off about the assassination plans, although Stannard had alerted the bodyguards and police.

> I ran sources everywhere in those days, absolutely everywhere – that was my forte. And those sources included people who knew about the various assassination plots against Mugabe at that time. I knew Dan was a good guy. I had heard that Mugabe wanted me to head the Central Intelligence Organisation (CIO) in place of the incumbent Ken Flower and, thinking he might be upset about my leaving the country, I had picked Dan to help fill the gap.

---

[1] Dan Stannard described the attempt on Mugabe's life thus: 'I was a chief superintendent in the CID/Special Branch, Salisbury and Mashonaland, at the time of receiving this information. I knew it was true because it had come from a member of the group who were determined to "destroy Zimbabwe" at the handover ceremony scheduled for 18 April 1980 at the Rufaro Stadium, Salisbury.

'The information was to the effect that a group of SA Special Forces had infiltrated Salisbury from South Africa, armed with a large quantity of explosives. These were very sophisticated and consisted of several traffic light control boxes filled with explosives and shrapnel, several claymores and two Strela (ground-to-air missiles). The plan was to install the traffic light control boxes along the route to be taken by Mugabe, Prince Charles and other heads of state to the Rufaro Stadium. At a given time these would have been activated by remote control at the same time as those installed inside the stadium. Ground-to-air missiles were to be used by some of the team at Harare Airport to shoot down aircraft taking dignitaries who had survived away from the capital.

'The intention was that the backlash would have precipitated a "blood bath" against whites and hurled Zimbabwe into a state of chaos and bloodshed. Unbeknown to me at that time was a plan by the South African Defence Force to enter Zimbabwe in the Beitbridge/ Messina area using tanks, armed personnel carriers, choppers and shock troops in order to re-establish law and order and at the same time annex Zimbabwe into South Africa's republic. It was known as "Operation Barnacle".

'I received this information two days before 18 April 1980 and was able to mount an operation. We raided a house in the Mount Pleasant suburb of Salisbury and made enough noise to alert the group so that they could escape, thus ensuring the safety of my source. I had the names of those involved but decided, rightly or wrongly, to let them escape. We recovered all the material, which was ready for installation, thus foiling the operation and pre-empting what would have plunged the new country into complete turmoil. I was awarded the Gold Cross of Zimbabwe 10 years later in 1990 by President Mugabe at State House.'

Mugabe thanked us for what we had done for him, for keeping him alive. Then he asked me what I was going to do in the future. That's when I told him the wife wanted to go. He urged me to stay, saying, 'We need people like you; people we can trust. Please stay.' But I told him that if Maggie wants to go, we go. I said, 'I am sorry, sir. I leave you in good hands. Dan will look after you.' He said impatiently, 'Yes, I know that, but I need you. I trust you.' Finally, I told him firmly, 'Well, my wife is senior to you, sir, and she wants to leave, so that's it.' He laughed then and accepted my decision.

Quickly reconsidering the situation, Mugabe leaned across the desk and invited McGuiness to continue working for Zimbabwean intelligence in South Africa. He summoned his security minister Emmerson Mnangagwa, a former guerrilla who had been captured and severely tortured by Rhodesian security forces. McGuiness remembered that Mnangagwa's first call on the day he had taken up his ministerial appointment a few months earlier was to visit the police interrogation room where he had been tortured. Nevertheless, meeting Mnangagwa proved entirely agreeable, says McGuiness. Mugabe seemed pleased with the compromise deal they had struck. 'At the end when I was leaving his office, Mugabe called after me, "Remember that I owe you a lunch, Mac. One day I will repay you. Remember that!"'

According to McGuiness, Mugabe finds it difficult to trust people because he is 'an insular sort of guy, who keeps his own counsel by preference'. Firmly believing that Mugabe grew to trust him, however, McGuiness appears to have attempted to humanise himself in Mugabe's eyes during the journey from Gwelo to Salisbury. 'I told Mugabe that I am a professional. I serve the master who pays me but I won't work for just anybody. I choose my masters. I would never sell my soul. Mugabe knew I had warmed to him as one man to another on that journey. We had become friends. Later on, he discovered that Joshua Nkomo had planned to make me the commissioner of police if he had come to power in Zimbabwe instead of Mugabe. Nkomo trusted me and so did Mugabe, as I did him.'

Far from trusting McGuiness as a friend, Mugabe probably wanted the former policeman to head his own intelligence network because he knew McGuiness as a ruthless person who was good at his dastardly job. Perhaps it was because he knew just how good McGuiness was at forcing one man to turn against another that Mugabe wanted McGuiness on his team. The new president had, after all, lived for years with prison punishment, the cruel effects of which were bound to have rubbed off on him. Uppermost in Mugabe's mind once he had power, perhaps, was not only to ensure that he was never at the mercy of men like Mac McGuiness again, but also that his enemies were as brutally and effectively controlled as he had been.

Mugabe's idea for an ongoing intelligence relationship with McGuiness in South Africa was for the former Selous Scout mastermind to persuade the South African military not to go across the border and make trouble in Zimbabwe, which was at the time considered a Marxist threat in Pretoria – the last bastion of white rule in Africa. Zimbabwe, in return, would not provide a sanctuary for African National Congress guerrillas intent on liberating its southern neighbour.

> It worked for a while but then the military hierarchy in Pretoria changed. The army began sending in their special forces to blow up this and blow up that. I told the South Africans they were crazy, that they would regret it, but it was like talking to a brick wall. So I went to Harare before my contract was up and told Flower and Mnangagwa that I couldn't make it work any more.
>
> It was unfortunate because Mugabe is the only politician among the many I have met who kept his word. He undertook at independence to let bygones be bygones and he never lifted a finger against his former enemies, including Ian Smith, who was allowed to live in Zimbabwe as long as he pleased and to criticise Mugabe whenever he chose for the rest of his life. He was more generous to Smith than Smith was to him, that's for sure. Mugabe would have honoured the undertakings given to the South Africans, I believe, but they did not trust him. That's why it all went wrong. I think that had the promises made to Mugabe been kept by the South Africans, as well as the British and others, Zimbabwe would not be in the state it is in today.

During the two years McGuiness lived in Pretoria, the South Africans recruited into their own forces some 5 000 disaffected former Rhodesian military personnel and established a network of agents, informers, spies and saboteurs inside Zimbabwe. Their objective was to keep Mugabe's government in a weak and defensive position so as to prevent Zimbabwe from becoming either a security threat to its southern neighbour by providing bases for anti-apartheid insurgents, or an example of a stable African state to the world.

In mid-1982, when a large proportion of the white population had emigrated from Zimbabwe but while I was still living there, South Africa's ongoing sabotage campaign hit its latest target. The destruction of 13 aircraft in a raid on Thornhill, Zimbabwe's main air force base near Gweru, formerly Gwelo, was the work of an assault team of three Rhodesian saboteurs recruited by South African military intelligence and assisted by a white air force officer stationed at the base, who provided crucial information. With no leads at the time, police randomly accused and arrested several senior officers, including deputy commander Air Vice Marshall Hugh Slatter. Held incommunicado and denied legal representation, Slatter and five others were subjected to electric shock torture until they admitted involvement in the raid.

One of the lawyers retained by the airmen's families had been struggling for days to obtain permission to see the prisoners when it was suddenly granted by the high court late one Friday afternoon in the week they had made their confessions. My husband George Patrikios was among several medical doctors approached by the lawyer to go immediately to the jail in order to examine the airmen for evidence of torture before visiting hours were over for the week and their incriminating wounds had the chance to heal over the weekend. Unlike the other doctors, who feared that they might become scapegoats, George agreed. His report confirming the puncture marks left by electrodes on the prisoners' bodies formed the basis of the airmen's defence and acquittal on charges based entirely on confessions obtained by torture. But while they were embracing their families as free men at the end of the trial in 1983, they were rearrested, prompting an international outcry.

Mugabe did not deny that the airmen had been tortured. 'Unfortunately, our interrogators used irregular methods. We admit they were irregular. They did use torture,' the Zimbabwean leader told reporters. But he did not see any reason why the airmen should not be re-detained after their acquittal. His government believed they were South African agents, he said, and it would not be responsible to let them 'float about committing acts of destruction'.

Later, at a press conference in Dublin during one of his many overseas trips, Mugabe asked: 'Why is there so much concern about these men? They are not the only ones in detention. Is it because they are white; because they are Mrs Thatcher's kith and kin?'

The airmen were eventually released. When my husband died some years later, Slatter sent me a letter of condolence from the United States, where he lived after the ordeal, saying he believed that George had saved his life. The episode proved to be one of the earliest nails in Zimbabwe's coffin because Mugabe's reputation abroad was severely damaged by the contempt he had shown for legal procedures. The London *Times* commented: 'Mr Mugabe's government substitutes its writ for the courts and is scornful of "legal technicalities". Thus the protection all Zimbabwean citizens deserve from arbitrary arrest and imprisonment without due process disappears; liberty depends on the whim of an individual.'

Mugabe's response was to criticise the legal system in Zimbabwe for disallowing evidence obtained through torture. 'The law of evidence and the criminal procedure we have inherited is a stupid ass,' he told journalists grandly, his elegant hands sweeping the air like a maestro.

Mac McGuiness believes Zimbabwe's new premier was, in fact, floundering. 'He was trying to put on a brave face in response to South Africa's determination to keep the war going. Mugabe had hoped that it would somehow go the other way after independence,' says the former intelligence chief. 'But the problem was that there was no dialogue at all between the leaders of the two countries. Nobody of any substance ever went from Pretoria to Harare for talks with Mugabe. And he knew only too well after several assassination attempts that they were after him personally; that they were trying to kill him. He was not only personally and as a country the target of a damaging military campaign from his ruthless southern neighbour, but in earlier years he had also been the focus of a great deal of dissent among powerful people inside his own party.'

What Mugabe had not at first realised was that he was a pawn in the bigger southern African power game. Once it became clear that the formidable force of South Africa was waged against him, and that his attempts to build a new country out of war-ravaged Rhodesia were therefore going to be fragile, Mugabe's paranoia began to mount. McGuiness agrees that it is sad, looking back, to reflect on what might have been had apartheid South Africa not been fighting for its survival at the very moment when Zimbabwe achieved its independence.

'It was a lot for one inexperienced prime minister to deal with, and he was well and truly distrustful by the time his suspicion of former rival Joshua Nkomo's intentions set in, which led to the first really big blunder of his presidency – the Matabeleland massacres known as Gukurahundi.[2] Mugabe simply did not know where to turn or who he could trust and, indeed, that was not imagined but a real concern,' says McGuiness.

---

[2] Gukurahundi, meaning 'the sweeping away of rubbish' in Shona, is the name given to the development in Matabeleland during the early 80s of a special army unit known as the Fifth Brigade. Trained by North Koreans and drawn almost entirely from former guerrilla forces loyal to Mugabe, its chain of command bypassed the rest of the country's military. Answering directly to the premier, the Fifth Brigade's purpose was to root out the dissidents responsible for random acts of sabotage that occurred in the years following independence. Its methods were brutal and were aimed at the civilian population that supported Mugabe's rival Joshua Nkomo, as well as at disaffected former fighters. Massacres occurred, the full extent of which may never be known. Estimates of murders committed by the Fifth Brigade range between 8 000 and 20 000. Little about the deaths or the cruel beatings and widespread destruction of homesteads was reported by the local or the foreign media. A Catholic dossier containing damning evidence of Fifth Brigade atrocities was scathingly refuted by Mugabe, despite his uncompromising attitude towards counter-insurgency. 'We have to deal with this problem quite ruthlessly,' he told a rural audience in Matabeleland in 1983. 'Don't cry if your relatives get killed in the process.'

Four

Comrades in arms

Surprisingly few people had a positive influence on Robert Mugabe in his early years. Some promoted him to the hilt, but for their own needs rather than for his benefit. Bona was unable to help the ordinary little boy as he struggled to find his way because she could only relate to the special child God had supposedly chosen for greatness. Even the kindly Father O'Hea viewed clever little Robert as a school trophy. Later on, Sally saw him as a way of realising her own political ambitions by proxy. Nobody loved him for who he was.

Once he became involved in politics, Mugabe's colleagues ranged from thoughtful revolutionaries to outright thugs. The man who had the most influence on him before he became premier of Zimbabwe is a vivid character called Edgar Tekere, a co-founder with Mugabe of Zanu. Tekere's face is deeply lined with determination, his mouth set in a semi-sneer. He walks surprisingly quickly for a person aged 69, recounting how he earned the nickname 'Two Boy' on the soccer field at school because he played so hard that he was considered more like two members of the team than one.

Tekere's mother, a teacher and high-ranking princess of the Makoni people of eastern Zimbabwe, was a descendant of the famous Chief Chingaira who took part in the 1896 rebellion or so-called First Chimurenga against British colonialists. She actively encouraged her son to fight against whites: on one occasion, when told by police during a raid on the home she shared with Edgar that he had shot dead a white farmer, she fell to her knees, kissing Tekere's feet in thanks for the death of a settler. Bizarrely, she and her relatives believed that Chief Chingaira's head was severed in battle and taken back to England as a trophy. Tekere tells me that he travelled to the UK a few years ago with a view to retrieving his great-grandfather's head but failed to locate it in the museums he visited.

Having long ago been sidelined by Mugabe, Tekere has nothing good to say about Zimbabwe's leader. However, he was Mugabe's biggest supporter in the run-up to the election that brought Zanu to power in 1980. While in Mozambique during the war years that preceded independence, Tekere was devoted to Mugabe. 'Then, as now, I loved Mugabe,' he told a reporter, referring to their escape together across the border from Rhodesia into Mozambique in 1975. 'I owed so much to him. He had taught me so much; he had made me study during the years in detention.'

The two formed a bond while imprisoned in Rhodesia with Enos Nkala and Maurice Nyagumbo, a foursome that became known as Super-Zanu after deposing their original Zanu leader Ndabaningi Sithole in prison. Tekere remembers the plot to overthrow Sithole, a seminal event in Mugabe's political career, as a victory for himself but an ignominious defeat for Mugabe:

> Whenever we got the chance, we used to talk quietly in prison among ourselves – Nyagumbo, Nkala, Mugabe and me – about getting rid of Sithole because, after being arrested for plotting to assassinate Ian Smith, he had told the Rhodesians he was willing to abandon the armed struggle. At that exact time, we were setting up our war council in exile, so Sithole had clearly betrayed us. Then, to our surprise, it became clear that Mugabe didn't want anything to do with our plan. He said it was wrong to depose our leader and he wouldn't go along with us. He was quite firm about that. So then, instead of four in favour of Sithole going and two against, it was three in favour of the motion – Tekere, Nyagumbo and Nkala – and three against – Mugabe, Sithole and Moton Malianga. Thereafter, the three of us conspired without Mugabe.

The plotting trio reasoned that Sithole would obviously be voting against his own dismissal while Malianga could be appointed chairman, thereby freezing him because he would not have a vote in that capacity, Tekere explains.

Then Nyagumbo was sent to Mugabe's cell to tell him, 'All right, okay, here's the picture: Tekere, Nkala and Nyagumbo are for the motion; one is against and one is neutralised. That leaves you, Mugabe. If you vote with Sithole against the motion, we three are going to carry it anyhow. Once that happens, you'll know that you are at political war with us. Do you want that? We will throw you in the same dustbin we are now throwing Sithole.' That's how we negotiated with Mugabe to abstain. It was blackmail, sure. We accused Sithole as the commander-in-chief of Zanu's newly formed military wing Zanla (Zimbabwe African National Liberation Army) of treason and, when the vote came, Mugabe abstained.

He sat silently throughout the meeting when we deposed Sithole. His abstention was total. This was the occasion when we appointed him to head the party because the next in line to Sithole had recently died in prison. Mugabe was our secretary general, the third in seniority, so he was naturally invited to head the party in the circumstances, though not to be its leader as such. I tell you this to show that there were absolutely no attempts on Mugabe's part to wrest the leadership from Sithole, as is often claimed. Indeed, he actively resisted the sacking of Sithole, just as earlier on in 1962 he had not wanted Nkomo to be deposed as leader of Zapu when we decided to get rid of him for lying to his colleagues.

Tekere sees Mugabe's attempt to stand up for what he believed as a lack of leadership resolve, whereas allowing himself to be bullied into condoning Sithole's dismissal was actually the beginning of Mugabe's moral decline. It showed how easily compromised he was. Having initially resisted the move because he did not believe it was right, Mugabe capitulated under thuggish pressure. He sat on the fence and chose survival rather than continuing to stand up for his principles. What the episode suggests is that Mugabe may well have entered the political arena as an ethical man wanting to make things right for his country, just as he had earlier wanted to make things right for his mother, but when faced with self-preservation, he was vulnerable to corruption.

Having fallen in with a bad crowd in Zanu, Mugabe was surrounded by self-involved bullies like Tekere who, with Enos Nkala and Maurice Nyagumbo, had been at the forefront of Zimbabwean nationalism's violent history. Their turf wars had begun way back in the early 60s, shortly after Mugabe joined them, with pitched battles against Zapu at a time when Nkomo's party was still the most popular of the two and in firm control of the country's main towns. No doubt Nkomo's lieutenants were equally eager to hurl petrol bombs and engage in the bloody attacks that have always been Zimbabwe's preferred method of resolving political dissent. But far from viewing the period as destructive in retrospect, Tekere tells me he is proud of having helped to orchestrate Zanu's early internecine fighting.

By the time Herbert Chitepo, the head of Zanu's exiled war council, was assassinated in Zambia in 1975 in mysterious circumstances that shook Zimbabwe's fractured nationalism and marked another decisive moment in Mugabe's rise to power, Zanu's leadership was in turmoil. Tekere insists that those responsible for the killing were Chitepo's colleagues in Lusaka, not the Rhodesian security forces as was widely believed, although he agrees that Ian Smith's forces may have been involved. At any rate, Zambian president Kenneth Kaunda, also suspecting Zanu, ordered an inquiry into the murder and subsequently arrested the party's military commander Josiah Tongogara and a number of key political office bearers.

The imprisonment of Zanu's hierarchy in Zambia meant there was no one left to coordinate the war effort, Tekere explains. As a result, barely a fortnight after Chitepo's murder, he and Mugabe were selected to fill the vacuum immediately after they were released from detention in Rhodesia on the understanding that they would work towards a negotiated settlement with a new party called the United African National Congress (UANC) led by Bishop Abel Muzorewa, a stooge of the white government.

I was told by the central committee in Salisbury that I was one of the people chosen to go across the border to help salvage the situation. Being one of Zanu's youth leaders and keen to go to war, I was eager to get to Mozambique, where we had decided to relocate the war effort because Kaunda did not want Zanu or its military wing operating from Zambia any more.

Several others were approached ahead of me to go across the border but they declined because of the violence in our ranks: they felt the mission was a death warrant. The party was very controversial at the time. We had sacked our leader Sithole and the charismatic alternative leader Chitepo had been murdered. There had been other internal killings too.

So we needed a good political and diplomatic spokesman for the party, who would obviously have to be very senior in the leadership. The central committee of Zanu chose Mugabe for the job, which he did not hesitate to accept.

We were told to be at the Kambazuma service station in one of Salisbury's townships at 6pm in the evening. I was driven there by my girlfriend. When we arrived we spotted a parked Peugeot 404. The driver ushered me into the back seat. I watched as a figure climbed over a security fence nearby, dropped to the ground and walked towards us. It was Robert Mugabe. He sat down beside me and the car, driven by a party loyalist, immediately moved off.

Edgar Tekere, the son of an Anglican priest, speaks elegant English and exhibits no signs of his drunken history. The description of his escape to Mozambique with Mugabe is long and detailed. Interesting because it contradicts in almost every respect other supposedly authoritative accounts of the same journey as related by several well-respected authors, it is a reminder that much of what is accepted as fact in Zimbabwe's history may actually be fiction.

Mugabe and Tekere were driven to Rusape in the eastern highlands, making their way slowly along back roads. All they discussed on the journey was how well organised it had been, Tekere recalls. When they arrived at a farm called Nyafaro, they were handed over to Chief Rekayi Tangwena, a local leader who had noticed unusual security force activity along the main roads. When Tangwena climbed up a hill to scan the area, he confirmed the Rhodesian army's presence and quickly escorted Mugabe and Tekere into thick bush behind his house, where his wife, a traditional healer, was waiting for them in a hideout.

Mbuya Tangwena lit a fire. The helpful mist descended and hid the smoke. She cooked for us. It was drizzling but not too wet. We slept on the grass for a while and then she said prayers, asking us to join in. Suddenly, the spirit of Rekayi's late father came to her. She got agitated and then calm, agitated again and quiet again. Rekayi came and talked to her for a long time before disappearing again.

That night, Mbuya Tangwena began to speak in somebody else's voice. The things she was talking about with her late father-in-law were clearly out of this world. She said to her husband as soon as he arrived, 'You must take these people now, take them now. Go now.' She insisted we must walk throughout the night. There were a number of routes to Mozambique and he asked her which way we must go. She then described the route exactly. He argued that it was the most difficult of various paths but she got very agitated and warned him of dire consequences if he disobeyed. 'These people are the property of the country,' she told him, 'and if they fall into enemy hands it will be a serious crime for you to commit, Rekayi.'

Tangwena asked his wife for some snuff to ward off inauspicious spirits, recalls Tekere. Then he told Mugabe and Tekere to follow him through the bush on the last leg of their journey into Mozambique.

Tekere goes on to describe the six hours he and Mugabe spent walking in single file behind Rekayi Tangwena, who was smoking a pipe. 'You could only feel the path with your feet on the trampled grass,' he remembers. 'Mugabe was behind Rekayi and in front of me. On either side, the grass was very tall after the rainy season. Suddenly, alongside me, close enough for me to touch if I stretched out my hand, came a growl.' He imitates the deep sound, his face contorted with the effort, and goes on to describe at length how Rekayi heard it, but significantly, Mugabe did not.

Tangwena indicated that the lion's presence alongside them was protection provided by the *mhondoro*, Tekere says. This is a reference to Zimbabwe's spirits of royal lineage who are believed to be the real owners of the country's land. Literally meaning lion, *mhondoro* refers to the belief that a deceased chief's spirit makes its way into the body of the king of beasts while the late royal ancestor is living in the bush for a period immediately following death. Tekere's purpose in relating the anecdote to me is clear: he wants to point out that Robert Mugabe did not hear the lion roaring because he did not enjoy the patronage of royal ancestors, unlike Tekere, whose mother was a princess, and especially Tangwena, a chief. The implication is that Mugabe would not have been viewed as a legitimate liberator – in a country where many believe past and present to be mediated by the ancestral spirit world of the living dead – if Tekere and Tangwena had not established a dialogue with these supernatural forces in order to win popular support for their cause.

The story is intended as a devastating put-down of Mugabe's

personal liberation history. Any Westerner wondering at this juncture how much Mugabe's lack of validity among the royal ancestors matters in Zimbabwean politics today might try to grasp an indisputable truth that even the most cursory investigation among Zimbabweans will confirm: it matters. When the accusation was first stated publicly by Tekere a few weeks after our interview in the autobiography he published in January 2007, it made the country's ageing president furious. Calling for Tekere's immediate expulsion from the party, Mugabe said he regarded these and other debunking claims in Tekere's book as part of a plot to unseat him.

However, the *mhondoro* was not the most significant revelation to dawn on Edgar Tekere as they crossed into Mozambique. He says it was his quarrel with Mugabe towards the end of their hazardous journey that shook him to the core.

The confrontation occurred soon after they had entered Mozambique:

> We were both completely naked, bathing in a flowing stream on the other side, nice and cool and very relieved to be safely over the border. I said to Mugabe, 'We are going into the camps among the recruits now, Robert, what gospel are we going to preach to them?' I was already quite clear about this in my own mind but I wanted to make sure that Mugabe, as our chief spokesman, had got the picture straight. He considered carefully and then replied, 'The UANC is our gospel', meaning Bishop Muzorewa's unity movement. It made me very, very angry. I yelled at him, 'What the hell are you talking about? Are you unaware that it was exclusively Zanu who sent us here?' I was ready to hit him and Rekayi had to intervene to calm me down. I wanted to cross straight back home and tell the central committee that they had picked the wrong man for the job.

This anecdote, also included in Tekere's book, is acutely damaging to Robert Mugabe's struggle credentials, if the Zimbabwe premier's furious reaction to it is any indicator. Mugabe feels his reputation as an uncompromising warrior is being challenged. For Tekere's part, as the spurned politician hell-bent on revenge, the purpose of the story is also to augment his own tarnished reputation. What it indicates about Mugabe is his political naivety. Without much political experience apart from his years in prison, but with an intellectual image at a time when Zanu needed a respectable front man, Mugabe had been chosen to represent a ruthless organisation whose aims and motives he did not really understand.

It is hard to imagine what it must have been like for Mugabe – a shy, thin-skinned teacher and scholar all his life, including the years spent in prison – to put himself into the hands of faceless people who are going to pick him up at a garage, walk him into the bush in the middle of the night, judge him unfavourably for not noticing a lion that may or may not have been lurking inches away, and scorn him for failing to realise that his organisation would automatically renege on the prisoner-release deal he had signed.

Tekere's account of what must have been a terrifying journey is impossibly idealised and magical. Presumably, had they been eaten by the lion, it would not have been a *mhondoro* representing the ancestors, after all. There is no sense in his ramblings of a bigger picture; no apparent enquiry in Tekere's mind about what they were actually trying to achieve. His repertoire involves scorning people who do not agree with him and bullying his way forward. He trots out words like democracy and phrases like 'freedom to the people' without any apparent understanding of what they mean.

Listening to Tekere, you do not feel you are engaging with a live mind. It seems all too concrete, linear and empty. You have to walk the entire route through the bush with him, plodding along one step at a time. It is hard to imagine sharp-witted Mugabe having anything at all in common with Tekere, assuming Zimbabwe's president is as intellectual a person as his seven academic degrees suggest.

However, an intellectual veneer does not necessarily imply a thinking mind. Book knowledge has to be linked to life and living to become creative: it needs to come from the heart if it is to be integrated within lived reality. Although children from the most deprived backgrounds can be successful adults in every respect, they need to be positively parented. It is parents who help children to understand the real world, without which emotional support the child can be clever but lack the ability to think about another person's interests in addition to its own. Well-rounded individuals learn from relationships as well as books. Had Mugabe been able to integrate his knowledge from the heart, he might not have needed to commit gross human rights abuses in later years.

Tekere goes on to ridicule Mugabe's military pretensions.

I was the Zanu politician who went among the guerrillas once we got to Mozambique, not Mugabe. Once in a while, I'd bring him into the camps and he would sit around talking about the political guidelines. Many years later, I said to him: 'Don't you boast about having been to war, Robert. You want to personalise the war but remember, we went together to that war. When we returned, you had not learnt how to fire even a pistol or how to salute back when a junior acknowledged you. You had not even learnt to put on a military uniform.'

Mugabe wore a suit whenever he went into the camps, according to Tekere. Although Tongogara thought this ridiculous and tried to put him into military uniform, Mugabe dressed in fatigues only once or twice, Tekere says.

Mugabe is a very strange man in a number of ways but mainly for his detachment. You would think he would have wanted to wear an army uniform to be part of the guerrillas, but he didn't. I never understood that. In a similar sense, he was never part of the various political campaigns that carried him to the top. Even in 1963 at our first Zanu congress in Gwelo there was quite a strong lobby to elect Mugabe president. A lot of people were impressed by his scholarly eloquence. It was Ndabaningi Sithole who got the job though, because he, unlike Mugabe, was so busy holding meetings with district leaders that he barely slept. Mugabe, on the other hand, had quite a campaign team that organised itself around him but he barely participated. He didn't campaign for himself. He appeared almost disinterested. It was as if the campaigners supporting Mugabe were pushing a donkey to go and drink.

At no stage do you find him doing anything to promote himself to a position of leadership. It's very strange. Even in Mozambique and at Lancaster House he seemed to be almost unambitious. He has this terrible early record, frustrating our attempts to remove Nkomo, then hampering our attempts to get rid of Sithole. He was the obstacle in both of these major events that moved him closer to power, not the activist. I never understood it. Maybe it was something in his nature, just the way he was. People who knew him as a young boy say he was always a loner and I think it must have something to do with that.

I ask Tekere if he thinks Mugabe's apparent indifference to climbing the power ladder might have been a ruse to win confidence in Zanu. 'Ah no,' he replies firmly. 'Nobody can be that crafty. It was too long ago for him to begin such a strategy in 1962, when we broke away from Nkomo without his help.' However, Mugabe's apparent modesty did earn him a legacy of trust within the nest of vipers, which played no small part in propelling him upward over the following 20 years, says Tekere. In his opinion, Mugabe was indeed the man he purported to be in those early days: a provincial schoolmaster who desired justice for all and was prepared to play a role in achieving it, but not at the expense of the colleagues he admired. It seems that Mugabe was a man of personal integrity in those days, however much Tekere scowls at the summation.

> What first spoilt Mugabe was the team in Zambia who had been working with Herbert Chitepo. They came through to Mozambique and joined up with us after Kaunda rejected them. That's when bad things started happening. You had characters like Henry Hamadzaripi, who was very ambitious, among the external leaders who had been based in Zambia. Once they joined the internal leaders, there was suddenly intense jostling for position within Zanu in Mozambique, which led to insurrection during one of the doomed British settlement initiatives.

'I want to single out one man in particular who spoilt Mugabe – Rugare Gumbo – who is still in the government. He had been in charge of publicity in the Chitepo-led external group before Mugabe left Rhodesia. He was a very effective propagandist, an ideologue. He began by preaching Marxism. Mugabe liked the sound of this ideology and before long, he had completely fallen for it and begun to sing the Marxism/Leninism song. But that's all it was – rhetoric. There was no genuine vision or belief behind it,' Tekere maintains.

> In Mozambique, Rugare Gumbo was our publicity spokesman. He became particularly fond of democratic centralism. He preached it a lot and it got into the head of Mugabe. Put simply, it was the idea that numerous as the people are and as welcome as they are to express their views, what matters finally is only the view of the leader. It's a recipe for dictatorship. During the Geneva conference, I clashed badly with Gumbo. I remember

chasing him out of the room on one occasion, saying, 'Get out from under Mugabe's feet!' I couldn't tolerate him telling Mugabe to say this and say that about democratic centralism. 'Don't let him dance around you like a fly around faeces,' I said to Mugabe, telling him to think on his own for a change.

Gumbo's philosophy would have fed Mugabe's subconscious belief that he was special, someone apart from ordinary people. But why, given Mugabe's intellect, would he mindlessly adopt the ideas of those around him? That doesn't make sense, I suggest to Tekere. Surely such a clever man made up his own mind? Tekere replies without hesitation:

> Mugabe himself did not feel strongly about anything. He was strangely indifferent – that was the problem. He was just being swept along at that time.
>
> The problem was that Gumbo – and later many, many others – kept telling Mugabe, 'You are the leader: what you say is final.' It was seductive and Mugabe got used to it. He became corrupted by it. At the same time, Mozambique's President Samora Machel was continually preaching central control. And the whole of Africa under its earlier chieftain system of governance was used to the idea of centralised control anyway. I remember Mugabe telling me just before we went back home after Lancaster House that Machel had urged him to keep tight centralised control over the whole country once he was in power. These were the bad influences on Mugabe at that crucial time.
>
> Men like Simon Muzenda, who became Mugabe's deputy in government, would stand up quite unashamedly and state during a debate: 'Why are we still talking about this? The president has stated his opinion; the president has spoken. What is there to discuss any more?' Or they'd turn to Mugabe and say, 'What does the president believe?' They pandered to Mugabe's vanity, even though he still enjoyed debate in those days and was prepared to listen to others. He didn't expect his word to be final in the beginning. But he grew to like the idea. It was the start of the Mugabe personality cult.

Once Mugabe became premier of the country he began to identify his supporters and reward their loyalty, says Tekere. 'He knew how to parcel out favours to those who supported him uncritically. Quietly, he gave to some and withheld from others, rewarding the bootlickers all the time, manipulating everybody around him. And soon that became the prevailing culture of Mugabe's court.'

One of the consequences of Robert Mugabe having grown up in a dysfunctional family is his fragile self-image. He absorbed his information about political concepts like Marxism from dogmatic advisers and books, not from humanity and human relations. His own mother dealt exclusively in abstractions – her idea of the man Robert would become had nothing at all to do with him as a person. If he was as easily influenced by others as Tekere suggests, it was because a frail sense of self made him so vulnerable that he listened to anybody who acted like a parent and seemed to offer valuable guidance.

Tekere points out that he began pouring cold water on the idea of centralised control as early as 1980. He says he was also virtually alone among Zanu stalwarts in decrying corruption as early as the following year. Nevertheless, I remember Tekere being asked at a press conference shortly after Zanu assumed power in Zimbabwe why a socialist fresh from the liberation struggle was driving an expensive blue Jaguar. Tekere's straight-faced answer was that the new government had so many social ills to address that it needed to move around fast. I remember, too, that it was Tekere who denounced the reconciliation speech for which Mugabe was hailed throughout the world following his 1980 election victory.

Tekere has his own interpretation of the post-independence period. 'As soon as we were elected, I realised, "This man Mugabe, oh no ..."' It soon became clear that Mugabe's biggest fault was his inability to tolerate criticism, he says. 'Mugabe was the one who caused me to say, right from the beginning of Zanu's rule, "criticism nourishes leadership". I used to say that a lot because it reflected the increasingly obvious fact that Mugabe did not like advice or criticism. It was my response to his intolerance of the views of others once he was in office. He still listened because it gave him time to think, but he didn't hear or learn any more.'

He is a very insecure man so he needs to be surrounded by admirers. It makes him feel stronger and more assured. James Chikerema, who grew up with him, used to say he was a very lonely, isolated child and that's how he has remained lifelong. When you criticise or threaten him, he gets rid of you. The threesome of what was called Super-Zanu – myself, Maurice Nyagumbo and Enos Nkala – who should have been Mugabe's lifelong friends because we went through detention together and we deposed Sithole together, were nothing but a threat to him. We had to go.

Robert Mugabe is a man without ethics. He is entirely expedient. What made him so uncomfortable about me is that as secretary general of Zanu, I saw it as my duty to remind and rebuke when necessary those who were betraying the party's principles. I saw myself as the custodian of Zanu's integrity. So when I spoke against the worm of corruption, saying way back in 1981 that we'd better do something about it, he abolished the post of secretary general to shut me up. He never forgave me for continually pointing out to people who said our high-minded Roman Catholic prime minister was not personally guilty of corruption that Mugabe was in fact the leader surrounded by plunderers, so how should we define him? Was he not the *chef* (a Portuguese word meaning chief) of the thieves, the principal thief surrounded by thieves?

With his poor childhood development record, even minor criticism would be experienced as a wound by Mugabe. He is a person who cannot tolerate difference. Being profoundly doubtful about himself, he is oversensitive to the idea that he is not as good as everyone else. People are either with him or against him. Differences of opinion are provocative and hurtful to Mugabe, who may think that compromise reduces him. The closer a compromise comes to his emotional self, the more he resists it.

Describing him as aloof and haughty, Tekere claims that Zimbabwe's president has never made any friends. He says Mugabe's sister Sabina once told him that had her brother died, 'we would have been unable to call out anybody as friends' at his funeral. Tekere, ever the self-promoter, then lists his own numerous friendships and the lengths to which people have gone to help him in troubled times. Among them, he says, is Victoria, the widow of Herbert Chitepo, a senior member of Zanu's Women's League at the time she bared her bottom to colleagues in protest at Tekere's expulsion from a party post in 1983.

He leans back in his chair, panting slightly after the tirade. Suddenly remembering other examples of Mugabe's dishonour, his eyes light up and his voice rises:

The man who made the arrangements in Ghana for Mugabe's little son's burial in 1966, who represented Mugabe at the funeral of his only child while the father was in prison, died in Harare about three years ago. Because he was not a supporter of Mugabe, not a word of sympathy came to his family from the president. That's the kind of man Mugabe is.

He goes on indignantly:

When the invasions of white-owned farms began on a large scale in 2000, Mugabe was presented with a political fait accompli. Others had organised it, not him. He tried at first to find out what was going on but he was asked bluntly which side he was on: the war veterans or the white farmers? So he blessed it instead of stopping it because he would otherwise have found himself at war with the guerrilla veterans and whoever was organising them. Subsequently, he pretended that it had all been his idea, which was not true. That's the kind of man Mugabe is.

The kind of man Tekere is, meanwhile, had been made clear to me shortly before I visited the rundown eastern city of Mutare to interview him. Quite by chance in Harare, I met the brother of a white farmer murdered in 1980 by Tekere and a group of former guerrillas. The killing happened shortly after independence when Christopher Johnson was setting a plough on his Goromonzi farm Bellview. Gunned down for no apparent reason at lunchtime while his wife was talking on the phone to her brother-in-law, Dave Johnson told me: 'She suddenly heard a noise in the lands and said, "I'd better go and see what's going on." Not far from the house, she found Chris lying dead beside his plough.'

The case was never solved or adequately prosecuted, explains Johnson, one of Zimbabwe's most successful farmers at the time. His brother's murder occurred a few months after Tekere and seven of what he called his 'security companions' had killed another white farmer named Adams on apparently spurious grounds. Charged with murder on that occasion, they were acquitted through an amnesty loophole.

When I go back to Tekere's shabby home in a Mutare suburb for our second interview, he recalls the Adams case, admits his guilt and remembers indignantly that Zimbabwe's recently elected premier had sent a representative to court to monitor the proceedings:

Mugabe requested briefings from our defence team and promised them that if we pleaded guilty and were convicted, he would immediately pardon me. I refused angrily when this was put to me by the lawyers, saying I did not want to owe my life and soul to Mugabe. No! 'We do not plead guilty,' I said. 'We plod on.'

He offers this anecdote both as an example of how lawless Mugabe was from the beginning of his premiership and how vigilant, by contrast, Tekere was in defeating corruption. Both assertions may be true but Tekere's ready recourse to violence after independence, when the war was quite clearly over, is so indelibly imprinted on his CV that it makes him an unlikely candidate to spearhead a moral campaign against Mugabe.

Although Tekere remained secretary general of the party even after the Adams case, he notes bitterly that his name was missing from the honours list announced by Mugabe's office at the end of 1980. He ascribes this slight to Mugabe's fear of him and his powerful influence within Zanu rather than to his own murderous behaviour. It is one of many examples of Tekere's equivocal code of ethics, a widespread malaise that is as evident in Zimbabwe in 2007 as it was in the former Rhodesia. Throughout my interview with him, and while reading his book, I have the impression that Tekere cannot distinguish right from wrong because his entire moral code is based on his own political aspirations. To have been sidelined by Mugabe, albeit for murder, is a reproach he considers both unjustifiable and unforgivable.

Suddenly, into Tekere's office leaps a man with glistening black hair that looks like a cheap wig. His eyes are ablaze and he is shouting incoherently. My tape recorder on the desk is the conspicuous tool of a trade virtually banned in Zimbabwe and I reach out to switch it off. My heart is racing as he glowers at me. 'Have you got permission?' he demands repeatedly, while addressing Tekere in Shona, a language I do not understand.

Tekere laughs heartily as the man lunges towards him and the two clasp hands. I am half expecting scary retributive measures for being caught asking political questions without a permit, but the intruder lingers only long enough to discuss something earnestly with Tekere before swinging around theatrically, hovering on his heels as if auditioning for a circus act, and marching out. Seeing that I am looking nonplussed, Tekere chuckles sympathetically and explains, 'He is one of our former guerrillas, who is now an army officer.'

Was he pretending to be hostile towards me?

Tekere shrugs. 'I know him very well,' he replies enigmatically.

As a result of this disconcerting encounter, and having seen a green military vehicle parked in Tekere's driveway on my way out, I decide not to return to Tekere's house as arranged the following day. I have already recorded two lengthy interviews with him and, needing little more, I phone his home. Waiting for Tekere to answer, I look around my threadbare room at the once-stylish Mutare Club, where the membership remains almost exclusively white and where a strict dress code is taped crookedly to the wall despite the place's pathetically depleted condition. I wonder what it must have been like for Robert Mugabe, circa 1975, to have been mentored by such an uncompromising man at a time when he was, according to Tekere, unequal to the task of leading a radical political group. What lessons would Mugabe have taken from that experience?

Freud described a mob-like group such as Zanu as 'impulsive, changeable and irritable ... Though it may desire things passionately, yet this is never so for long, for it is incapable of perseverance. It cannot tolerate any delay between its desire and the fulfilment of what it desires. It has a sense of omnipotence; the notion of impossibility disappears for the individual in a group ... a group knows neither doubt nor uncertainty.

'(These) groups have never thirsted after truth,' Freud goes on. 'They demand illusions, and cannot do without them. They constantly give what is unreal precedence over what is real; they are almost as strongly influenced by what is untrue as by what is true. They have an evident tendency not to distinguish between the two.' Anyone aspiring to lead such a group must sustain and embody the group's belief in its own omnipotence. 'If a leader bows to this iron rule, the group will follow him anywhere. As soon as he ceases to do so, he is liquidated as a leader, and replaced with someone more suitable.'

When Tekere eventually answers the phone, I hear him yawning as I ask without much preamble if, as is widely believed, Robert Mugabe arranged for Zanu's military leader Josiah Tongogara to be murdered on Christmas Eve in 1979.

'I believe Tongogara's death was a straightforward car accident, although I wasn't there,' he replies. 'I do not believe in the theory of a plot by Mugabe to kill Tongogara, although I'm sure Mugabe was jealous of Tongogara's popularity. I strongly believe that if my friend Tongogara had been assassinated, he would have come to me in my sleep and said, "*Chef*, I was killed."'

One has only to study the police reports of the accident to know that it could not have been plotted, Tekere explains. 'Tongogara and his friends, travelling in the dark, rammed into a stationary truck with a steel back. Tongogara, in the front passenger seat, was killed; the others survived. They had been rushing to the guerrilla camps in Mozambique to brief the fighters on the outcome of the Lancaster House talks. There was an urgent need for our most senior army commander to tell the troops that they were to surrender their weapons and proceed to British-monitored assembly points inside Rhodesia. It was a sensitive matter which Tongogara wanted to address personally. Unless this order came from Tongogara himself, there was likely to be a mutiny as our troops had made many military advances around that time and firmly believed they were winning the war. This is why he was in such a hurry to reach the camps before the guerrillas heard the news from any other source.'

Tekere explains that he travelled to Maputo immediately after the accident to examine Tongogara's remains. He and Sydney Sekeramayi, who is one of Mugabe's longest-serving ministers, saw the corpse in the morgue:

> His body was horribly damaged, almost split in half, and I asked Sekeramayi, a medical doctor, what we should do. He said that he knew some plastic surgeons in South Africa who would be able to make it look presentable for the hero's burial that Tongogara deserved. We flew in a team of specialists who restored him well enough to be viewed in a sealed casket.

Perhaps it was the unusual recourse to cosmetic surgery which ignited the rumours that grew into startling allegations of foul play. You meet people all over Zimbabwe who claim to know somebody who received an anonymous tip-off via an undertaker that Tongogara's body was riddled with bullets. Or perhaps it is the ruling party's appalling record of rivalry and assassination that provokes such suspicion, acute mistrust having been the dominant feature of Zimbabwe's political history.

What Edgar Tekere's account of Mugabe's early career highlights is the ruthlessness to which he was expected to conform by many of his political colleagues and mentors.

Five

A surprise agreement

Just when Robert Mugabe's party was confident of a military victory in Rhodesia, the war was suddenly forestalled by a new initiative that envisaged independence via the ballot rather than the bullet. The unconventional diplomacy that took place in London in 1979 at Lancaster House, the venue of the all-party conference called to solve 'the Rhodesia problem', was both manipulative and bullying, but it achieved its purpose. Described in unprintable terms by Robert Mugabe, it was conducted by British foreign secretary Peter Alexander Rupert, the 6th Baron Carrington of Bulcot Lodge, privy counsellor and holder of the Military Cross – a formidable figure. Even in 2005, as an elderly though active public speaker, the urbane Carrington is a striking man. His face is lined with deep vertical cracks that look more granite than human, and he has a reputation for clear, courageous analysis seasoned with a wit that was capable of swinging even hard-headed Margaret Thatcher round to his way of thinking.

It was Lord Carrington's distinctive style that produced consensus between Ian Smith's government under the leadership of his black puppet Bishop Abel Muzorewa and the Patriotic Front, formed for the purpose of negotiation and led jointly by Robert Mugabe and Joshua Nkomo. Hailed as a diplomatic miracle, the Lancaster House agreement was signed a few days before Christmas in 1979. It ended not only an African civil war but the long-running British constitutional crisis that Mrs Thatcher, who had come to power in May of the same year, wanted solved.

Carrington lives in an elegant pied-à-terre behind Harrods in London, where I am invited for coffee one morning in October 2005. I tell him I am hoping to construct a portrait of Robert Mugabe the man because the prevailing image of him as a monster is not helpful in understanding the decline and fall of Zimbabwe. The view of Mugabe as a madman implies that as an aberration what happened to him in his leadership role will not occur again. In truth though, there have been a number of similarly erratic leaders in post-colonial Africa. If there is no discussion, we do not learn anything from the Mugabe story, I suggest. Aren't we more likely to learn from the catastrophe if we try to understand Mugabe reacting, and indeed overreacting, to his experiences, rather than simply viewing him as a villain hell-bent on destruction?

Carrington nods enthusiastically while attending to his wife, who has her leg in plaster after a fall. She listens keenly to our conversation as she sits in the drawing room waiting for a taxi to take her shopping. Dark-eyed and handsome, she wants me to know that Mugabe's first wife Sally was a charming woman. 'Yes, a very good eggette,' Lord Carrington adds, as he makes sure that his wife is comfortable and then takes the seat opposite me. 'Mugabe's new wife is a thoroughly bad influence on him,' he confirms. Shouting at the dog yapping at his feet, he adjusts his jacket and sits up straight. 'Off you go then,' he commands, ever the ringmaster.

We discuss Carrington's illustrious political career, beginning as a junior minister under Winston Churchill. He explains that he often travelled to Rhodesia and South Africa as a director of various mining companies during his years as a backbencher in the 70s. He made a point of meeting leading nationalists, including Joshua Nkomo and Ndabaningi Sithole, but he never met Mugabe.

He had no interest in meeting capitalists like me, I suppose. The first time I ever met him, although I knew all about him – that he was the Marxist and so on – was when he came to Lancaster House. I gave him dinner.

   I knew that he'd been treated very badly by Ian Smith; locked up for 11 years and not even allowed out to attend his child's funeral, and so on. I said to him, 'Are you bitter?' And he said, 'I'm not bitter about people. I am bitter about the system.' And I thought that was a very interesting remark. He appeared to be quite genuine and open about it.

Carrington's initially favourable impression of Mugabe was short-lived. It soon became clear to him that the tension and distrust exhibited at Lancaster House were dauntingly obstructive, particularly from Mugabe. 'I didn't think there was a hope of getting an agreement because you can never get agreement on complicated issues like that – Palestine in the Middle East is a perfect case – unless everybody wants one,' he explains.

> At that moment, everybody did want one for their own reasons, and they all thought they were going to get their own way – except Mugabe.
>
> The South Africans were fed up spending so much money to prop up Smith, and poor old Joshua was getting on and wanted to become the president of Zimbabwe. White Rhodesians were dying and sanctions were at last beginning to bite. So everyone wanted some sort of solution, except Mugabe, who didn't think it was necessary. And he was probably right. There is no doubt that Mugabe would not have signed the Lancaster House agreement if presidents Julius Nyerere of Tanzania and Samora Machel of Mozambique hadn't prompted him to. He knew he was going to win militarily anyway, so what was the point of it? But once the conference was launched, it was quite difficult even for him to walk out because he was being pressed by Nyerere and Machel, whose countries were both suffering as a result of the war.

The sides involved in the conflict – the former Rhodesian government and the nationalists – were diametrically opposed to each other, which convinced the British that the only way forward was to dictate the agreement. Having personally failed in various negotiations as first lord of the Admiralty and as defence secretary, and being acutely aware that the new British premier considered the Rhodesia problem a threat both to Britain's economic relations in sub-Saharan Africa and to Tory party unity, Carrington regarded the elusive Rhodesian settlement as his top priority. He knew from the outgoing Labour foreign secretary that 80 per cent of his staff's work would concern Rhodesia if the matter was not 'lanced' immediately, so he announced on his first morning in the Foreign Office: 'We're going to settle it.'

Although the Conservative manifesto decreed that Britain was prepared to recognise the rebel country provided Rhodesia met certain principles – and indeed many Tories were in favour of immediately endorsing Ian Smith's regime – a sudden warning against leniency towards Rhodesia by the Australian prime minister Malcolm Fraser a few months after Thatcher came to power persuaded Carrington to get a mandate from the Commonwealth in order to strengthen his hand.

So it was that the parties concerned found themselves forced to the conference table at Lancaster House in September 1979. All of them were apprehensive. 'Who gave authority to the Commonwealth to settle the future for us?' demanded Nkomo. Mugabe began to refer to Carrington as 'the good lord'. Neither the Patriotic Front nor the Rhodesian delegation liked Carrington's step-by-step approach, all of them demanding to see the entire deal. But they were obliged to go along with him because self-governing Rhodesia had by then reverted to the status of a British colony.

The Patriotic Front believed the war had been about 'the total liquidation of colonialism in Zimbabwe' but its leaders had conflicting priorities and lacked unity, which played into Carrington's coercive tactics. With Mugabe presenting himself as a committed Marxist and Nkomo trying to remain moderate, Carrington was able to expose their vulnerabilities. On one occasion when Nkomo slammed his fist down on to a coffee table during an informal meeting with Carrington, Zanu's legal adviser Professor Walter Kamba remembers Mugabe having to nudge his outraged ally into shaking Carrington's outstretched hand at the end of the session. The next day they returned to find that the coffee table had been removed because, as Carrington joked, the British government feared it would be smashed to smithereens.

The British foreign secretary's mocking, aggressive style angered all the delegates. Once, when Smith told Carrington that the Lancaster House terms were the worst he had ever been offered, the British peer replied, 'Well, of course they bloody well are! You've turned down everything since the talks on *HMS Tiger* and *Fearless*, and ever since the 1960s.'

In response to Britain's ultimatums, Mugabe remarked that Carrington could 'go to hell'. The *Times* of London claimed that Carrington had all the delegates' rooms bugged so that he would know exactly where to apply pressure. Some in the Patriotic Front contingent believed the British had deliberately housed the black delegates in cheap hotels. Not surprisingly, the players did not trust Thatcher's foreign secretary, who made constant taunting reference to a 'second-class solution' in which Britain would have no choice but to recognise Rhodesia in the event that the Patriotic Front left the negotiations. In the end, though, it was Ian Smith who left the table, saying, 'To me, British diplomacy is a polite word for deceit.'

What Robert Mugabe had in common with Lord Carrington was his sense of superiority. The big difference though, was in the British aristocrat's effortless loftiness as opposed to Mugabe's version, which had been constructed as a shield. Carrington's manner is in the blood, a subtle form of intimidation that leaves outsiders feeling wrong-footed and, to a greater or lesser extent, inferior. He is superior, acts it, believes it and achieves it. Mugabe's constructed variety is a means of protection against the humiliation he feels when dealing with those who habitually belittle or denigrate.

The boy from Kutama who grew up in abject poverty lingers life-long and can be made to feel second rate simply by another's way of being. He gets bitter and uncommunicative when he is made to feel inadequate; when he does not know which knife and fork to use, for example. So he hides behind a mask of grandiosity. Mugabe gives the appearance of disdain because he wants to be acknowledged as superior, perhaps to get as far away as possible from the opposite, inferiority, which he dreads.

No doubt immense pressure of all sorts was brought to bear on Mugabe by Lord Carrington at Lancaster House, seeing everyone else had already been manipulated on to the British side. Mugabe stood alone. A particular source of anxiety to him were the cordial relationships he saw developing between Zanu's army commander Josiah Tongogara and various players at Lancaster House, including even Ian Smith.

Democracy and land were the key issues. Carrington held out the bait of elections in return for the Patriotic Front acceding to the agreement. His aim was to give Mugabe and Nkomo the main concession on the creation of democracy to allow black majority rule in exchange for compromise on land. Mugabe was furious that Smith's puppet Muzorewa would not support him in speaking out for African land claims. He recalled later:

I said, 'But you are Africans, how dare you accept the position on land shall be governed by the Bill of Rights? We can't get anywhere with the Bill of Rights. Don't you remember our history? The land was never bought from us. Support our position on this one!' They said no, they could not. So at one time I said to Lord Carrington, 'Look at them! What are they? Baa baa black sheep, have you any wool!' It took him time to unravel that but finally he got it ... They were black sheep, just saying baa baa to the master!'

After many delays and following assurances that funding for land resettlement would come from America as well as Britain, Mugabe eventually caved in and agreed to Carrington's insistence on guaranteed property rights.

Far from being impartial during the negotiations, Carrington was an obvious manipulator. His strategy was to persuade each of the leading players that he was going to win at the polls. Nkomo compared him with a spider that 'creates a round web and parks itself in the centre. Then it darts out to pick up a fly ... That's what he was doing.' Concerned primarily with ending the Rhodesia problem's domination of British foreign policy, Carrington used all his authority to force the parties into a particular settlement. The carrot of a second-class solution was always dangling in front of the Rhodesian government, while the stick of the frontline states was constantly behind the Patriotic Front. Carrington's use of power was evident not only in his decision to 'keep it in the family' by appointing his personal friend Lord Soames as governor, but also in Soames' subsequent arrival in Rhodesia before the ceasefire had even been agreed upon at Lancaster House.

Mugabe was cold and distant throughout the conference, recalls Carrington:

He didn't take much part in Lancaster House. Some of his people did but he didn't. Even when he was being polite there was a sort of reptilian quality about him. I didn't ever warm to him as I did to Joshua, who was a frightful old rogue but very human. Mugabe wasn't human at all. You couldn't warm to him as a person. You could admire his skills and intellect and so on, but he was an awfully slippery sort of person – reptilian, as I say.

'The little bishop was an absurd figure in his Gucci shoes and belt, although I remember talking to Peter Walls, the Rhodesian general, about him,' says Carrington, referring to Bishop Abel Muzorewa, the moderate African leader on whom white Rhodesians had pinned their hopes. 'I said to Walls, "I don't think I've ever sat in a room with so many thugs and murderers in my life. I suppose the only exception is the Bishop." And Walls exclaimed, "Muzorewa! He's killed more than any of them."'

> If I absolutely had to choose, I would take Mugabe in preference to Smith, though. I couldn't stand Smith. I thought he was a man who saw every tree in the wood but couldn't see the wood. He said to me once in front of everyone at Lancaster House, after I had missed a few sessions or something, that the trouble with the conference was that I was not really taking any trouble because I was continuing to do my job as foreign secretary. 'And while you're ignoring this conference,' he said, 'people are being killed in Rhodesia.' It was the only time I lost my temper. I said, 'Mr Smith, but for you nobody would be being killed.' The day afterwards he left the conference, thank God. He was a really stupid man, Smith; a bigoted, stupid man.

The person Carrington commends for having a good influence on every-body at Lancaster House, particularly the white Rhodesians, is the head of Smith's army at the time, General Peter Walls. 'He wanted a solution. He was a nice man but he got very upset at the end of it all. I don't know why,' muses Carrington. The reason for Walls' disenchantment, according to several sources, was that having cooperated fully with Carrington and taken everything he was told on trust, he subsequently believed that he had been manipulated into supporting Mugabe's electoral victory.

The other man who made a good impression at Lancaster House was Walls' opposite number, Zanu's Che Guevara, the tall, bearded and charismatic Josiah Tongogara. Many expected him to become the president of Zimbabwe, with Mugabe as the prime minister. He was the crucial 'moderating' force in the nationalists' ranks, according to Carrington, one of whose ploys was to play the military men off against the politicians.

The Foreign Office strategy with Walls, a vain man, had been simple and effective: invite him to London, make a fuss of him, 'my dear fellow', get him to steer the Rhodesians towards a settlement and then help the British achieve a ceasefire on the ground. After several intimate chats with Carrington, in which they slapped each others' backs and called one another Peter, Walls met Margaret Thatcher at Downing Street and the Queen Mother at Kensington Palace. When he left London for Salisbury shortly before the Lancaster House talks ended, he was convinced that the British government had given him 'all sorts of assurances' that Mugabe would not come to power. Whether Walls had become confused by Carrington's elliptical way of speaking or had been deliberately duped by the British was never clear.

Carrington says he always knew Mugabe was going to win:

The South Africans and the Rhodesians thought Lancaster House was going to result in a sort of hung election and that Joshua Nkomo would join up with Muzorewa and they would form a front against Mugabe, which if you looked at the figures, was quite clearly rubbish. I must say, I did have quite some misgivings about Mugabe because he had played very little part in the negotiations except to be rather obstructive. So I thought, what with him being a Marxist and one thing and another, he was going to be very difficult indeed in office. But then of course he didn't actually practise what he preached, did he? Once in office, he became a capitalist, didn't he?

I think it didn't turn out badly initially in Zimbabwe because during his exile in Tanzania and Mozambique, Mugabe had seen exactly what had happened to the economies of those two countries as a result of kicking out the whites and generally introducing pan-African socialism or whatever it was called. Being a highly intelligent man, I think he saw that this was going to be quite the wrong thing to do. He didn't want to be the prime minister of a bankrupt country as a result of kicking everybody out.

Referring back to Mugabe's comment about being bitter with the system rather than with people, Carrington says:

He was extremely magnanimous in allowing Smith to go on in Zimbabwe – I wouldn't have, I really wouldn't – and I think that was partly because he didn't want to alienate whites. That attitude lasted for quite a long time, 15 years or so. And then I think what happened is the economy started to go wrong.

Like so many people – not just Africans but people like Galtieri of Argentina, for example – when they are in domestic difficulty, they find some sort of cause behind which to rally their supporters. Mugabe chose to kick out the white farmers. There's no doubt about it, he's been awfully stupid about that and the whole land situation. By giving the land that became available to his cronies, he dried up the contributions from us and the Americans. And then, in more difficulty but in order to stay there, he did more and more things which were totally against the interests of the people of Zimbabwe. This is what happens to all dictators in the end.

I ask Lord Carrington what he thinks Mugabe learnt from the fact that he got away with the massacre of thousands of people in Matabeleland in the early 80s. The mass slaughter known as Gukurahundi was barely noticed, let alone condemned, by the British. Did Mugabe get a sense of his own invincibility from Britain's failure to condemn the outrage convincingly?

'Did we sweep it under the carpet?' asks Carrington incredulously. 'I suspect we did, didn't we? That happened after I stopped being foreign secretary so I didn't have anything to do with it. I don't know how I would have reacted. We've always been rather powerless, haven't we? That was the trouble. I was at that time preoccupied with the Falklands and resigning from my post and one thing and another so I don't have a very clear recollection. I expect we wished it would all go away, didn't we? So I suppose Mugabe did get away with it and perhaps that did make him feel he could get away with anything.'

Carrington's explanation for the failure of Britain and much of the international media to condemn Mugabe's slaughter unequivocally is that everybody wanted Zimbabwe to succeed, not least because apartheid South Africa was next on the world's salvation agenda. 'I think that's probably the answer,' he says.

It's a pathetic answer, isn't it?

'Terrible,' he agrees, laughing. 'I think it's terrible but it's probably the answer. But other than the killing of the Ndebele, it went tolerably well under Mugabe at first, didn't it? He wasn't running a fascist state. He didn't appear to be a bad dictator. But then of course we all wanted him not to be. That's perfectly true. But nevertheless, I don't think he did all that badly in the first 15 years. The judges and the police were not corrupt. But gradually he bought the army and the police with spoils from the Congo; he bought them all, didn't he?'

Carrington visited Mugabe at State House in Harare in his private capacity in 1998. 'I had quite a long chat with him then. Nothing important, just chit-chat. He was not mad at all. People say he's mad but he isn't at all.' Mugabe kept Carrington waiting far too long, according to a member of the British party, but then gave him tea and quipped as he passed a plate of biscuits around that there had been no snacks on offer at Lancaster House. Carrington joked in return that the British could hardly have made biscuits available because Joshua Nkomo, an enormously fat man, would have eaten them out of house and home.

'He treated Joshua very badly, didn't he?' says Carrington, suddenly reminded of the fate Nkomo suffered following his attempts at a coalition with Mugabe. Recalling the defeated Joshua Nkomo sitting with his back to the proceedings during Zimbabwe's independence celebrations in 1980, he says, 'I remember I was talking to the South African author and friend of Prince Charles, Laurens van der Post, who told me that in Ndebele custom, you sit with your back to the ceremonies if you don't agree with them. Nkomo made his feelings quite obvious, which probably wasn't a good idea.

'He's a puzzle, isn't he?' muses Carrington about Mugabe. 'There are some people you disagree with but still respect but I didn't find Mugabe a good man ever. Joshua in a way was, you see. He was the man who started the whole nationalist opposition; a man of some quality. He wasn't an intellectual like Mugabe but he was a human being.'

Carrington's description of Mugabe as a puzzle reflects the contradictory features many people notice in Zimbabwe's president. His initial claim to Carrington that he was not bitter with people but only with the system is typical of his intellectual responses to personal questions. Mugabe was out of touch with the emotional bitterness that was to emerge in his later actions. While becoming Bona's good boy during his childhood, he had learnt to hide his feelings, which is perhaps why Carrington noticed a discrepancy between what Mugabe said he believed and what he really believed. When Carrington describes Mugabe as 'reptilian', he is observing a man cut off from his feelings, devoid of ordinary warmth and humanity.

His assertion that Mugabe is not mad is an acknowledgement that Zimbabwe's president makes sense intellectually. Virtually everything Mugabe says is rooted in fact. However, sanity and maturity involve coming to terms with reality: we cannot have things our own way indefinitely; no one is going to be the king of the castle forever. Mugabe is cut off from the reality of being an ordinary person limited by the humanness that acknowledges his vulnerability and mortality. Once he creates the illusion of being beyond ordinary humanness, elevating himself to a place where he is answerable to no one, he is out of touch, which is a form of madness.

Carrington notes that Mugabe was not widely favoured by the international community before he won the election in 1980. I tell him that Zimbabwean historian Lawrence Vambe, an old school friend of Mugabe's, accuses Western governments, especially Britain, of having hastily constructed an image of Mugabe as a good man simply because they wanted the Rhodesia problem to go away. Carrington shrugs and concedes distractedly, 'That may be right.'

Then he changes course abruptly:

> The other thing that was important was how avuncular Christopher Soames, the British governor, who was very large and solid, sort of put his arm around Mugabe and jollied him along. It was a brilliant performance. If not for Christopher and, I must say, me, the civil servants in Rhodesia were all going to say that the election was not free and fair because there had been intimidation, which of course there had been, but on all sides. They wanted us to declare the election not free and fair, which would have been catastrophic. Christopher said, and I supported him, 'No, we must allow it to go forward.'
>
> Christopher's great achievement was to get Mugabe on side at that time. He did it by appealing to him as a person, as a man; by being his friend. It was a brilliant performance. It was really very good of Christopher; otherwise, it wouldn't have worked.

When it was all over and Lord Carrington was congratulating himself for allowing the most popular candidate to win against his own prime minister's instincts, the ephemeral nature of African democracy suddenly became clearer to him. While attending Zimbabwe's independence celebrations in Harare, Carrington explains, he was given a message by Tanzania's foreign minister.

> Julius Nyerere had earlier told me in London during Lancaster House that his man Robert Mugabe had better win because if he didn't, the frontline

states were not going to accept it. Nyerere's foreign minister had been sent to me after the election to say, 'Julius wants you to know he is pleased that Mugabe won, but why did you let him win by so much?'

In retrospect, considering that Nyerere believed Lord Carrington would manipulate not only agreement between the warring parties at Lancaster House but the election result that followed, and considering that Carrington was under orders from his own prime minister to solve 'the Rhodesia problem' no matter what, Zimbabwe's best interests seem to have been of secondary importance to the settlement sponsors. That Robert Mugabe subsequently developed a warm – and genuine – relationship with the last British governor of Rhodesia, Lord Soames, was the most positive surprise of all in the closing chapter of southern African colonialism.

Six

Tea with Lady Soames

Mary Soames, the widow of Britain's last governor in Rhodesia, Lord Christopher Soames, is sitting in an armchair behind an ever-ready tea tray in her cheerful London parlour in Holland Park. She is wearing a crisp cotton blouse and a large World War 2 gong that was awarded to her father, Winston Churchill. Her attractively animated face smiles youthfully from a couple of framed photographs nearby. A wartime portrait of Churchill looks incongruously haughty amid the clutter of chintz upholstery, a large frilly lampshade and embroidered satin cushions proclaiming, 'Forget me not' and 'My dog is not spoilt'. An overflowing box of Scrabble has been stuffed under a cherry wood table beneath a large painting of an 18th-century garden party that dominates the room.

'I am very interested to know what happened to old Bob,' Mary Soames enthuses. When I remark that Mugabe seems to have been particularly fond of her, she admits: 'I suppose I'm far too mealy-mouthed where he is concerned because I liked him very much too. People have said to me since he started doing all these terrible things, "You ought to write to him, Mary." And I say, "That's not going to achieve anything." Anyhow, I haven't written to him but I have crossed him off my Christmas card list. I've applied my own sanctions and if that hasn't worked, I don't know what will.'

Lady Soames first met Robert Mugabe on the night he won Zimbabwe's inaugural democratic election in 1980. She was walking up the passage at Government House in Highlands, Salisbury, when he and her husband emerged from a meeting.

Christopher said, 'You must meet Mr Mugabe, the new prime minister. Mugabe was looking very prim and proper in a suit and tie. I thought what a nice-looking man he was, with good bones, and he hasn't really changed that much. I suppose he's touched the hair up, don't we all, but he doesn't look sort of grizzled and fallen away.

I sat next to him once or twice after that first meeting and I always found him interesting and very nice to talk to. I remember telling him that my daughter and I had been sent to Bulawayo on the day of the election, to get us out of the way, I think. We wanted to do some sightseeing and I was telling him that we had wanted to see Rhodes' burial place at Matopos. Then I stopped and said, 'Oh dear, I suppose that is tactless of me.' And he replied, 'No, no, it's history.' He didn't mind at all. I said, 'Anyhow, we couldn't see it because there were guerrillas wandering around so we had to spend the whole day by the Holiday Inn pool, which is like any pool in the world.' And he laughed quite easily.

On another occasion, sitting beside Mugabe at a dinner after returning from Mozambique, Lady Soames remarked on the neighbouring country's appearance of poverty and stagnation, 'in marked contrast to Zimbabwe, whatever its problems. I told him it looked like everything had completely ground to a halt on the morrow of independence there. And he said, "Well, we had the very good fortune to have been colonised by the British, with all that that implies." It sounds very odd speaks today, doesn't it? Did he mean it, I wonder, or was it said just to pull me along? Did he fool Christopher, who was quite a canny bird and who came to like Mugabe very much indeed, despite having had some tough days with him in the beginning?'

We discuss the good and bad faces Mugabe has shown to the world over the past three decades. On the one hand, he did more to educate his people during his early years in office than any other leader in Africa. But on the other, his later actions against Zimbabwe's urban poor, whose shacks and shops he destroyed with a callousness reminiscent of apartheid's worst excesses, paint a picture of a cruel and arrogant tyrant. He has likened Britain's premier Tony Blair to Hitler, calling him a liar and a puppet of the United States. Baffled by Mugabe's attitude to her country, Mary Soames says that in 18 years of friendship with Zimbabwe's president she never saw even a hint of the hostility that was to become his trademark. On the contrary, there were occasions when one could not but believe his honesty, generosity and sincerity, she insists.

A week before Zimbabwe's first democratic election, for example, she remembers Lord Soames summoning Mugabe to Government House to warn him that if he failed to curb the intimidation taking place among his guerrillas in the run-up to the polls, it would be difficult or impossible for the British to declare him the winner.

> Christopher told him, 'Please, let's not argue about this because, come on, we know and you know ... And if it goes on,' said Christopher, 'I will be forced to act against you.' They had this long and reasonable talk and it was then that Mugabe said to him, 'How long will it be between the election result and independence – several months, I hope?' And Christopher said, 'Oh no, days, well, perhaps weeks, but certainly not months.' I'm obviously paraphrasing but I had it from the horse's mouth, as they say. And Mugabe then said, 'I want you to stay because I need to be able to talk to somebody. I don't know anything about governing a country and none of my people do either.'
>
> He was quite frank about having nobody trained in anything except guerrilla warfare. And Christopher said, 'No, I shall not be able to do that.' He said to Robert, 'You know it wouldn't work because you would want to do things that I would not approve of, and I would have the responsibility. So we would fall out. I promise you, with all the goodwill in the world that I bear you, it wouldn't work out. You have to accept that independence will come within the month.'

'Now, if Mugabe hadn't liked Christopher and if he hadn't had a real feeling of confidence in him, surely he wouldn't have admitted his vulnerability? He was admitting that he couldn't do the job he had fought so hard to get,' she says with an air of disbelief. 'It was rather touching.'

We discuss how unfortunate it is that Mugabe and his lieutenants could not possibly have acquired the qualifications to run a country during Ian Smith's oppressive years. Lady Soames nods thoughtfully as I recall how the Rhodesians – or 'white rhododendrons' as she called the country's former rulers while she was living briefly in Salisbury as the governor's wife – had deliberately failed to employ black people in anything but menial roles. Mugabe, unlike most of his political colleagues, had achieved an advanced education yet, as Lady Soames notes, it was not of 'the feet on the ground' variety but strictly academic. Neither he nor any in his party had ever been offered the opportunity inside Rhodesia to acquire the complicated range of practical skills that would have helped them to manage a modern economy. It is probably this extraordinary short-sightedness, based on the Rhodesians' outlandish belief that they would rule forever, that accounts more than anything else for the chaos that prevails in Zimbabwe today and, for that matter, on much of the African continent.

One might argue forlornly, Lady Soames and I agree, that instead of Africanising the entire civil service so soon after independence, regardless of the skills deficit in his ranks, Mugabe could have left a lot more whites in their specialist public sector jobs in the hope that they would find the enlightened self-interest to train black successors. However, Mugabe was not just a political leader but a revolutionary one, pledged to righting the economic wrongs of the past, namely, access to jobs. How could he have withheld employment opportunities from his supporters at the very moment of their liberation?

We sip tea and ponder the insoluble skills deficit Mugabe faced when taking office. Then Lady Soames begins fulsomely, 'Now, do you know an extraordinary thing ...' Her vowels are drawn out through trumpet-shaped lips to dramatise the revelation.

Christopher always kept in touch with Robert. He'd said to him after independence, 'Rely on me. I will do everything I can to help you personally and to help Zimbabwe.' Then shortly afterwards, there was a big economic conference in Harare to which Christopher was sent as the representative of the British government. It was an official thing to try and muster up investment in the country. Christopher got to know Mugabe much better during that conference because he saw him then like anything, whereas I was doing other things with Sally.

After he returned to London, Soames offered to host a dinner of highly motivated investors for Mugabe, who accepted enthusiastically, she continues. 'He and Sally arrived in London and came to lunch at the flat to discuss the dinner, and it then took place. Christopher had asked the Irish businessman Tony O'Reilly, who subsequently put a lot of money into Zimbabwe, as well as Rothschild and every kind of person you can imagine who could really put investment into the country. (Christopher paid for the dinner himself, by the way; given gladly, I'm sure. His heart was really in it, you know.)'

As she was eager to hear how her husband's investment evening had gone, Lady Soames sat up waiting for him to return from the dinner. 'Christopher came in with a look of doom on his face. I said to him, "What's happened?" He replied angrily, "I could wring his neck! There were all those business people and he gets up after dinner and he makes a purely Marxist speech."'

> Afterwards, when the dinner guests had all gone, Christopher said to Robert, 'What do you mean by spouting all that frightful Marxist tripe?' (I'm sure Christopher did not mince his words.) And Robert replied quite simply, 'But it's what I believe.' Christopher felt terribly let down, actually. In the eyes of all those business people, he must have seemed as mad as Mugabe.
>
> Now, can you beat that? It made us realise that all along he had been a Marxist utopian. He was determined to promote state socialism even if he knew he couldn't practise it. He did seem genuinely to mind about the poor in those days. And in fact, realising Mugabe was a socialist, Christopher had pointedly said to him at the flat when they were discussing the investors' dinner, 'You *know* that these people are going to have to get a profit from their investments; you *do* realise that, *don't* you, Robert?'

Mugabe's inappropriate speech at the dinner is puzzling, as Lady Soames says, but poignant, too, in the divide it reveals between the man who valued Christopher Soames as his friend on the one hand, and the intellectual Robert Mugabe on the other. The intellectual made the Marxist speech as if the friendship did not exist. Mugabe so lacked emotional understanding of social interaction that he could not see what the speech meant for the friendship. His poor judgement embarrassed Lord Soames, a friend who had gone the extra mile for him. It was as if Mugabe did not have the emotional capacity to understand the complexity of the situation he was in.

The gaffe seems not to have happened deliberately but naively, like an adolescent putting his foot in it. Mugabe appears not to have understood why Soames was so upset with him afterwards because he was unable to see how the issues of friendship and intellectual integrity were linked. Having become a utopian Marxist but without his feet on the ground, as Lady Soames says, Mugabe had taken in a lot of ideas which made sense of his deprivation. Yet he had never worked out what it meant to be a human being with a friend who held different views. He did not know how to reconcile contradictory positions in himself, much less in the world. Like an adolescent wanting to borrow his father's car but hating the capitalist bastard who had bought the vehicle, he was not emotionally mature enough to integrate the two. Instead of reasoning that he could not accept the dinner because it compromised his beliefs, or else rationalising that the world is full of contradictions and he sometimes had to accept help from those he disagreed with, he tried to do both.

The English lord was a good friend to middle-aged Mugabe but he could not be enough of a mentor to compensate for the deprivations that had characterised Mugabe's life. Soames seems to have had a way of guiding Mugabe that did not threaten him. In the absence of a father of his own, Mugabe seemed to value the gentle though unequivocal hand of his British friend. He invested with Soames hopes and fantasies of what one might want from a parental figure. But what Mugabe lacked was someone from his own culture whom he could trust completely; someone who understood his interests and supported him in a thoughtful rather than a blind way, helping him to learn to negotiate the contradictions and complexity of life. What Mugabe most needed was someone who could help him see himself in a realistic way, not in the inflated view reflected to him by his mother or the utter insignificance implied by his father's indifference. He needed a sane 'parent' who would help him face reality.

Despite the dinner debacle, Soames forgave Mugabe and they remained friends. The Zimbabwean premier continued to consult Soames on a range of issues and to heed his advice, as he had done at the time of independence when the British peer implored him not to incorporate an image of two assault rifles on the national flag. This would have been another example of Mugabe's immaturity, like an adolescent waving a banner of his football hero. 'Christopher simply told Robert that his greatest claim to legitimacy was the ballot box, not the gun, and he listened,' recalls Lady Soames.

She became as fond of Mugabe's wife Sally as her husband was of Robert, though she recalls her initial encounter with Zimbabwe's first lady shortly after the election with a shudder. 'Christopher had suggested it would be a good idea to ask Mrs M to tea – to receive her.' She rolls the 'r' to make light of the formal term. 'I said, "Oh, goodie" and invitations were duly launched.'

When Sally Mugabe arrived at Government House, however, she brought with her a young woman guerrilla who was reluctant to leave her weapon under the tree in front of the British governor's stately residence. With the regimental sergeant major of the Commonwealth Monitoring Force standing over the two protesting women, pointing insistently to AK rifles and revolvers already piled there, Sally's bodyguard realised that she was not going to be allowed over the threshold unless she obliged.

It was not an auspicious start to the relationship between Mary and Sally.

> I was sitting with the tea tray in front of me and this furious-looking woman was perched on the edge of her chair, glaring at me. Mrs M was sitting next to me looking unrelenting too. I had to make all the going. Wielding the tea cups, I started on small talk – very small talk. Mrs M was quite disagreeable. At one moment, when I said something or other didn't happen, 'thank God', Sally snapped, 'I don't see what God has to do with it.'

Mary Soames rattles the tea tray to show me how nervous she became. It was the most unpleasant official encounter of her career, she says.

They soon became firm friends, however. In subsequent years, Mary Soames says the two women spent as much time as they could together. Sally, who had begun to suffer from renal failure, travelled increasingly often to England for treatment until Lord Soames arranged for her to be given a dialysis machine of her own. I interrupt to mention the unkind criticism Soames' gift gave rise to in Zimbabwe at the time. I remember hearing repeatedly that Mugabe's wife had commandeered a dialysis machine for her own use at home while ordinary Zimbabweans suffering from the same disease went without treatment. It was cited by embittered former white Rhodesians as an example of Mugabe's corruption and indifference to the needs of his people at a time when he was neither corrupt not indifferent. Lady Soames shakes her head. 'They were quite ghastly in their attitudes, weren't they?' she agrees.

> Sally used to come down to the Mill to have tea with me. We lived an hour out of London and I sometimes offered to come up and meet her, but she insisted. She always brought me lots of lovely presents, fresh fruit and tea, mainly, lots of Zim tea. It was a bit like the things people brought you in wartime. The children liked her too. It was hard to think she was the same angry woman I had received at independence.

Mary and Sally did not see each other at all in the last year of Lord Soames' life.

> He was so ill, and so was she, actually. Then to my astonishment, when Christopher died on a Wednesday afternoon, my son Nicholas took a phone call after it had been on the 6pm news and announced, 'Mama, Robert and Sally Mugabe are coming to Papa's funeral.' I simply couldn't believe it.
>
> They flew over specially. They came to the Mill straight from the airport. It was September 1987. We were having a private luncheon for about 30 people, mostly family, before the funeral. The village was absolutely gobsmacked. There was Prince Charles and Princess Diana with the Mugabes! I can only put it down to genuine friendship. Christopher had been out of politics for ages by then: Mrs T had sacked him way back in 1981 so I don't think there was any mileage in it for Robert.
>
> After luncheon, I had to get rid of everybody. Family belted away and the Waleses went off. I was supposed to be at home alone with my children. But the Mugabes stayed too. I suppose they had nowhere to go while they waited for the church service. Sally was looking around everywhere. I realised she expected Christopher to be lying there. I asked her to come upstairs with me because I didn't know what else to do. I had to get ready. She sat on the bed and asked straight out, 'Where is he?' I said, 'Christopher is in his coffin in the church. Now, Sally dear, we must go soon and I have to get my hat on.' But she sat there and streamed with tears. I was mopping her up and saying, 'Sally, dear, please ...' But she was undone. I was deeply touched. Perhaps it meant nothing, I don't know, but it seemed so utterly sincere. And Robert was so very dear and sweet that day too.

She calls her secretary on the intercom, asking for photographs of the funeral to be brought downstairs. The woman arrives with several large albums. I stand beside Mary Soames' chair as she pages through them. 'Here we all are outside the church. There's Prince Charles and the back of Diana. And here's Sally. Look how she is looking at me – and Robert too. Look how sad they are. And there they are waving at the coffin as it is being driven away.'

Mary Soames' recollection of Robert and Sally coming to Christopher's funeral lunch uninvited resonates with her generosity and open-mindedness. Both Mugabe and his wife seem naive and innocent, as if they were able to reveal themselves fully because they knew Mary and Christopher were not judgemental. Knowing that the Soameses were genuine and that they were never going to be used or patronised by them, it had become a straightforward friendship. Mary had accepted their varying behaviours over the years, including Sally's initial rudeness as the guerrilla queen and then her frank curiosity about the whereabouts of Christopher's body at the funeral. She seems to have been intrigued by their idiosyncrasies and her understanding of the cultural divide. The sudden arrival at her home of the Mugabes in the midst of her family's grief and against the rigid rules of aristocratic protocol did not offend her: she simply set two extra places at the table alongside Prince Charles and Princess Diana.

Having been back to Zimbabwe twice with her husband since independence, Mary Soames returned to the country several times after Christopher's death:

> Successive high commissioners would simply inform State House that I was going to be there and leave it at that. On each occasion, Robert received me. The High Commission people were always amazed because they had very little to do with Mugabe themselves.
>
> Then Sally ups and dies. I decided that if I had to walk there I was going to Harare for her funeral. I was just about to book my own flight, having rung the high commissioner in Zimbabwe and asked if I could come and stay, when somehow the palace got to hear that I was going out. The Queen, via her private secretary, asked me if I would represent her and Prince Philip.

'So immediately,' she says in an excited girlish voice, clapping her hands, 'my fare was paid and it became an official visit.'

Mary Soames had always liked Robert Mugabe. She found him interesting and mysterious, noticing in him a warmth and an ability to relate that few others had experienced. There was clearly some trust between them from the start, which she valued. Her determination to be at Sally's funeral was not for any ulterior motive but because it was a matter of the heart. The loyalty between the controversial African politician from a background of dire poverty and the unusually tolerant British aristocrat was genuine.

On Lady Soames' arrival in Harare, the high commissioner informed her that they were due that afternoon to see Zimbabwe's late first lady as she lay in state.

> There was an outer tent at State House crammed with people, all of them black. Inside was a smaller group of people and this huge brass bed – which I understand was flown in from Ghana – with my friend Sally laid out on it like a kipper in what seemed to be her bridal dress. She looked awful as she had been there for quite some time. Mugabe was sitting on the other side of the bed with a Bible in his hand. A funeral Mass was to take place shortly beside her death bed. We all had to file by, quite close. I was so sad, genuinely sad, and I didn't want to do the wrong thing so I kissed her hand or something. It was very moving. And all the time Robert was sitting there looking absolutely heartbroken.

Sally was very important to Robert, says Lady Soames. Acknowledging that he already had children by Grace when his first wife died, she insists he always loved Sally. That he had children by another woman once he knew Sally was dying may have been more about having the children that Sally could not give him after their first child's death, and possibly also a reflection of the prevalence and acceptability of polygamy in Africa, than about disloyalty to Sally, she believes.

> They had been through such a lot together. I mean, she told me once that she used to sit in a library somewhere in London day after day, week after week, writing out his study notes for all those degrees he took while he was in prison in Rhodesia because he wasn't allowed to have books. At her burial in Heroes Acre, Mugabe made a speech in which he talked very lovingly about Sally and of course, the struggle. Well, it had been a

struggle, hadn't it?

On my last visit to Zimbabwe, Mugabe gave me a wonderful party, when he made the most moving speech about Christopher that I have ever heard. He said, 'I regarded Lord Soames as my friend. He did great things for this country.' There is no record of that speech unfortunately, so I can't tell you exactly what he said but it sounded so genuine. That was as recently as 1998 and there was absolutely no mileage in it for Mugabe by that time.

He was wonderfully friendly that night. He introduced me to Grace and he had me sit on the sofa beside him. I had been milling around and he called me. 'Come and sit here, Mary,' he said. He made people come up and meet me. Then he got up and gave this really touching speech. It was similar to what he had said about Christopher on the morning of Independence Day in 1980 at a party he gave then at State House, which he asked us to attend. We were busy packing up to get the hell out of it but we went along. Robert stood up and made a speech in which he said, 'I love Lord Soames.' It was wonderfully engaging, although there were some very long white faces listening to it, including some in our own entourage, I can tell you.

Lady Soames' account of her husband's relationship with Robert Mugabe shows not only the real affection that existed between unlikely allies but what was possible for Mugabe when he was in an accepting, loving environment. It reveals the person Mugabe could be when he had a friend, demonstrating that being genuinely loved brings out the best in all of us. Virtually everyone around Mugabe had related to him in a self-interested way since his childhood. That he lapped up the little bit of generous warmth he got from Lord and Lady Soames makes you wonder what might have been had he had more real interest and affection in his life.

The Soameses had put their hearts into the official job they were called upon to do in Zimbabwe in 1980. Their resultant relationship with Mugabe was not just an expedient one. His feelings for them were genuinely warm, too, because they seem to have touched each others' hearts in a way that seldom occurs in the ruthless world of international politics.

Throughout our interview, Mary Soames asked rhetorically whether Mugabe was always a bad person or if something happened to change him. The answer, perhaps, is that the two possibilities ran parallel. While the seed of what Mugabe has become may always have been there, he may well have developed differently had he been surrounded by more people like the Soameses, who had his interests at heart and whom he could trust. Even at the time of Mary Soames' last visit to Zimbabwe in 1998, when Mugabe was about 70, he had the potential to remain a good leader. But a twisting of his being took place subsequently and he then moved inexorably in a destructive direction. The tragedy is that he had the capacity to go either way.

Seven

I told you so

One of the earliest challenges facing Robert Mugabe when he became the premier of Zimbabwe was how to deal with his predecessor and arch enemy, the wily Ian Smith. The country's former prime minister remained convinced that he had a role to play in protecting white interests after independence, even though many of his troopers had either left Zimbabwe or aligned themselves with the new order. A gloom merchant who had always denigrated black empowerment, Smith was so oblivious to the hurt caused by racism that he sang the Afrikaans song 'Bobbejaan, klim die berg' ('Baboon, climb the mountain') in front of black university students at an election meeting in 1970, claiming in the resultant uproar that it was just an old South African rugby song and completely non-political. 'Sixty years ago Africans here were uncivilised savages, walking around in skins,' he remarked the same year, while Mugabe and other nationalist leaders were locked away in his prisons. 'They have made tremendous progress but they have an awful long way to go.'

Zimbabwe, a small country shaped like a teapot in the heart of Africa, has had only two leaders over the past four decades (although Bishop Abel Muzorewa was briefly at the helm during the transition from Rhodesia to Zimbabwe). Ian Smith and Robert Mugabe both defied international opinion, giving the finger to the whole world in much the same belligerent way – Smith when he joined the United States of America as the only territory in history to separate successfully from the British Empire without its consent, and Mugabe with a sustained campaign of human rights violations. Both presided confidently over repressive regimes while mouthing lofty moral delusions.

The similarities between the famously cantankerous Ian Smith and his irascible successor are so numerous that one suspects an uncanny synergy in their make-up as well as leadership styles. Like Ian Smith, Mugabe chose the lawless tradition of leadership inherited from Cecil John Rhodes, after whom the country was named in the colonial era. Repression of one sort or another, so characteristic of Mugabe's presidency, was also a marked feature of Smith's regime. Neither Smith nor Mugabe wanted democracy: both had it forced upon them. And the violence that characterised Mugabe's leadership from the earliest years was endemic in Smith's Rhodesia. Both men were racist or xenophobic. Neither of them could tolerate criticism, the response to which was almost as dire in Rhodesia as in Zimbabwe. Both blamed others, and particularly Britain, for ongoing crises of their own creation.

Zimbabwe's unfolding fate has always sounded familiar to those of us who have watched the country's fortunes rise and fall over many years. Mugabe constantly reminds us that he learnt about land seizure from his predecessors. It was Britain's governors who inaugurated the country's tradition of autocratic rule, allowing leaders to pursue their own interests rather than those of the nation and thereby heralding endemic instability and aggression. After obtaining a mineral concession from Lobengula, the king of the Ndebele, in 1889, for example, Rhodes began a far-reaching land grab. Four years later, the colonialists attacked and defeated the Ndebele kingdom, seizing land and livestock and distributing it among the white settlers.

Although Smith and Mugabe were coerced into a transition to democracy that ended the bush war, their primary identification remained ethnic. Neither had ever had any real commitment to the will of the people as a whole. Smith often stated his opposition to democracy, most memorably when he declared that majority rule would 'never in a thousand years' occur in Rhodesia.

Like the abused child who risks becoming an abusive parent, the politically oppressed have regularly turned into oppressors in countries all over Africa. Mugabe furthered his rule with the despotic strategies employed by the colonial settlers he so derided. His drive towards centralised control, for example, was facilitated by Smith's 15-year 'state of emergency'. It offended every basic human right and included the enduring system of propaganda inherent in Smith's attempts to control the media.

Despite his powerful hold over the white electorate, Smith remained blind to the dangerous cul-de-sac into which he was leading his country. Mugabe was similarly empowered to change course but he too lacked vision, being oblivious or indifferent to the damage his policies were inflicting on the Zimbabwean people. Both out-manoeuvred a host of international politicians who were seeking solutions to the country's problems.

Theirs was a catastrophic relationship. Mugabe became committed to armed struggle primarily because of Smith's intransigence. The two men became each other's most bitter enemies. Ironically, their deeds complemented one another in their mutual rule by lawlessness and violence, each being driven to his excesses by the other.

Perhaps the most intriguing similarity between Robert Mugabe and Ian Smith is their marked emotional immaturity, which I am hoping to explore when I track down Smith. (Most human beings operate in the world in an immature way, maturity being a rare developmental achievement. The psychological perspectives that regard early child-hood as formative of later personality – such as the views expressed throughout these pages in the analysis of Robert Mugabe's behaviour – focus on childhood experience as it impacts on adult functioning, not on 'childishness', literally.) Ian Smith has been living in South Africa since early 2005, following medical treatment after a fall which left him unable to fend for himself, says his daughter Jean Tholet. My hopes are initially dashed when she as his gatekeeper tells me in no uncertain terms to let her 86-year-old father rest in peace. 'He is an old man and he's done all that; leave him alone,' she barks. Only at the last minute, when I suggest very quickly as she is saying good-bye that her father might care to talk to me for the sake of his legacy, seeing that I am writing a book rather than a newspaper article, does she relent. 'I expect he wouldn't mind saying, "I told you so" once more,' she admits with a laugh.

So I get on a plane to Cape Town in August 2005 to meet the man who pioneered Zimbabwe's politics of international isolation. Sitting in his room at a retirement hotel near St James, I ask Smith where he thinks Mugabe went wrong. 'Mugabe is like a lot of political people,' he begins. 'He asks himself one question, "Is it going to help me win the next election or not?" Simple as that.'

Smith blames everybody but himself for the fact that it was Robert Mugabe the Marxist radical who succeeded him rather than one of the more moderate nationalists with whom he tried to negotiate a power-sharing deal. 'I have often been asked if I have any regrets. At the time and in the circumstances, I believe I made the correct decisions. If anyone wants to convince me otherwise I am always open to being convinced. I think I am a decent, honest, straightforward person. I like to do what is best for my country. But it was other people who determined our fate, unfortunately.'

The British betrayed his trust time and again, according to Smith. 'Harold Wilson, who was the best of all the British politicians, was the only one who was truthful to me; he was honest. He said to me on *HMS Tiger* (the British warship on which the most favourable of Britain's offers to white Rhodesia was negotiated in 1966 and later rejected by Smith), "You know, Ian, there is nothing that would give me greater satisfaction than to come to an agreement with you. But I want to tell you that four or five of my ministers have said that if I make an agreement with Ian Smith that will be treachery, against the wishes of the Labour Party, and we will stand up in public and condemn you, and walk out on you." That's what Wilson said and then he asked me, "So what do I do?"'

Years later, Smith recalls, he was waiting in the VIP lounge at Heathrow on his way to America, 'having a quiet drink, although I am not a great drinker but occasionally I don't mind a whisky', when the attendant at the door came to tell him that someone claiming to be an old friend was waiting outside to see him. 'I said, "Ask him what his name is." The doorman came back and said, "He says he is Harold Wilson." I replied, "Bring him in". Then Wilson walked up and put his arms around me.'

Smith's bitterness is reserved for the South African premier who brought Rhodesia's rebellion to a halt. 'I got a message from John Vorster in about 1975, saying, "Speak to these chaps and make a plan. We want to solve this problem, whether you like it or not." So we met on a train on the Victoria Falls Bridge between Zambia and Rhodesia in 1975. That's when the farce began. I told my side, "Now listen, you chaps, nobody has a drink until the whole show is over." By the end, one of my ministers came to me with a film he had taken, saying "Look what I have got in my pocket. They (the black delegates) were all drunk and falling over themselves trying to get back across the bridge into Zambia."'

Although the smooth-talking American Henry Kissinger played a key role in the events that brought Robert Mugabe to power, Smith tells me he respected the US secretary of state. 'A lot of people said he was a Marxist and a communist and so on but I thought he was a good chap.'

Kissinger damaged his international standing when he lied to Smith at their Pretoria meeting in 1976, telling the Rhodesian leader that presidents Julius Nyerere of Tanzania and Kenneth Kaunda of Zambia had already accepted his proposals when, in fact, they had refused to accept anything that did not put the guerrillas in power. A state department spokesman blustered at the time, 'Well, if it (getting Smith to capitulate) took lies, it took lies.' Nevertheless, Smith chuckles as he recalls the kiss and hug he got from Kissinger's wife Nancy when she was introduced to him by her husband as 'my wife's hero' shortly before Kissinger delivered his coup de grâce. He also remembers the tear in Kissinger's eye when the American broke the news while watching a rugby match that Rhodesia's political game was up.

Ian Smith remembers vividly the day Mugabe won the election that brought him to power in 1980. It was the worst day of Smith's political life. Still in shock after hearing of Zanu-PF's landslide victory, he received a phone call from a member of Mugabe's staff inviting him to meet the country's new leader. 'I said, "Is he there at his house? Will he be there if I come?" The aide said yes and I said, "Okay, I'm on my way."'

Sitting on the edge of his bed, brown suede shoes together, hands on his knees, Ian Smith resembles an old schoolmaster in appearance and demeanour. He looks pained whenever I mention Mugabe's name, sounding puritanical and apparently unaware of any contribution he might have made to the misfortunes of Zimbabwe.

Describing how he drove alone ('I never needed bodyguards', he scoffs) in his Peugeot station wagon to Mugabe's private residence in Mount Pleasant, a suburb of Harare, Smith recalls: 'The bloke at the gate was expecting me. In I went. Mugabe said, "Come and sit next to me," and he showed me to the sofa. I sat down. He then sat right up close to me and held my hand.'

I glance at Smith's daughter, who is sitting in on the interview to make sure that I don't upset her father. It was her late husband Clem Tholet who wrote the song 'Rhodesians Never Die' that was virtually an anthem for whites during the bush war. She is smiling at Smith's hand-holding revelation and I laugh heartily, unable to conceal my amusement at the thought of Ian Smith and Robert Mugabe, two infamous African dictators, holding hands on the sofa. The banality of evil, indeed.

Our amusement irritates Smith. 'Well, I don't like people holding my hand. So I got my hand out of his hand and moved to the other end of the sofa,' he grumbles, showing how he wrenched his hand free.

The moment on the sofa turned out to be prophetic: the black man steels himself to extend a hand of friendship and the white man spurns it. Many observers say that a toxic turning point in Mugabe's presidency followed his discovery that white farmers – including Smith himself, as he confirms to me – had begun to fund the opposition Movement for Democratic Change (MDC) in 1999. Mugabe believed he had been kinder to white Rhodesians than they deserved and deeply resented what he saw as their betrayal rather than their democratic right. Sydney Sekeramayi, who has been in Mugabe's Cabinet since independence, told a journalist in 1999 that Mugabe felt utterly rejected by the white community and vowed to get his revenge.

The gesture on the sofa may at the time have been Mugabe's cultural style of extending the hand of friendship, literally, in the way you often see black men holding hands in Africa. It is clear, however, that he was trying to forge a link between the two in a very complex situation. The tables have turned. Mugabe is now in the position of power against a backdrop of denigration, cruelty and imprisonment. Neither of them knows how to manage the moment. If it were Nelson Mandela, the Xhosa prince, instead of Mugabe, the barefoot boy from a dirt-poor village, there would be no ambiguity about who was in authority because Mandela does not have to prove he is the better person – he knows it. Not so Mugabe, a man who doubts himself despite his bluster and who is acutely vulnerable to the self-righteousness of Ian Smith, a person incapable of self-doubt.

The two are worlds apart. Smith is still in denial, slightly aggrieved, like someone who has had something taken from him. Not forgiving or open, he provokes a slightly appeasing attitude in Mugabe, as if the new leader is asking to be liked. Mugabe seems sincere and naive, like the lonely child wanting to be friends. 'Come, sit next to me and hold my hand.' It is noticeably not a formal handshake, man to man. Perhaps Mugabe was hoping that the unexpected intimacy established with Lord Soames would work with Smith too. But this was unlikely between Smith and Mugabe because both seem too immature to field the complexities of their relationship. The scene on the sofa seems a little like schooldays: Are you going to be my friend? You were the prefect last year, now it's my turn. But Smith pulls his hand away and moves to the other end of the sofa.

According to Smith – who was in fact eager to cooperate with Mugabe and subsequently asked to be included in Mugabe's Cabinet once he realised that other, less confrontational whites were to be in the new government – the two worked well together in the beginning. But the cordiality did not last.

All of a sudden, early one morning – it was after 18 months – Mugabe announced that the government was now going to embark on its true course and create a one-party Marxist state. He actually used the term Marxist. Nobody could believe it. So I went to see him. Every time I had gone to see him before, he welcomed me, thanked me for coming, for giving him the benefit of my experience, for telling him what the white people were thinking. We had an incredibly amicable relationship.

I reminded him that since he came to power I had not raised one word of criticism against him, and I said I had asked my backbenchers to be reasonable, to give him a chance to do the right thing. So I said to him, 'Why are you doing this? You're breaking confidence in the future of the country. I haven't criticised you up to now but I have to tell you that if you carry on like this I will have to criticise you in public for the first time since you came to power.' I could see he was displeased; in fact, incensed. From that day on, he refused to talk to me. Under a one-party Marxist dictatorship, you agree. You don't disagree.

He was a very clever bloke and he worked with me for as long as he thought it was going to help him. Once again, it was just to keep himself in power. I give that answer to all questions about Mugabe because that is all there is to it. Everything he has ever done is about keeping himself in power. Dictators and fascists all over the world think like that.

I smile at Smith, the dictator who put his country through an unnecessary war rather than surrender power. I have always loathed his sanctimony and crooked, bullying ways. I remember how much the pregnant mother of my godchild suffered after Smith ordered the arrest and solitary confinement of her husband Peter Niesewand, a BBC journalist who had dared to stand up to the tyrannical Rhodesian leader during a press conference broadcast on national television in 1972. Smith smiles back uncertainly, an old man at the end of his life, trying to retain his dignity as a nurse pats him on the shoulder.

Later, paging through the picture section of his autobiography, he finds a photograph of a prize Brahmin bull he reared on his Rhodesian farm long ago. He holds it up for me to admire and then flicks to an earlier page. 'That's me as captain of the cricket team at Chaplin High School in 1937,' he says proudly. 'I was captain of everything.'

Smith is a simple person, a schoolboy rather than a schoolmaster at heart. It matters to him that he is the captain of this and the captain of that. He aspires to be the head boy and is always looking for glory, gold stars and gleaming badges. Paradoxically, it may be that immature men like Smith and Mugabe end up in positions of power precisely because they do not understand the complexity of what lies ahead. A mature person would surely have been affected by and suffered amid all the killing and destruction entailed in the war fought by Smith and Mugabe, but the two of them appear to have strode on, both cut off from their feelings and from a cruel reality. In the same way, children are capable of hurting animals and tormenting each other without being aware of the pain and damage they are inflicting.

'I was vice president of the Royal Air Force Association, which held some of its meetings at the Albert Hall in London,' Smith tells me. 'I used to meet up with all those chaps who had Victoria Crosses and bars and gongs galore. I didn't have anything like that but they still wanted to elect Ian Smith, this bloke with horns growing out of his head, as their vice president.' Many in the United Kingdom admired Smith, not only because as a fighter pilot during World War 2 he was shot down in 1944 and bore the scars of an earlier Hurricane crash on his lopsided face, but because he was the son of ordinary, lower middle-class Scottish parents and a most unlikely challenger of world opinion.

A biographical note supplied in 1964 by aides to Britain's Tory premier Sir Alec Douglas-Home outlined Smith's career and concluded: 'He is a simple-minded, politically naive and uncomprehending charac- ter. His political approach has been described as schoolboy. He possesses a strong vein of schoolboy obstinacy and there is a mixture of schoolboy stubbornness, cunning and imperception about his speeches. Likewise, there is a *Boy's Own* ring about his patriotic utterances. Nevertheless, his pedestrian and humourless manner often conceals a shrewder assessment of a particular situation than at first appears on the surface and he should not be underrated.' Surprisingly, this damning description appears in the introduction to Smith's autobiography as an example of how misunderstood he was by the British government.

He says he always resented being called a racist. 'I know I am not a racist. How can I be when I have lived here all my life among these people? I have no racism anywhere in my system. I think it is a sterile policy and it doesn't help. I have always asked myself: is it going to help me and my country? I am a practical and above all a fair and honest man.'

Smith has evidently forgotten the time he was caught in full racist cry giving only the number of white deaths when asked how many Rhodesians had died in the bush war. And his autobiography, published more than 15 years after he left office, contains at least one of the whopping lies he told himself and his followers during his premiership. Variations of it still crop up in his conversation and fly in the face of his well-known assertion that black rule would 'never in a thousand years' come to Rhodesia. 'At no time in the history of our country was there any attempt to interfere with free access to the voters roll and the principle of unimpeded progress to majority rule. But right up to the present day one still comes across articles accusing Rhodesians of trying to perpetuate white minority rule – such is the power of the communist propaganda machine.'

Having been out of the limelight for many years, Smith is clearly enjoying the interview. He describes how he watched the growing disappointment in Mugabe's government, mixed with growing nostalgia for his own regime. 'People in Zimbabwe, black people, greeted me all the time while I was still living there and told me how much better things were for them in the old days.' He seems to think this exonerates his disastrous politics, whereas all it proves is that Zimbabweans are left with mixed feelings. 'I once challenged Mugabe to join me in a walk through an African township in Harare, to see which of us was the most popular,' Smith recalls. 'He declined to take me up on it, and I think that speaks for itself.

'I think I can correctly say, "I told you so",' Smith continues. He has, in fact, been saying this since 1998. 'History records that my predictions have materialised,' he wrote in his autobiography. 'Never did I think that I would ever be able to claim that Mugabe had helped me. I was wrong. He has proved my case conclusively. It is public knowledge that he and his close relatives and friends have succeeded in making themselves instant multimillionaires. They own the biggest and best houses in the capital city. They have secured a controlling interest in many of the country's largest and most important industrial and commercial enterprises, and stolen most of the farms and ranches in the country. At the same time, the standard of living of the great mass of the people has deteriorated alarmingly. There are frequent complaints from parents that their biggest problem is that their children go to bed hungry at night – something which never happened before Mugabe came to power.'

Since Smith wrote those sentences about Mugabe's corruption and economic mismanagement almost a decade ago when the country was still stable, 'things have gone unbelievably wrong in Zimbabwe,' he says. 'Never in my wildest dreams did I think it would become as bad as it is. I thought we were far too civilised and that we would manage to retain a certain amount of sanity. But I was wrong. Nothing matters to Mugabe except staying in power. He is clever, so he survives. When he travels, he has six big Mercedes Benzes with their windows blackened so you don't know which one he is in.'

I ask Ian Smith what he thinks about as he looks out to sea from his retirement home window in South Africa. He talks wistfully of his farm Gwenoro, inherited from his father and situated in a rural mining town called Selukwe while he was growing up and renamed Shurugwi after independence. He tells me it has been partially occupied by squatters for some time but still produces pedigree cattle, sweet potatoes and oranges. 'We grow some of the best seed potatoes in the world, with added carotene, because it is lacking in the indigenous diet. These have been patented by my son. We've got big tractors and trailers that cart the oranges ...'

Smith's eyes go glassy as he gulps back his nostalgia. He makes no secret of his frustration at being in Cape Town at his daughter's protective insistence rather than home in Zimbabwe.

> It's my life. I want to go back there. That's all I want to do now – go back. It was the greatest country in the world, Rhodesia. We had the best civilisation in the world. We had freedom and that's what I want again more than anything; to see if I can help restore a little bit of freedom for the people of Zimbabwe.
>
> Land requires dedicated people who believe in the maxim that we do not inherit from our fathers but borrow from our great-great-grandchildren. Each generation is honour-bound to pass it on in a better condition. I just want to do as much as I can to keep my farm going and hope that when this madness is all over I will still have it. That's my last great hope in life.

If there is a sense of reasonableness about Smith, it is precisely because he does not understand what he did to black people in Rhodesia. His denial of his own racism even in his dying days shows how lacking in self-knowledge he was all along. Foolish enough to assume the leadership of the whites after independence despite being reviled by the majority of black Zimbabweans, he perpetuated the white community's shallow attitudes instead of stepping aside for a leader, informal or otherwise, who might have encouraged whites to regret the painful past.

Mugabe spent more than a decade behind bars at Smith's behest. He was prevented by Smith from attending his only child's funeral, a fact which Smith confirms calmly to me as if, despite the benefit of hindsight and hopefully a glimmer of guilt, it was a reasonable thing for one man to do to another. It is hard to imagine someone like Robert Mugabe meeting an unrepentant man like Ian Smith and not becoming overwhelmed by the pain and the anger of the past, unless of course Mugabe was completely out of touch with his own feelings when the two sat together on the sofa.

With so much unacknowledged beneath the surface, Mugabe's hand-holding gesture on the sofa with Smith was not, as Smith insists, an insincere moment, but more likely a wishful one. Mugabe was unrealistic, a poor judge of character, in hoping that Ian Smith would work with him. Once he realised that Smith was not the person he wanted him to be in the new country, Mugabe became exaggeratedly disillusioned and bitter. When Smith won most of the white seats guaranteed under the Lancaster House constitution five years after independence, Mugabe reacted spitefully as well as racially by firing his loyal white agriculture minister – who was no fan of Smith's – and appointing a black man in his place because he wanted to punish the white community.

Unable to see any middle ground in a conflict, Mugabe's instinct is to contemplate stark alternatives – never complex possibilities. People are either for him or against him. His initial disillusionment with the white community arose, not from Smith's actions in implementing the terms of the Lancaster House agreement, but from his own immature idealisation of who Smith was going to be and his subsequent failure to deal with who Smith actually was. Too emotionally immature to read Smith accurately, too inexperienced in relationships of any kind to know that Smith was not going to meet his expectations, Mugabe was involved in a form of self-deception that was to repeat itself over and over again during his presidency. Unfortunately, it fed his growing paranoia by convincing him with each passing disillusionment that there was absolutely nobody he could trust.

Eight

Britain's diplomatic blunder

During the first decade of his premiership, Robert Mugabe was regarded as one of Africa's most inspiring leaders. His education, public health and social welfare programmes were widely applauded. He worked a 16-hour day, rubbed shoulders with international royalty and basked in the adulation of his people. Over the following 10 years, however, the success to which he had become accustomed began to diminish. He was travelling so extensively abroad that students at the University of Zimbabwe, calling him Vasco da Mugabe after the early European explorer, began to joke about their president being the only person flying regularly from Harare to the neighbouring Namibian capital of Windhoek via London. The bountiful nation he had inherited from Ian Smith, though ravaged by war, had been in good shape economically at independence but was beginning to falter by the 90s. Zimbabwe's pivotal agriculture industry had gone from strength to strength under Mugabe but much of the donor money that should have been spent on land reform was being squandered by the president's cronies.

The country that Nyerere had dubbed 'the jewel of Africa' in 1980, which Mugabe had promised to protect, was slowly becoming tarnished. By 1994, when it was revealed to the president's evident embarrassment that 98 previously white-owned farms had been leased to Mugabe's senior officials at minimal cost, alarm bells began to ring in donor agencies across the world.

Mugabe, at the height of his power, believed that the entire state was at his disposal – which was true, thanks partly to the repressive legislation inherited intact from Rhodesia, as well as to his own autocratic instincts. If he decided to wipe out his political opponents, he could do so. If he felt like taking donor money and dishing it out to his closest supporters in order to secure their loyalty and admiration, that was his prerogative. His portrait hung everywhere. Everything that happened in Zimbabwe was about Robert Mugabe. The lonely boy, who believed himself special and aspired to greatness, had achieved his goal. Dissenting voices warned of a looming economic crisis and the country agreed to drastic World Bank policies designed to curb government spending but Mugabe remained secure in the knowledge that he was the king of the castle.

It was a letter written in 1997 by Britain's international development secretary, Clare Short, that forced Mugabe to confront the fact that he was not, after all, omnipotent. She wrote it following a disagreement between Mugabe and Tony Blair over Zimbabwe's land redistribution plans during a meeting at the Commonwealth Conference in Edinburgh earlier that year. In it, Clare Short dismissed Zimbabwe's contention that Britain had an obligation to fund land redistribution in the former Rhodesia. 'I should make it clear that we do not accept that Britain has a special responsibility to meet the costs of land purchase in Zimbabwe,' she said. 'We are a new government from diverse backgrounds without links to former colonial interests. My own origins are Irish, and as you know, we were colonised not colonisers.'

Clare Short's attitude so incensed Mugabe that the letter led not only to the recipient, agriculture minister Kumbirai Kangai, accusing the British government of bad faith in disowning land compensation claims, but also to Mugabe damning the newly elected Labour administration as 'worse than the Tories'. It accounted in part for the Zimbabwean president's open hatred of Tony Blair a few years later. After Mugabe's attempts to bolster his sagging economy by audacious plunder in the DRC in 1998, and following his vicious attacks against the judiciary, press and human rights activists at home, the Zimbabwean president was no longer the respected African statesman of former years. Relations with Britain declined further in the wake of the 'arrest' by a gay rights campaigner of homophobic Mugabe while he was on his way to shop at Harrods in London in 1999. The opening of British diplomatic mailbags at Harare airport the following year might have been calculated to infuriate Blair's Foreign Office. The resultant condemnation of Zimbabwe's government sent Mugabe into an anti-British campaign of verbal abuse on a scale and at an unseemly level never before encountered by the former colonial power. Describing Blair's government as 'little men' who used 'gay gangsters' against him, he hurled insults at 'B-liar', as he called the British prime minister.

When I met the Rt Hon Clare Short MP at Portcullis House on the Victoria Embankment, London, in June 2006 and embarked on a summary of Mugabe's road to ruin, she immediately scoffed at the suggestion that land ownership was always an issue for him:

> I don't believe land redistribution was close to his heart at all because the progress on it from independence until the recent troubles was so weak.[3] Of course, the allocation of land was grossly unfair and there was resentment in the country, quite reasonably, amongst politicians and peasants alike that the whites had all the land. There had been an agreement on support for land redistribution by Britain at the time of Lancaster House, which was negotiated by a Tory government. The deal, I think, was that we offered some money provided there was no compulsory purchase.

Her party came to power at a time when there was some money left of the funds originally allocated by the Tories to land redistribution in Zimbabwe, 'which the Zimbabweans had not bothered to take up', Short explains. She says she remembers looking at it and telling her staff that seeing there were so many very poor Zimbabweans on collective lands who had little support and needed more, she disapproved – like Mugabe – of the policy of 'no compulsory purchase'. Instead, she believed there should be a properly planned land redistribution policy because, from the point of view of her department's vision, the new British government was interested only in assisting poor people. 'I had nothing to do with Lancaster House: that was all played out, done or not done. We as new Labour were looking at everything Britain did in

---

[3] According to Father Fidelis Mukonori, head of the Jesuits in Zimbabwe and a confidant of Mugabe, part ot the reason so little progress had been made on land redistribution was, firstly, because the Lancaster House agreement made the purchase of white-owned farms difficult during the first 10 years after independence. Secondly, he claims, the Organisation for African Unity, forerunner of the African Union, had implored Mugabe to desist from radical land reform on the grounds that it would prejudice progress towards black rule in South Africa.

the world and focusing on the systematic reduction of poverty.'

According to Clare Short, her intention in writing to Mugabe's government was to point out that Britain was happy to support land redistribution provided it was for the benefit of the poor. This is not the impression her words conveyed to Mugabe, however. On reading the letter, Minister Kumbirai Kangai complained that Zimbabwe had expected a more sympathetic hearing from a Labour administration in Britain. 'We are still paying for debts incurred by Ian Smith,' he noted. 'Some were to borrow money to buy guns to kill us while we were fighting for liberation. If we recognise we have an obligation under international law to pay the previous government's debts, the British government is obliged to meet obligations made by Mrs Thatcher.'

Short flatly dismisses the suggestion that the former colonial power had an ongoing moral obligation to Zimbabwe:

> Britain was needing to be seen in Zimbabwe as the enemy and the guilty party, the supporter of white farmers, at a time when their economy was in trouble. I was trying to move on from the colonial baggage and get us off to a fresh start. I wanted us to act as a development agency, not as the former colonial power. I wasn't trying to be clever or anything. Aid budgets had been used throughout the Cold War for political reasons. I was stopping that right across the board. No more aid for a dictator like the Congo's Mobutu because he's serving some or other Western interest. Our money was for poor people and their development. Whatever Zimbabwe is claiming about my letter, I doubt very much that if it hadn't been written we wouldn't have ended up exactly where we are today.

Despite her bluster, Clare Short finds the subject stressful. Although repeatedly scorning suggestions that her letter flew in the face of acute African sensitivity to British dictates, she wears a deep frown, irritably breaking the wooden spatula accompanying her coffee into shards to pick her teeth with as she talks. Known as 'Bomber' Short in Ireland, she has been a controversial figure throughout her career, notably when she called for the legalisation of cannabis in the UK and later when despite having voted for the war and sat in the Cabinet throughout the invasion, she resigned from Blair's Cabinet over the 2003 war in Iraq. At the time of her appointment to Britain's Department for International Development (DFID), she was asked by journalists if she would behave diplomatically and avoid embarrassing the government. 'I'm going to try to be good,' she replied, 'but I can't help it; I have to be me.' Within a few months, she was accused of making insulting remarks in response to a request for help from the volcano-damaged island of Montserrat, one of Britain's few remaining overseas territories. A Labour colleague commented that Short 'sounds like a mouthpiece for an old 19th-century colonial and Conservative government'. Then came the long-running row with Robert Mugabe.

Britain's previous government had also quarrelled with Mugabe over his land policies. The Conservatives had cut off support for land redistribution in 1994 after spending £44 million, on the grounds that some of the farms purchased were being given to Mugabe's cronies in a generally corrupt exercise. Substantive discussions between Zimbabwean and British officials did not recommence until two years later. An Overseas Development Administration (ODA) appraisal mission despatched to Harare in 1996 proposed a land redistribution project to resettle up to 35 000 rural households at an estimated cost of up to £145 million. Funding pledges were to follow a donor's conference.

Clare Short's dramatically different attitude to Mugabe's claims on the British taxpayer came as a shock to him. His initial strategy, Short believes, was simply to win the argument with the incoming British administration and get his money supply restored. 'I don't think at the beginning of this mess Mugabe really planned to wreck his economy and his country in this terrible way,' she reflects. 'I think he just became power-crazed and in hubris scratched at an old sore that hadn't healed. But I think he was doing it with an ulterior motive rather than with the intention to get energy behind a new phase of land redistribution – which he could have achieved. Having made the fuss, which was fair enough in terms of crude politics, everyone wanted to help. A lot of international support would have flowed into a properly organised land programme.'

Mugabe's fuss was so intense that the retired Tory doyen of Lancaster House, Lord Carrington, was asked by the new government to call on Zimbabwe's premier in Harare in an attempt to repair relations. Carrington declined the invitation. Like many observers, he could see that Mugabe was already in deep trouble when Clare Short's letter arrived, and that it had given a failing politician the means to deflect criticism.

A donor conference on land reform organised by the United Nations Development Programme took place in 1998, but relations between the Zimbabwean government and the donors subsequently broke down. A further British mission was sent to Zimbabwe the following year to examine the case for UK and European Union assistance to the proposed land redistribution programme. All the prospective donors, including the Netherlands, Norway, Sweden and the United States, were concerned – like Britain – with governance issues as well as the high cost of doing nothing at a time when the Zimbabwean government had clearly stated its intention to proceed with resettlement irrespective of the donors' decisions on support. Significantly, says Clare Short, the UK was the only donor willing to consider funding further land purchase.

Mugabe's pronouncements on the matter had become ever more strident and anti-white. Portraying the land issue as a historic score that needed to be settled between the land-hungry majority and 'a greedy bunch of racist usurpers', he had repeatedly declared his intention to disregard any legal challenges to his threatened land grab. 'I, Robert Mugabe, cannot be dragged to court by a settler,' he blustered. Calling constantly for the 'indigenisation of the economy', he inflamed race relations by adding that some Zimbabweans were 'more indigenous than others'.

Mugabe reacted bitterly whenever Western governments criticised his land policies. 'How can these countries who have stolen land from the Red Indians, the Aborigines and the Eskimos dare to tell us what to do with our land?' he demanded. Time and again, he threatened to seize white-owned farms without paying compensation. 'If white settlers just took the land from us without paying for it, we can in a similar way just take it from them without paying for it or entertaining any ideas of legality and constitutionality. Perhaps our weakness has been the fact that we have tried to act morally and legally, when they acted immorally and illegally.'

When Clare Short's ministry finally announced in January 2000 that it would allocate an initial paltry sum of £5 million for land resettlement projects to be administered through non-governmental channels, Mugabe was 'beside himself with rage', according to one of his ministers, Nathan Shamuyarira. After what the Zimbabwean government saw as the international community's lengthy and unnecessary interruption of its own plans, Britain's decision to sideline the state's redistribution programme in favour of civil society initiatives was seen as a major rebuff in Harare. A summary of these events by Amnesty International concluded: 'Apart from derailing the entire donor-supported programme, it gave support to civil society at a time when civil society movements (NGOs) were taken as a significant threat to Zanu-PF's chances of retaining power, a point underlined by the government's defeat, just one month later, in the February referendum on changing Zimbabwe's constitution.'

Clare Short's decision to channel Britain's land funding through civil society rather than the Zimbabwean government also implied the unthinkable, from Mugabe's point of view: that a central promise of the liberation struggle could be realised without the direct involvement of Zanu-PF. Indeed, by the end of February 2000, war veterans, youth 'militia' and an assortment of Zanu-PF supporters had started to invade commercial farms.

Provocative and insensitive as Clare Short's letter and subsequent British actions were to a chip-on-the-shoulder character like Robert Mugabe, part of what she was telling him was that Britain did not like the way he had been dishing out its money to his cronies. Short was saying, in effect, that Mugabe could not have it all ways. If Britain's government was going to support him, the British were entitled to insist on having some say over how he used their money. Even if Britain had robbed him in the past, the former colonial power's decision to help Mugabe in the present was conditional on his government being prevented from using donor money to enhance either his own importance or his cronies' lifestyles. It was not an unreasonable position for Britain to take.

Dark-haired and flamboyantly dressed in red, Clare Short's firm chin and no-nonsense body language suggest a confrontation even when you are looking for a chat. She laments:

> I can't believe Mugabe didn't want a sensible solution to the land problem when it was on offer (at the UN-led land conference). It has resulted in such a tragedy ... it's almost unbelievable. My own view is that after the referendum on a new constitution went against him in 2000, Mugabe got the shock of his life. Power makes people so arrogant, as we've seen recently with Thatcher and Blair over here. Mugabe had been in charge for a heck of a long time by then. He had forgotten about land redistribution

when he should have been dealing with it during the first 20 years of his rule, but then he went back to it when he was becoming unpopular. And he reached such a point of anger in the atmosphere he revived of the past when he was at his greatest, that while wallowing in his glory days and his grievances, he utterly wrecked his country.

The deeper source of Mugabe's grievances was the fact that his omnipotence was being thwarted by the British government. Mugabe's furious response to Clare Short's letter became typical of his behaviour in subsequent years: he lashed out at anyone who delineated the acceptable line of conduct and dared to tell him he had crossed it. His descent into tyranny, beginning with his attacks on the judiciary and the media in Zimbabwe and his vilification of the British government, was all about blows to his omnipotence.

What Short was conveying to Mugabe was that he was not the king of the castle. He could not do as he fancied, regardless of his mother's long-held belief that God was behind him. Mugabe's response, typical of a spoilt child when told he cannot do as he pleases, was to vow, 'I'll do what I want and you see if you can stop me. I want it my way and if you won't give it to me, I'll show you! You'll see what I can do!'

Terrifyingly, the emotionally underdeveloped Mugabe had the power of an adult man with a vast violent force at his disposal. 'I will do what I want and nobody is going to stop me' became his demonstrable attitude. Before long, it had become the reality because nobody stopped him. With no containment from any of the parental forces in his life – the British government, the African community of nations or the Catholic Church – a petulant Robert Mugabe proceeded to run amok.

Having grown up in a family without a father to set personal boundaries at important moments in his development, Mugabe had no clear limits and no male role models outside the church. There was no father figure to tell him to go to his room until he acted like a more reasonable human being, willing to compromise with other people. Tragically, the less he was stopped, the more it fuelled his omnipotence. Once he had realised the extent of his power in the nationwide land grab, and knowing that he really could do anything he liked, there was no looking back. Despite pushing his luck time and again, there were no serious consequences. So where was it going to end? How much damage did he have to do before someone told him, 'Here's the limit'?

Whether or not Mugabe's power could, in practice, have been curbed is an open-ended question. It is not possible to police a person who does not recognise an external authority. Mugabe also lacked an internal 'father' to help him develop a conscience and a sense of concern for others. Still operating with the maturity level of a young child, where there is no responsibility for the consequences of his actions, he was saying to himself, 'I have replaced my father so I'll do what I want and get rid of anybody who is in my way.' He lacked the capacity to see the consequences of his actions from any mature perspective.

Clare Short tried to curtail Mugabe's excesses but her methods were spectacularly unsuccessful. In arrogantly discarding what most Africans saw as Britain's moral responsibility to Zimbabwe, she fuelled the anti-imperialist sentiment that Mugabe subsequently manipulated to his own advantage among his African peers.

Short is not inclined to acknowledge her damagingly incautious role in what history will surely record as a disastrous chapter for British diplomacy. Instead, she is quick to condemn Peter Hain, Britain's minister of state responsible for Africa at the time and a man with a long history of opposition to white domination in Africa. 'I think the rhetoric of the UK was badly handled by Hain, of all people. I remember being in my bedroom in Birmingham and hearing him on the radio. I thought, "Peter, you sound like a colonial master speaking up for white farmers." And of course the media here loved that.'

The media also loved the underlying truth of some of Mugabe's charges against Britain. He argued that the sole reason he had been persuaded to sign the Lancaster House agreement, which guaranteed minority property rights for the first 10 years of his rule, was the promise of funding for land redistribution from Britain and the US. Mugabe disputed Clare Short's assertion that the Lancaster House deal had been binding only on the Tories. Some commentators noted that Short's ill-considered letter confirmed what Robert Mugabe had long believed: that the Conservatives understood the consequences of imperialism better than Labour because it was they who had conducted the colonial era and might be better trusted to deliver redress.

Short seizes the mention of historic amnesia as an opportunity to denigrate Tony Blair. 'He hasn't much knowledge of history anywhere in the world; he's just not a well-read man,' she argues. 'But I'm steeped in it.' She describes her Irish lineage and its role in the troubles there, culminating in the inevitability of civil war when the British, having partitioned the country, tried to force key Republicans to swear an oath of allegiance to the Crown. 'It was asking too much and some people just couldn't do it. That was another of the tragic moments in history we live to regret, like Tony Blair deciding to take Britain to war with Iraq, and Mugabe seizing the land.'

Having shown little insight into Mugabe's fury at her own actions, Clare Short reveals an unexpected understanding of his support among fellow African leaders. It is as if her digression into Irish nationalism has awakened a more sensitive view.

I understand why sophisticated people in South Africa, for instance, took a pro-Mugabe position. Land was the point of colonialism and all the ugly power issues that went with it. Mugabe was a giant of history who had liberated his country from oppression, so of course he was a massive icon in South Africa. I think this is part of the reason why South African President Thabo Mbeki has handled it all so badly.

The rhetoric of the British by Peter Hain got things off to a bad start in the neighbouring African states. I was arguing at the time that we should give out all the documentation of all the options on land redistribution and then keep our head down because the emotiveness of it all was affecting everybody. In that sense, Mugabe stirring up the land issue worked very well for him. But now, looking back, whatever they are saying today, all the leaders of Africa must know that they've helped wreck Zimbabwe so there must be some sort of a blame game. They're not going to say, 'Oh, if only we'd gone along with what was offered at the UN conference, we might not be here now.' No, they've got to blame somebody. Britain's the obvious historical figure, although they did business with Britain at Lancaster House. Mugabe says things went wrong because he couldn't get another phase of Lancaster House: he wanted to rewrite history.

It's one of the terrible tragedies of history, as I say. It's completely understandable why Mbeki couldn't or wouldn't; why neighbouring states in Africa couldn't or wouldn't. It was too difficult for them politically; the symbolism was just too strong. But I don't think any of them could have imagined, when deciding not to make a stand, that we'd end up here. If they'd known, they'd have done something earlier.

And if she had known where Zimbabwe was heading, what would Clare Short have done differently?

> One of Britain's errors was the noisy rhetoric. We should have kept it right down, not tried to take a leading position, and we should have made sure that the neighbouring countries were absolutely clear as to how much money was on offer and how strongly the case for redistribution was supported internationally. We should have made that our rhetoric. I absolutely don't accept that the letter I wrote was seminal, although of course I would take it away if that could stop the destruction and suffering that has gone on in Zimbabwe. But it is definitely Mugabe who is responsible.

Undoubtedly, Mugabe is to blame for wrecking Zimbabwe – with the unwitting collusion of his weak 'parents', Britain and Africa. Clare Short rapped him on the knuckles in a clumsy way but then, intimidated by his fury, Britain withdrew. Mugabe was quite obviously not listening to anybody. His power clearly needed to be limited but Britain simply said to Africa: 'He is a difficult child – you deal with him.' What the British failed to take into account was the extent of Africa's loyalty to Mugabe. Because the leaders of African nations had watched Britain condone Mugabe's Gukurahundi massacre of thousands of black people 15 years earlier, they thought Mugabe could be forgiven for assuming that the former colonial power would be equally indifferent to the brutal eviction of a much smaller number of white farmers from land which many Africans considered to be illegitimately occupied. Perhaps the only exception was Nelson Mandela, who made no secret of his condemnation of Mugabe's excesses and once clashed heatedly with Zimbabwe's president at a SADC meeting in Angola in 1997.

Clare Short insists that Britain has been more or less powerless in the region for at least half a century:

> All we can do now in watching the tragedy that is still unfolding in Zimbabwe is reflect on what happened. Through books like yours, we need to keep revisiting history. We need to capture all the details and interpretations of what happened and write it all down so that we can consider and perhaps understand the events more clearly with hindsight, and so that if we have failed to stop a tragedy or prevented it from happening in the first place, we can at least learn from it.

Some time after my interview with Clare Short I met Rajan Soni, an independent London-based consultant in the field of international development. He had been employed by the ODA to investigate land redistribution in Zimbabwe on a number of occasions, initially while the Conservatives were in power and again for DFID under Clare Short. Once the latter was calling the shots, he told me, it was absolutely clear from the attitude of her staff towards his recommendations that Labour's strategy was to accelerate Mugabe's unpopularity by failing to provide him with funding for land redistribution. 'They thought if they didn't give him the money for land reform his people in the rural areas would start to turn against him. That was their position; they wanted him out and they were going to do whatever they could to hasten his demise,' according to Soni.

Far from Britain feeling powerless in Zimbabwe, as Clare Short claims in the wake of Mugabe's destruction, it appears that Mugabe was correct in his belief that the former colonist was aiding and abetting the forces that opposed him, namely the MDC in cahoots with the predominantly white Zimbabweans who had organised and financed the party. Nothing was going to strengthen Mugabe's hand in Africa more than evidence of British attempts to topple an African head of state. Ironically, given Clare Short's high-minded though belated opposition to Britain's disastrous invasion of Iraq in the years that followed, her government's attempt to bring about a change of regime in Zimbabwe was based on remarkably similar foreign policy failures to those bedevilling Iraq. These included ignoring local history and the realities of power on the ground, failing to seek the advice of neighbouring countries in the region and failure to think about the long-term consequences of their actions.

Ultimately though, there is a sense of inevitability in Robert Mugabe's decline. Sooner or later he was bound to feel aggrieved because he was surely going to reach a point where he could not have his own way. A basic rule of the world, that we will all meet resistance somewhere along the line, forces most of us to find the wisdom to get on with our fellow humans without killing those who stand in our way. However painful our disappointments, we learn to come to terms with the loss of our dreams and the defeat of our plans through compromise and emotional maturity.

Not so Robert Mugabe. Clare Short's letter was a test of his character, which he failed miserably. He became enraged and aggrieved, justifying himself while blaming others in the classic response of the immature individual. Whether Short had provoked him or not, Mugabe had a choice. It may have been especially difficult for him to be constructive, having grown up in an environment that did not help him to develop emotionally, but he had the intellectual capacity as an adult to recognise this and rise above his upbringing. In dealing with colonialism and its aftermath, he had the choice of spending his time indulging his grievances and plotting his revenge, or he could try to get over it and build an alternative that worked. Although he had enough resources left in Zimbabwe in 2000 to start afresh, Mugabe was so busy scoring points against his enemies that he undermined his own possibilities for progress.

Nine

A reluctant politician

One person who brought out the best in Mugabe was, surprisingly, a white farmer called Denis Norman. Tall, humorous and hard-working, he was Zimbabwe's first agriculture minister and a forthright individual to whom the president often turned for help when he needed a problem solved. An affable Englishman who managed to avoid being contaminated by the racism that poisoned Zimbabwe as surely as it had done Rhodesia, he still speaks with an Oxfordshire burr more than half a century after migrating to the southern African country as a humble farm assistant.

Had Denis Norman rather than Ian Smith led Zimbabwe's white community, the country's recent history might have been dramatically different. But Norman was not a politician at heart, although he served in Mugabe's Cabinet four times. 'He brought me in whenever there was a mess,' explains Norman. 'He seemed to have confidence that I would sort things out for him.' More recently, the British government has also put its faith in Denis Norman. It is with Norman that Foreign Office officials consult periodically in the hope of eventually mending relations between the two countries.

As the Zimbabwean leader's favourite travel companion, as well as Mugabe's preferred troubleshooter, Norman accompanied the president on state visits all over the world in the first two decades after independence.

He always seemed to want me along, except once when he said he wasn't going to take me behind the Iron Curtain. I asked why not and he told me he didn't think I'd enjoy it and he didn't think they'd understand me. I said, 'Fine, I'll stay on this side then.' I was one of the few people who could make Mugabe laugh and I was always able to talk to him frankly. I owed nothing to him or anybody else and I never wanted to be a politician in the first place so my attitude was that if he didn't like what I was saying or doing, he could take my job and give it to someone else.

Known among Zimbabwe's white farmers as 'Nothing's Wrong Norman', the burly Englishman-turned-African owned seven farms when Mugabe came to power, and he headed the Commercial Farmers' Union (CFU) in the days when Zimbabwe grew most of the world's tobacco.

I first met Mugabe a few weeks before the election in 1980. He was the last of the contending nationalist leaders to come back to the country from exile and he arrived on a tumultuous wave of support. He sent a message to say he wanted to meet me as one of the leaders of the private sector. I went to his house, where he had an office, with some trepidation because we'd been fed a diet of horror stories that he was the man with horns and a tail. He was welcoming and charming but none of us thought he was going to win at that stage.

Mugabe suggested he send some of his staff to the CFU's offices for a crash course in agriculture during the few weeks remaining before the election, and Norman was happy to oblige. The day after Zanu's victory, Norman was summoned to the British governor's residence and told by Lord Soames that he was the new agriculture minister.

I said, 'No, I can't be.' Soames replied that Mugabe was forming a best-man government and had nobody with any knowledge of commercial agriculture so I was the one who was going to help him. I said, 'No, I'm not', very firmly. It was the last job I wanted. But he insisted that we couldn't afford to let the opportunity slip. Saying things like, 'It won't be forever' and 'Surely you can give a bit of time to save your country', he got me to agree to think about it.

The next day, when the undecided Norman reported back to Soames, he was sent to see Mugabe, who greeted him warmly and said how delighted he was to hear that Norman would be joining Zanu's government.

I told him I hadn't even made my mind up yet and I definitely wasn't going to join his party, to which he replied, 'I'm not asking you to. All I'm asking is if you'll join the government as deputy minister of mines and help me out.' I told him, 'No, that can't be. I don't know a thing about mining,' made my excuses and stormed back to Soames' office, where I pulled him out of a meeting and said, 'Count me out.' But that evening, I got another call from Soames, advising me to listen to the 6pm news. I asked him why and he replied, 'Because you're in – you're the minister of agriculture.'

We are talking in the study of Denis Norman's relatively modest home in West Sussex, England. The walls are adorned with framed photographs of him posing with the famous, among them the Queen and an assortment of world leaders, including a smiling Robert Mugabe. In pride of place is a large oil painting of the Normans' magnificent farm residence in Norton, Zimbabwe – a Cape Dutch mansion surrounded by prize-winning gardens. He says he visited Zimbabwe on business in 2006, but not his former home on the farm. 'I'll never go back. I couldn't bear to see it again,' he mutters.

Norman's memory of the early part of Mugabe's premiership is of a man in quiet command, listening carefully to everybody and never cutting off even the most verbose of his ministers; a leader who did not raise his voice and was unfailingly polite to everyone.

He was a very disciplined man. He treated people with respect. He wasn't lavish in his lifestyle but he did have clear standards. He dressed well, invariably in a dark suit with a silk tie and matching handkerchief, but without ostentation. He wore a good watch but nothing flashy. You could tell that money and acquisitiveness were not part of his motivation. There was another motive that drove him.

He always seemed to value my opinion and I'm sure he gave the rest of his Cabinet that impression as well. He came to my defence a few times because in the beginning some of the other blokes clearly saw me and the only other white minister, David Smith, as usurpers. One of them warned me that he'd personally see that I was out within eight weeks.

At the first Cabinet meeting, the blokes turned up in all kinds of gear

– Hawaiian shirts, Mao uniforms and bush camouflage. After about four hours when everybody had had his say, Mugabe summed up, saying the new government had got off to a good start and we'd be meeting every Tuesday. 'There's just one more thing,' he added quietly. 'If you want to be Cabinet ministers, I expect you to dress like Cabinet ministers.' That set the tone for his leadership straight away, calmly authoritative, and the following Tuesday every one of them was in a sober suit and tie.

Norman's anecdote about Zimbabwe's first Cabinet meeting illustrates not only the new prime minister's quiet authority but Mugabe's apparent preference for a Cabinet full of immaculately dressed Anglophiles. In this example of his ambiguous identity, Mugabe did not seem to accept his ministers as African parliamentarians with their own distinctive style, nor himself as an essentially African leader. His own dress and manners tended to mirror English rather than African norms. Indeed, in adopting Rhodesia's laws and institutions virtually intact, he seems to have been intent on recreating a colonial picture from the very beginning.

Norman well remembers his first disagreement with Mugabe in Cabinet. There had been a debate for 14 weeks over the price of cattle and Norman had prepared a schedule to support his claim for a 30 per cent increase. Each time he presented it, his colleagues argued for a lower rate and Norman withdrew the paper, only to present it afresh the following week. Eventually, when there was agreement on 29 per cent and Norman was about to withdraw his request again, Mugabe stepped in:

'That's it,' he said. 'I'm sick and tired of this nonsense. Twenty-nine per cent it is.' And I said, 'No.' He was annoyed and told me, 'We've come all this way with you and you haven't budged an inch. Surely you'll give us just the one per cent difference?' I told him, 'No, I won't.' He looked surprised and asked why not and I replied, 'Because my paper was detailed. I went to a lot of trouble to prepare it and I can justify 30 per cent. The only justification for your 29 per cent is that it's less than 30.' So he sighed and said, 'Okay, 30.'

Somebody then asked when the increase became operative and Mugabe replied, 'Tomorrow.' I said, 'No, no, three months back when I started the negotiation.' Mugabe refused to shift at that point but so did

I. Knowing how wary he was of upsetting the farmers in those days, I said, 'Who's going to tell the CFU that the government's let them down – is it going to be you or me?' He looked at me for a long time and finally relented, 'All right,' he said, 'but don't you ever do that to me again.'

Interestingly, Mugabe was not rigid in his dealings with Denis Norman. They had a head-on confrontation in full view of the entire Cabinet yet the premier was able to back down, having considered Norman's position. The two adults had their differences, discussed them and resolved them. Theirs was a mature relationship because Norman talked to Mugabe respectfully yet firmly, having done his homework thoroughly. Uncompromising in the best sense, Norman was not out to triumph, humiliate, or score points – and Mugabe knew the farmer was no threat to him. Norman cut a swathe through power relations by making it clear that he was not a politician playing games, and Mugabe appreciated that. The two men trusted each other.

Norman's relationship with the Zimbabwean president was unlike any other in Mugabe's life. For a start, Norman was his own person: he could not be corrupted because he was not driven by self-interest. Neither obsequious nor manipulative, he had preconceptions about Mugabe in the beginning but after meeting him man to man considered the president to be a thoughtful, intelligent person and was thereafter completely fair-minded in his dealings with Mugabe. Norman understood communal culture and, in accomplishing a shift to African values, was able to plan his projects appropriately. Though extremely wealthy, he had no airs and graces. When asked by Mugabe to help out, he always obliged. Mugabe was then able to hand over to Norman, giving him the support and the space to do what needed to be done. When undertaking a mission, Norman engaged fully, learnt voraciously but then let go. His generosity and unusually strong sense of self exerted a positive influence on Zimbabwe's president, making Norman an admirable asset to Mugabe at a time when the new premier was feeling his way. It was a good relationship in every respect. Unfortunately, though, there were few others like Norman in Mugabe's court.

Over the next five years Norman accompanied Mugabe on several tours of the country. The prime minister, as he was at the time, related well to the mainly white commercial farmers and was always willing to meet agricultural leaders. Some land was being purchased by the government on a willing buyer-willing seller basis but as Norman points out, the easy part of land reform is acquiring it. The difficult proposition is making the land productive and Zimbabwe was providing scant support to peasant farmers in the mid-80s.

> Nevertheless, as a result of our projects to make the markets more accessible, peasant agriculture went up 1400 per cent in the first four years alone. I defy any country to better that. This prosperity in far-flung areas had a knock-on effect. The whole emphasis of development began to change and Mugabe loved the new mood of empowerment in the rural areas. People began to insist on having a say. When an NGO arrived and announced that they were going to build a school, the locals said, 'No, we don't want a school.' They already had a good school on the other side of the river: what they wanted was a bridge so that both their children and their goods could cross the river. I saw agriculture as the route to development and so did Mugabe. He was terribly enthusiastic.

In his dealings with Denis Norman, you see a side of Mugabe that was creative, passionate and flexible. The two men ignited something in each other that was grounded in their mutual commitment to Zimbabwe's progress. Working out solutions to development challenges, they formed a genuine partnership that had nothing to do with the patronage characterising Mugabe's power relations. Together they watched with pride as the country flourished in the first five years of Mugabe's rule.

> He very seldom went without a tie. He was always the prime minister visiting his people, which went down extremely well. He was very, very popular for the first 10 years. He was more interested in the projects than meeting actual people, though he always enjoyed talking to the ones in the know, the experts. He wasn't a people's person except when he had a large audience to address. On a one-to-one basis, he appeared to be embarrassed, awkward – shy, actually. He'd be obliged to go to official functions and banquets, which he never enjoyed. He sat there looking miserable with a glass of water or sipping wine that remained half-full at the end of the night. People like Mugabe's relative James Chikerema have told us over the years that he was a loner even in his school days, so that

was evidently a lifelong trend.

The only time he ever went to a minister's house was to express condolences, and he was particular about doing that sort of thing in person. He only once visited me at my home, which was to meet South African tycoon Anton Rupert for tea. He signed Zimbabwe up for Rupert's peace parks project as a result of that meeting. Anton thought he was superb, as he was in those days.

Mugabe took a great interest in the annual Harare Agricultural Show, recalls Norman, explaining that their Cabinet colleagues did not share the enthusiasm for what many considered 'a white man's colonial bang'. Having an obvious affinity for cattle, Mugabe attended with Norman every year and would rush past other exhibits to get to the livestock section, where he became quite knowledgeable over time and got to know some of the breeders by name.

Because it was considered poor form for the prime minister to visit the show without seeing at least one government exhibit, Mugabe would put in a token appearance at one of the state's stands.

On one occasion, we went to see the prison services' exhibit together. Walking through it, glancing at displays of the mailbags sewn by prisoners, that sort of thing, Mugabe was going at his usual brisk pace, hoping not to engage with anybody, when there appeared in front of us one of the biggest guys you've ever seen in your life, an Afrikaner built like a rugby lock, his chest and hat gleaming with brass. He threw the most extravagant salute as Mugabe was rushing past. All of a sudden, Mugabe stopped, his stride briefly suspended mid-air. 'My God,' he exclaimed, turning to face the prisons chief. 'It's Dupe!' And he clasped this mountainous bloke excitedly, introducing me to his former warder, a man named Du Plessis, who had become the chief of staff. 'Come on, Dupe, show us your stand,' Mugabe enthused and we wandered aimlessly around the exhibition as the two of them reminisced. When we left, Mugabe patted the officer's chest full of medals and said to me, 'He's risen all the way through the ranks. I always thought you'd make it, Dupe.' And this enormous white man replied, 'I always thought you had a good chance too, sir.' Mugabe couldn't stop laughing.

Their mutual love of cattle was not only a bond between Mugabe and

Norman but an indication of a shared aesthetic. Perhaps the sight of cows reminded Mugabe of an earlier time when he could escape his problems and read books alone amid the silent beauty of the countryside during his youth. It was a simple connection he had made early on with Norman, which reflected not only their mutual discomfort in the limelight but also the undemanding nature of animals as opposed to people. As a result of his affection for cattle, Mugabe took a keen interest in Norman's campaign to eradicate tsetse fly, one of several agricultural controls that had collapsed during the war years. Whenever Norman came to Mugabe's office, the prime minister would take the time to question him on the wider agricultural scene and, invariably, suggest that the two of them made another countrywide tour together.

Then he fired me. The results of an election for the 20 white seats that had been guaranteed for the first five years under Lancaster House had just been announced. Ian Smith had won most of them and, as a result, I got the chop. Mugabe was very, very upset. He wrote me a letter, thanking me for all my efforts but saying that the whites did not seem to appreciate what he had done for them 'and so I'm afraid they're going to get a black minister'.

It was a knee-jerk reaction on his part and a foolish move on theirs. They had had five excellent years. It was during that time that we negotiated our way into the European market for beef. They had it all going for them but there was still this 'good old Smithy: he'll see us right' thing, even though Smith was already history by then. Like Mugabe, I couldn't understand why they supported Smith when given the chance to endorse Mugabe, whose policies were definitely in their favour at the time. When Mugabe came into power, he had appointed a white man to head the army, a white man was in charge of police, I had agriculture and David Smith got commerce and industry. He did everything to appease white fear of black rule. He didn't put his own people into these key positions to start with. He was terribly disappointed and above all hurt, I think, when the whites voted for Smith in these circumstances, after all his efforts. In my opinion, that was the first big setback we suffered as a country under Mugabe.

The moment when whites voted racially marked, as Norman says, the beginning of the Zimbabwean tragedy. In telling the new president that like their old leader Ian Smith, white Zimbabweans as a group would not hold Mugabe's hand, they conveyed to him their decision to stick with their own kind – not because Mugabe had failed to do a good job but because he was black.

Mugabe saw their decision as a betrayal, which came as a major disillusionment to him. Since taking office and attempting to hold Smith's hand in 1980, he had nurtured the utopian idea that everyone would get together and make Zimbabwe a success. Although unrealistic, his vision of unstinting cooperation seemed to work as he had envisaged for the first five years. During that time, especially in his relationship with Denis Norman, Mugabe showed all of his positive attributes and potential. But he did not have the inner core of emotional development to overcome his disappointment when the whites failed to acknowledge the efforts he had made to reassure and accommodate them. His bitter response in firing Denis Norman was to convey a new mood in the country. 'You be white and we will be black,' he was telling the white community. 'You go your own white way and we will go ours.' He was deeply hurt by their racial rejection and hell-bent on revenge. Unable to see beyond himself and his feelings, he got rid of Denis Norman – someone who had helped him out constantly and was a real ally to him.

Unlike Mugabe, who lacked the emotional maturity to resist revenge, Denis Norman was not a man to bear grudges. Despite being punished by Zimbabwe's leader for his whiteness, he got over it and remained on good terms with the president. He did not get caught in the racial maelstrom, however distressing it was to be used by Mugabe as a pawn against the white community. Embracing life once more, he did not succumb to bitterness but found another project and got on with it.

After leaving the government, Norman became chairman of a new organisation called the Beira Corridor Group, which aimed to restore the various lines of communication between Zimbabwe and Mozambique that had been destroyed during successive wars in the region. Within 10 years, this private sector initiative had rebuilt the port of Beira, laid down railway tracks, resurfaced roads and opened up the oil pipeline between the two countries. Norman used to report personally to Mugabe on the project, their relationship having remained warm and courteous.

In 1987, there was another scheduled change to the Lancaster House constitution, this time abolishing the reserved white seats and holding an election for 10 seats in the senate. Mugabe asked me to stand and I declined and then, as usual, he persuaded me, saying I had to help him out. So I stood, and I topped the poll. However, after I had served for three years in the senate, he abolished it altogether in 1990, which I thought was a major mistake. The second chamber acted as a brake on legislation being pushed through on waves of emotion, as happened quite often in Zimbabwe.

But Norman was not to be out of government for long.

The day after he abolished the senate, Mugabe phoned and asked me to come and see him. When I sat down opposite him at State House, he said, 'You're the minister of transport.' I laughed and objected, saying I may not have known enough about agriculture but I knew absolutely nothing about transport. Citing the Beira Corridor successes as evidence to the contrary, he told me the transport portfolio wasn't going at all well and would I please help him out just one more time. Reluctantly, I agreed.

Once again, Denis Norman embarked on a tour of the country, this time looking at transport, roads, bridges, and so on. He was appalled to see that, 10 years after independence, there hadn't been a single major project in Matabeleland, the heartland of Zanu-PF's traditional opposition.

That's what I set about remedying first, among other problems. And surprisingly, we raised quite a lot of funding from the Japanese, the Germans and various others. Then came the new Harare airport project in 1988, a complete disaster.

We had called for international tenders, whittled them down to eight and then to three. Eventually, the contract was awarded to a French company. Next thing, a bunch of Arabs clutching worry beads arrived at my home at 10pm one night, telling me they'd been to see Mugabe and wanted to build the airport. They hadn't even tendered the first time around and they were quick to mention their involvement with Leo Mugabe, the president's nephew.

Norman sent them packing. Making enquiries about the tender irregularity at the next Cabinet meeting, he tried to find out who had been responsible for sponsoring the Arabs. His colleagues insisted the contract had been awarded too hastily, despite Norman pointing out that he had spent two years on the tender. Finally, he compromised by suggesting a re-tender process that would be restricted to the original semi-finalists but include the Arabs.

> We brought in international evaluators and the Arabs came last while the French company won it again. I assumed it would go ahead on that basis but by then I was in the process of moving back to my old agriculture portfolio because that had gone downhill meanwhile and Mugabe wanted me back in it. My successor approved the airport for the Arabs within a week of me going. I tried to warn Mugabe but he was waffling a lot by then and he told me, 'Ah well, we have to try and take everybody with us.' He wasn't anywhere near as tough or as principled as he had been 10 years earlier.

Norman attributes Mugabe's irresolute behaviour to the fact that there were increasing signs of dissatisfaction in some quarters:

> The Young Turks, the wealthy 40-year-olds, were beginning to push and agitate. They wanted their chance at the helm and the men around Mugabe were still very much to the fore and in the way. Money was beginning to change hands on things like tenders and Mugabe knew it but he didn't do anything about it because it meant challenging those loyal to him in an environment where more and more weren't on his side any more. It began slowly but you could detect in all sorts of ways that he wasn't totally hands on the wheel any more. We got an airport half the size for twice the price because the original Japanese funders pulled out of the Arab deal, the interest rate shot up and Mugabe just allowed it to happen because his concerns lay elsewhere.

After barely two years in the transport ministry, Denis Norman was returning to the country one night, waiting to collect his suitcase, when a baggage attendant at the airport informed him that his appointment as minister of energy had just been announced on the radio. 'He was congratulating me and I told him, "No, you're mistaken. I'm the minister of transport, not energy." He replied with a laugh, "Actually, you're the minister of both." And sure enough, another letter of appointment was waiting for me in my office.'

Within a few weeks, the lights had gone out in Zimbabwe – literally. Denis Norman asked around and everyone told him it was because the water was low at Kariba due to the drought. Nobody in the ministry was any the wiser so he went to Kariba himself to talk to the station manager:

> He told me the problem was not at Kariba but at Hwange, where five of the six generators had burnt out. When I got there, everybody in the power station blamed lack of money, which I didn't accept. Then a youngish black chap sidled up to me and said, 'If you want to get this all in working order, I know the man who can do it for you.' The person he had in mind was the former station manager, who had been sacked by an earlier minister. I asked him where the man was and, shrugging, he said 'Somewhere in England.' I managed to find his address and wrote him a letter, asking if he wanted his job back. His reply said he'd be arriving the following morning. But he didn't come to me in the ministry: he went straight to Hwange and within a fortnight he had a second generator going.

A few months later, Norman recalls with amusement, he received a request from the reinstated station manager at Hwange for a week's leave in the UK. When Norman asked how he could possibly justify time off so soon after taking up his appointment in Zimbabwe, the man explained that he had jumped on the first plane from London and now needed to return for his clothes. It is an example among several given by Norman of how keen individuals and corporations within the private sector were to come to the country's rescue in times of need – with some notable exceptions.

'Ian Smith lost the biggest opportunity of all in 1980,' explains Norman, adding that he blames Smith for squandering vital goodwill. 'He was in Parliament with 20 seats. Mugabe was very accommodating but Smith did not respond well. If he had told his followers to support Mugabe's efforts, you would have had more people pulling together much earlier.' The problem was that Smith resented losing power himself and he was not magnanimous enough to conquer his own disappointment in the interests of the country, says Norman.

Norman's wife June is a descendant of a member of Cecil John Rhodes' original Pioneer Column that trekked from Kimberley in South Africa to Rhodesia. She invites us to the dining room for a delicious lunch of trout, boiled new potatoes, homemade mayonnaise and fresh strawberry ice cream. Despite having lost a fortune in Zimbabwe and suffered the disintegration of their close family as two sons and a daughter settled in Australia and South Africa, while their parents went to live in England, the Normans do not appear to hold a grudge against Robert Mugabe.

Although June shakes her head when I ask if she is bitter, she shrugs helplessly and points out, with a wary glance at her husband, 'Mugabe always had the power to do something about it.' Norman considers her remark and adds slowly, 'I don't personally dislike him but I do think he should have retired 10 years ago. He was always good to me. I always found him personable and honourable in his dealings. He also had a warm side to him which I saw quite clearly sometimes.'

One evening while in Swaziland for a SADC (Southern African Development Community) meeting on agriculture, for example, a number of ministers were packing up after Mugabe had announced he was tired following numerous meetings. Norman asked casually if anyone had heard the news. 'I used to love throwing a pebble in and watching the ripples,' he recalls.

'What news?' they chorused and I told them that Margaret Thatcher had resigned. Well, what a rumpus ensued. They were cheering and clapping and whooping with delight. Mugabe just sat there looking stern until the din subsided and then he asked, 'What's all the hilarity about?' They squirmed a bit because you could see he was being sarcastic but they told him, 'The Iron Lady's gone – good riddance to her,' that sort of comment. He kept very quiet for a while and then asked, 'Well, is it really such a good thing that she's gone? Let me remind you of some facts. Who got us our independence; was it the Tory's Margaret Thatcher or Labour's James Callaghan? Who was the prime minister of Britain who sponsored Lancaster House?' He went on: 'Let me tell you all something important. I don't agree with her policies but I do respect her. I respect her for what she stands for in her own way. She deserved a better end than this and I'm going straight back to my room now to write her a letter. See you all tomorrow.'

Mugabe was a person who made up his own mind, notes Norman. He never socialised and he had no close friends with whom to discuss his own problems. But he took an interest in colleagues and often tried to help them resolve their own issues, according to Norman:

> During the early years of our independence, Mugabe approached me one day and said he needed a favour from me. He said all our colleagues in Cabinet had achieved something on their own steam, either at university or in their careers. 'But not Maurice Nyagumbo and I'm worried about him,' Mugabe said. Maurice hadn't gone further than waiting on hotel tables because he'd always been in a prison, either in South Africa or Rhodesia. But now Maurice had decided he wanted to be a farmer, Mugabe told me, and he had identified the farm he wanted in his area, Rusape. Could I perhaps arrange a loan for him to buy it? I looked doubtful but said I'd see what I could do.

Norman rang a friend at the Land Bank and in due course informed Mugabe that Maurice could borrow the money for his farm. Mugabe was delighted.

> Ten months later, it was Maurice who came to see me, saying he now needed a favour. 'Can you buy the farm back?' he pleaded, explaining that 50 of his relatives were living there and expecting him to look after them. 'They're costing me so much that I just can't afford to live on the farm any more,' he told me. So I went back to the Land Bank and the chairman arranged for the farm to be sold to someone else. We had a good laugh about it but the story illustrates a big problem in Africa. Maurice was successful among a lot of poor relatives and so he was expected to support them all. It's a recipe for disaster and feeds into corruption, nepotism and all sorts of problems not experienced by Westerners. Maurice eventually committed suicide after being found guilty of corruption in the Willowgate scandal involving the purchase of motor vehicles at discount prices. He told me shortly before he died that he hadn't kept a single one of those cars for himself.

When Norman decided to leave Zimbabwe in 2003 and went to say goodbye to Mugabe, Zimbabwe's premier looked baffled on hearing the news:

He asked where I was going and when I told him England, he said in disbelief, 'But you can't do that. Why?' I told him I'd taken a job as a conservation consultant. He asked how long a contract I'd signed and when I said it was for three years he looked relieved and said, 'Well okay, but don't stay away too long. Come back.' Telling him I'd think about it, I then asked, 'But there's a question I want to ask you: where did it all go wrong?' And he replied, 'You're being a bit impertinent aren't you? *Has* it all gone wrong?' I answered, 'I know it has and you know it has gone wrong so why don't we discuss it honestly?' And he looked at me wistfully for a while, mumbling about honesty being a commodity in very short supply around his office. Then he said slowly, 'Things aren't what they used to be, are they?' He reminisced about the trips we used to make around the country, saying, 'Those were good days, weren't they? I really enjoyed it all back then.'

Mugabe went on to answer Norman's question by listing the usual scapegoats, including Tony Blair. He said he had never got along with Labour leaders because they did not understand the consequences and responsibilities of colonialism. 'They just don't see things the way we do,' Mugabe complained.

I remember him getting that hostile letter from Clare Short soon after Labour took over. He was furious. 'Who are these people to tell me they're not involved?' he kept asking. His anger towards Britain built up from a starting point and her letter was that starting point. Mugabe couldn't solve the land issue without money and he didn't have the money. I do blame Britain for that. It was a diplomatic blunder whether it was the fault of the High Commission or the Foreign Office. They should have known how he would react, regardless of their own aims and constraints in respect of new ethical aid policies and commitments of their own. The NGO thing was extremely badly handled by Britain too. Why make such an issue of funnelling money through the non-governmental sector when there were plenty of good government agencies to work with in Zimbabwe at the time? It never failed to upset Mugabe. 'Don't they trust me with their money?' he'd ask constantly. Those two blunders by the British government soured relations not only with Britain but with the EU countries too, who all took the lead from Britain as far as Zimbabwe was concerned.

If his quarrels with Britain had occurred in isolation, they might not have amounted to much, says Norman.

> But at the same time as he was feeling let down by the Labour government in England, he was starting to lose influence and prestige at home. Not only was he well aware that the next generation was getting restive, but he'd also lost some of his aura when Nelson Mandela was released from prison in South Africa. That hit him hard because he'd always been the kingpin in SADC for example, and then the spotlight shifted pointedly to Mandela. I went all over Africa and the world with him and often saw his acute sensitivity to the intrusion of Mandela. He felt he'd been battling away against insuperable odds in Zimbabwe while Mandela languished in prison. That's how he saw it.

He bitterly resented South Africa surging ahead on Mandela's coat-tails, explains Norman, who sat in many meetings with the two leaders during the 90s.

> There was no banter between them at all; they were miles apart. Once, when we jointly opened a bridge at the border with South Africa, the two of them walked towards the middle from their respective sides, each carrying a pair of scissors to cut the ribbon – a bit like the pistols at dawn scene. Then some white students came across from the South African side to organise lunch for everybody. Mandela thanked the students and suddenly announced a photo opportunity with them and the two presidents. He referred to Zimbabwe's leader simply as Mugabe, not by his full title. Well, they rushed towards Mandela, a couple of kids sitting on each knee, while Mugabe was completely left out. He looked awkward and aggrieved while Mandela was enjoying himself, cameras flashing, everybody laughing. You could see that Mugabe felt upstaged by this flamboyant man.

Mugabe's jealousy of Mandela was akin to sibling rivalry. He had longed all his life to be recognised as the special one who was not like all the others. But just when he had ascended the castle steps, along came this worldly-wise older brother, who was on top of his game and who immediately hogged the limelight. Mandela was not in the least insecure. His easy confidence as he charmed absolutely everybody was hard for Mugabe to swallow. He felt he had overcome so much ... and now this! Even Mandela noticed his pique and quipped that Mugabe had been the star 'until the sun came out'. Coming on top of a lot of other disillusionments in the early 90s, Mandela's emergence as the king of the world was one too many disappointments for a weak man like Mugabe to bear graciously.

'So you have this sensitive man feeling deeply insecure,' explains Norman. 'He senses things are going wrong and starts tightening up around himself; his security tightens, his speeches become more threatening; he openly fears the media. Eventually the legislation starts becoming more repressive. And into this situation come the war veterans, opportunists who sense that things are less well defined than ever before.'

Led by a reckless man, Chenjerai Hunzvi, who called himself 'Hitler', the war veterans demanded a meeting with Mugabe in 1997. They complained bitterly, saying they had won the country's freedom but been overlooked since independence, and they demanded Z$2 000 each per month for life as well as an initial payout of $50 000.

I had resigned as minister of agriculture shortly before the war vets came on the scene but I know that Mugabe had two ministers with him at that first meeting when Hunzvi announced that they wanted to talk exclusively to the president. I was really surprised to hear that Mugabe obligingly asked his ministers to leave. In his heyday, he would have said, 'No, this is my team and they're staying.'

The result of the meeting was that a lot of money was awarded to the war vets. Mugabe thought there were around 27 000 of them but then the number grew to over 50 000 – many more jumped in on the racket. Inevitably, it didn't work because these guys quickly ran out of money so they came back for more – $2 000 a month became $4 000 and so on. Hunzvi had accurately sensed Mugabe's weakness setting in and thought he'd try his luck. He got away with it the first and the second time. Then they went back a third time and said what they really wanted was the land that he'd promised them during the war. Mugabe was in a situation where he was dealing with a blackmailer. You pay once, then he demands more; you pay again and suddenly he's got you.

Mugabe tried to deal with the war veterans' demands single-handedly, perhaps because he feared the land issue might provide one of his challengers with a powerful tool to use against him, speculates Norman.

Nobody knew what was going on. Nothing was budgeted for so finance kicked up but the minister was told by Mugabe, 'Just find it.' When it came to the third meeting and Mugabe knew the money couldn't just be found, he told the war veterans that they had indeed been promised land so perhaps they should simply take it. He had no solutions left so he made this throwaway remark, thinking it would get them off his back. He didn't say, 'I will introduce legislation to acquire the land which will eventually be distributed to you,' as he should have done. They went straight out of his office and undertook the first wave of mayhem on commercial farms. It was only then that Mugabe realised how urgently he had to get on top of the situation so he started legislating for what was actually a spontaneous land grab. In my opinion, that just made matters worse because my impression at the time, talking to everybody, was that the war veterans would have disappeared after a while. They'd come from nowhere and would fade away, I thought.

The rest is history now. The war vets moved on to commercial farms in mobs. I saw Mugabe almost daily when the grab began because I was representing various farming groups and individuals. He would always see me. I said, 'Look, do you realise what's happening at Anglo Estates or here or there?' And he would look shocked, genuinely, and say, 'But they can't do that; they're not allowed to do that. Phone the police chief or this regional officer or that CIO director.' You could see he felt completely impotent. I was always phoning somebody or other on Mugabe's instructions, trying to damp the fires down, but Mugabe knew it was out of control. He knew you couldn't put the genie back in the bottle. There were gangs springing up spontaneously all over the country, including his police and army officers. He had let them loose without realising it at the time. His own people weren't telling him what was going on any more because they were all getting involved. You had hundreds of warlords, including Mugabe's relatives, springing up all over Zimbabwe, each grabbing his own patch and saying 'I'm in charge – I'm the commander of this section or that section.'

On many farms, two groups would arrive at the same time and launch pitched battles to establish control. Many farmers got caught in the middle; some died. It was mayhem for a while and Mugabe's preoccupation was to position himself in such a way as to look like he was in charge. But it had definitely run away from him. It was absolutely clear to us – and to him – that he had lost control. From then on, the legislation became tougher and tougher. The curbs on journalists and the firing of judges were all purely to tighten the screws so that he could stay in power.

Whether it is true that Mugabe had no control over the farm invasions, as Denis Norman believes, or whether he simply wanted to give Norman this impression, remains unclear. Given that farm invasions were run from Zanu-PF offices with the active help of the police and local officials, it is hard to see how Mugabe could not have approved them.

Increasingly, Zimbabwe's president resorted to violence to counter his impotence and loss of power, bullying being his last resort. 'Mugabe isn't a flashy man driven by wealth but he does enjoy power,' summarises Denis Norman. 'That's always been his motivation. When he saw it beginning to slip due to what he believed were other people's failings, he started lashing out, an instinct that got the better of him and became unstoppable.'

Ten

The faithful priest

One man who knows Robert Mugabe better than most is Father Fidelis Mukonori, the head of the Jesuits in Zimbabwe. He says their relationship is 'respectable', based on a long history of trust and debate. 'I say what I want to him – straight. He knows I have no political ambitions; nothing to hide from him. And he is relaxed when he's talking to me. Am I his friend? Well, he is as old as my father and we have never gone for golf or swimming together, but there are things he can say to me which I don't think many people know.' Admitting that some of his dealings with Zimbabwe's president require his input 'from a Catholic priest's point of view', Father Mukonori says his church does not, however, talk in terms of 'confessions'. He concedes that Robert Mugabe uses him 'as a sounding board', but will not be drawn into a discussion on the president's regrets, which is fair enough. What is less understandable from a priest, however, is Father Mukonori's failure in several hours of discussion with me to condemn any of Mugabe's actions.

Their relationship began during Zimbabwe's war of liberation, when Brother Mukonori was one of few activists who was, as a cleric, able to travel freely around Rhodesia gathering sensitive information at a time when nationalist politicians were either in prison or under surveillance. He began to conduct briefings with Zanla's commanders at their bases in Mozambique, having become Mugabe's eyes and ears inside the country.

We met often. We'd talk very frankly. I'd give him a full report on the military situation inside the country as well as a general intelligence update. They would brief us from their side and we'd analyse all the information. Mugabe ran these meetings, which would sit for five hours non-stop. I'd tell him how the guerrillas were behaving inside the country. If he had been led to believe that a particular action had been carried out by Rhodesian soldiers when it hadn't, I'd say, 'No, it was Comrade so-and-so in command and this is what his men did.'

Mugabe relied on him for the truth, says Mukonori. 'He always knew he got it from me. It's my style. I tell it like it is. If God himself came to tell me something, I'd question him to make sure the information was correct.' He explains that Mugabe was aware that one of Brother Mukonori's tasks at the Catholic training institute Silveira House before and during the war was counselling young people who planned to enlist in the guerrilla forces. 'I used to sit down with them and ask why they were going to war and see if they really understood the meaning of war – that they would either kill or be killed. I would try to explain what they were in for; that there's more suffering in a guerrilla war than in a conventional one because nothing is provided, like food, discipline, medicine. The guerrilla has to manage for himself.'

Father Mukonori achieved a master's degree in theology at the elite University of California, Berkeley. He was well known in liberation circles for having acted as Mugabe's go-between on the international stage. It was he, working with another member of the respected Catholic Commission for Justice and Peace (CCJP), who conducted the shuttle diplomacy that kick-started Lancaster House, for example.

During my briefings with the guerrilla leaders in their camps outside the country in the 70s, Mugabe and Nkomo had often said they were willing to go to an all-party conference and I used to think about that a lot. After acting as researcher and adviser to the nationalists during various failed Anglo-American initiatives, I knew exactly where everyone's weaknesses and problems were. We drew up a plan and spent five weeks shuttling between the two leaders of the Patriotic Front. Nkomo thought it an excellent document and Mugabe did too. We asked them, 'Are you willing to attend an all-party conference?' Both said yes – anywhere, anytime.

The Patriotic Front stressed the need for Britain to accept its responsibility as the coloniser, recalls Father Mukonori.

> Never mind Smith's unilateral declaration of independence – that was illegal, null and void. The Patriotic Front, particularly Mugabe, wanted to avoid the Americans taking over the talks or even standing shoulder-to-shoulder with the British. They said, 'No, we don't know the Americans, we have no quarrel with them, but we do need their strength.' They should be the friend of the British in the negotiations but stand behind them, not alongside or in front. That was very important if we were to achieve and retain clarity. China, who had helped Mugabe fight the war, must stand behind Zanu, just as Russia, with whom Zapu had relations, must stand behind Nkomo. Psychologically, it was always a big issue for Mugabe to ensure that the principal players sorted it out among themselves.
>
> And he still feels that way today. It's why he's always pointing out that he doesn't have a problem with the UN or whoever: his problem is with the British. He is a principled person, whether you like to hear that or not. When he makes a point, he will split a hair down the middle to prove it. He is always very clear. He takes pride in knowing what the correct position is and sticking to it. You may disagree with him but he is clear and logical always. He's an excellent tactician for that reason.

And a poor strategist for the same reason, you might argue, given that only Mugabe's position can be the correct one. But Father Mukonori seldom draws breath, raising his voice whenever I try to question him on the issues he seems to have overlooked.

He goes on to explain how he used the powerful influence of his church to engineer constitutional talks in London. Having negotiated a detailed agreement on the structure of an all-party conference with the Patriotic Front in 1978, he handed the resultant document to the head of the Bishops Conference in Salisbury, who took it to Rome and gave it to the Pope. While it is hard to imagine that Lord Carrington called the Lancaster House conference because he was influenced by the Pope, Father Mukonori has no doubts on the matter. 'The Holy Father gave it to the British and American embassies in the Vatican, and that's how Lancaster House started. We even asked the Holy Father himself to stress to the Americans that they should stand behind the British, and he did that. After arranging for the plan to be hand-delivered in Rome, we flew to Washington and held talks with the State Department.'

As a prominent man of the cloth totally trusted by Mugabe, Father Mukonori has been in a unique position to influence the Zimbabwean president's decisions over the past 30 years. Before meeting the Jesuit supremo, I fully expected him to have been a positive influence on Mugabe, but his own moral judgement seems to have been questionable since the beginning of the relationship. Having secured his place at Mugabe's side by acting as a spy for him among Zanu's supporters during the liberation struggle, Father Mukonori obtained this intelligence as a priest taking advantage of the preferential rights accorded even black clergy in wartime Rhodesia. He counselled guerrilla recruits, not by taking a moral or spiritual position on killing and being killed, but by warning them of the discomfort they would have to endure in the bush. Later, he became a blatantly political player, setting up alliances at Lancaster House.

Film footage of Robert Mugabe's inauguration shows a fresh-faced Brother Mukonori standing beside the new prime minister in the cerise ceremonial robes of his order, Bible in hand. It is Father Mukonori, ordained in 1991, who has given the blessing at all Zimbabwe's independence celebrations since Mugabe came to power in 1980. It is he who has worn the moral badge but failed to invoke its authority. Admittedly, it was his intervention that helped halt the horrific Matabeleland killings conducted by Mugabe soon after he gained power. Father Mukonori also helped to compile the Catholic dossier on Gukurahundi that links Mugabe to the massacre. Thereafter, it was he, among others, who engaged in repeated efforts to find a solution to the occupation of commercial farms, and who brokered talks between Mugabe and the opposition MDC.

In recent years, his focus has been on trying to devise an exit plan for Zimbabwe's elderly president. Always careful not to offend Mugabe, according to fellow clergymen, Father Mukonori has won a concession here and there from the president, provided he posed no challenge. But his successful interventions are arguably diminished by the respectability accorded Zimbabwe's dictator in having so elevated a Catholic presence standing beside him throughout his tyranny.

During our meetings, the Jesuit uses his intellect and his brilliant education to show that Mugabe, with his seven degrees, is right. Even if he is wrong, he must be right, and everyone around them will agree that he is not only right but principled, because they have proven that he is right. Together, he and Mugabe have the correct view and will split hairs to endorse it, while paying lip service to working things out with others. If under pressure while justifying their own view, they will call on God. How does anyone argue with that tactic in a nation of deeply spiritual people who do not question the basis of organised religion? The Catholic Church becomes an alliance to the president; an enormously powerful ally that can silence a whole country for a time. Mugabe, being a selectively receptive, emotionally immature person, may well believe that Father Mukonori is his mentor, a 'good man' confirming his position from a Christian perspective.

Father Mukonori's ability to operate freely as a priest-turned-politician dates back to a confrontation he had with his Jesuit superior a few years before Lancaster House.

> Father McNamara said he appreciated my going to the war zones and asked, 'Can we talk about it?' I told him I did not think he would understand. It was difficult ... The superior nervously intensified his smoking. I assured him I did not wish to imply that I was planning to join the movement ... I felt my part was to continue as a Jesuit doing my work with the CCJP as my contribution to the liberation of Zimbabwe. If the Society of Jesus had a problem with my continuing in this way then I would have a problem staying in the Society. Father McNamara then gave me his blessing. If other Jesuits had a problem with what I was doing, he would support me. From that day, I did not look back.

No doubt the Jesuit superior, despite spiritual misgivings, struggled to weigh the advantages of keeping an unusually well-educated man like Father Mukonori on board against the obvious damage such a presence in Mugabe's guerrilla camps inflicted on the integrity of the Church. The superior was hypocritical, however, in choosing to ignore the holy commandment, 'Thou shalt not kill', let alone in sending confusing moral signals to Mugabe. Small wonder, perhaps, that Father Mukonori thereafter believed his position and Mugabe's to be the correct one.

Father Mukonori is a large, likeable man with receding hair. Dressed in a casual red shirt and worn brown trousers, he exudes warmth and curiosity. He relates a proverb, which sounds like an excuse for endorsing Mugabe's actions should he ever be called to account; a coded explanation of his continued good relations with a leader who has committed more sins against his people than a holy man should condone. We are sitting opposite each other, tape recorder and a tea tray between us, the sun streaming through the window, cocks crowing in the yard outside.

In Shona we say that when you punish a dog that has done something wrong, you can hit it with a stick or deprive it of its food, even its water, but don't ever close the door. Don't shut it out because the dog knows what it's done and it needs time to come back chastened. If you haven't left the door open, it will attack because there's no way out – or in. It is left to fight for survival. It has nothing left to lose. It's always better to leave some room for manoeuvre, no matter who or what you're dealing with.

I take this canine proverb to imply that Father Mukonori has been keeping the door ajar for Mugabe to come back chastened, although in not revealing what the dog has done wrong or why it is being punished, he seems to be keeping the door open purely as the unassailable moral authority on the scene.

He goes on to explain that what Mugabe saw in 1997 as an attempt by Britain's incoming Labour government to ditch its responsibility for land redistribution in Zimbabwe marked the start of the Zimbabwean president's disastrous fight for survival. The attack on him by British minister Peter Hain was as offensive to Mugabe's supporters as his simultaneous insults about Tony Blair were to the British government, Mukonori contends.

Mugabe felt under attack and he felt that he had no time to justify himself; to say, 'Look, this is what happened to the funds allocated for land purchase but this is what we believe can still be done.' The attackers were setting the timetable and he was constantly preparing for battle from then on, so he fought and fought and fought and ended up in the laager. If his attackers, like Clare Short and Peter Hain, never knew the truth about what was agreed at Lancaster House, only what they'd been told, they no doubt believed that they must be in the right while Mugabe also thought, or knew, that he was in the right.

According to Father Mukonori, one of the keys to understanding what has gone so horribly wrong in Zimbabwe is the fact that the land issue was left unresolved at Lancaster House.

> Land was exclusively dealt with after the rest of the Lancaster House deal
> had been agreed. It was left to the end because it was the crucial matter
> and everyone knew that. Over almost three and a half weeks there was
> virtually a stand-off on the issue. Then, just when Britain decided to take a
> strong stand on land, the Rhodesians suddenly launched a massive military
> campaign in Mozambique and Zambia. They hit those two countries so
> hard and I personally thought – and so did Robert, and many others, too
> – that there was a direct link between those Rhodesian military attacks
> and British frustration at Lancaster House.

The carnage brought Kaunda and Machel's foreign ministers to London with a stern warning for the Patriotic Front: settle the land issue immediately, or else. Mugabe was summoned to Tanzania, where Julius Nyerere underlined the demand. Father Mukonori's voice takes on a petulant pitch as he recalls Nyerere's words: '"Robert, you can't let those people destroy two countries. The land is a constitutional issue and you can change the constitution when you are in power." That's what Robert was told by his mentors but when he decided to change the constitution after the mandatory 10 years, everybody cried foul,' he says, with a bitter little laugh at what he sees as Nyerere's expediency and Western double standards.

This is a rather odd summary of events. Lancaster House enshrined the willing buyer-willing seller principle for 10 years – until 1990. Mugabe did not touch the concept until 1992 when he passed the Land Acquisition Act, making compulsory purchase a possibility, and no one except the white farmers cried foul. In the event, this Act laid down such complicated rules for acquiring a farm that nothing serious happened in respect of land redistribution until the farm invasions of 2000.

Father Mukonori goes on to point out that at the same time as African leaders were telling Mugabe to bide his time constitutionally during the Lancaster House conference, President Jimmy Carter pledged assistance over and above America's development aid to Zimbabwe in order to help Britain fund the purchase of commercial farms for eventual land redistribution. It was this offer as much as the threats from African leaders that broke the Lancaster House deadlock in 1979. Astonishingly, though, no documents exist today to prove the US's promise.

'When the land question started getting out of hand in 1992,' explains Father Mukonori, who at the time was on one of his numerous land claim missions to help Mugabe resolve what the churchman correctly identified as a looming catastrophe, 'I asked Edson Zvobgo, the official lawyer to the Patriotic Front at Lancaster House: "Where is the land document you signed with the British and the Americans? Does it say who the land must be given to? Does it stipulate peasant farmers as the only beneficiaries? Does it prevent land being redistributed to government ministers?" These are the sorts of questions I asked,' he explains, seeming to endorse Mugabe's disastrous cronyism on the basis that if not breaking the rules set at Lancaster House Mugabe could distribute the farms to his loyal followers by way of patronage rather than giving them to the poverty-stricken rural people who needed agricultural opportunities. In Father Mukonori's opinion, unless otherwise stated in a document, Mugabe could do whatever he liked with the land.

It was on requesting the vital land document from the lawyer that Mukonori and Mugabe realised that America's offer had never been committed to paper by their own team. When they hurriedly asked the State Department for a copy of the relevant document, convinced that American diplomats and negotiators at Lancaster House would have kept minutes, they were told that Washington had never seen it in writing either.

> Unfortunately, the memorandum of agreement regarding the land question at Lancaster House is not on the record. We remonstrated with Zvobgo but it was too late by then, of course. It was a chapter concluded in the heat of emotions with Kaunda, Machel and Nyerere breathing down the Patriotic Front's necks, saying, 'Sign up, sign up'. So they signed, but it was the constitutional agreement they had signed, which merely said land had to be bought on a willing buyer-willing seller basis for the first 10 years. The memorandum on the funding of land for redistribution, as discussed in the final weeks of Lancaster House, never existed – and that upset Robert a great deal.

Mugabe felt he had been made a fool of, tricked like Lobengula, the 19th-century Matabele king who was double-crossed by Cecil John Rhodes, I guess out loud, having cottoned on to the accusatory way

Father Mukonori thinks. He nods vigorously. It was his own side's legal lapse as well as the subsequent amnesia of the British and the Americans that were jointly responsible for the failure to formalise land boundaries at Lancaster House. Obvious questions were not asked, crucial documents were not drawn up and signed. Yet Father Mukonori ultimately blames the fact that his team was rushed by others, not that they were themselves gullible or incompetent.

In addition, he argues, a number of 'crucial conceptual misunderstandings, let's call them that', contributed to the decline and imminent collapse of the once-prosperous Zimbabwe.

> For example, most of what has been written about Lancaster House, based on press reports at the time, indicates that Robert was attending the conference reluctantly and that he would have preferred to shoot his way into Salisbury. No, that's not true. He had a strategy of looking stony-faced and saying he was going to fight his way to power but that was just his negotiating tactic. He knew very well that it was the Patriotic Front politicians who had to win the war, not their military commanders. He was very well aware that he was bargaining from a position of strength because of the weakening Rhodesian position, but he always wanted to win through the ballot box. He told me once, 'If we get in through the barrel of the gun we will also leave through the barrel of the gun. We are aiming for democracy but the war is necessary because Ian Smith has been so intransigent that we have to shoot back before they will respect us.'

Another damaging myth, according to Father Mukonori, is that the guerrilla commander Mugabe is often accused of having murdered, Josiah Tongogara, died because he was a threat to the leader of Zanu-PF.

> Mugabe always worked well with Tongogara. He announced once that anything Tongogara and Brother Mukonori could agree on could be implemented without further reference to him, and he remained true to that. Both of them were in favour of democracy. If they'd been left with no other option they'd have shot their way to power. But that was not their preference. What the Lancaster House strategy meant though, was that the land remained an outstanding issue.

The whites never understood that, any more than they understood how they'd acquired most of the land in the first place – and maybe the British didn't understand it either. Later they said, 'Oh, Mugabe's not such a bad guy, after all. If we knew he only wanted his flag and his motorcade we could long ago have given him independence. We're better off today on our farms, making more money than we did under Smith.' Now, is that not arrogance?

They never doubted their right to the land. Even when they had decided that Robert Mugabe was not such a bad guy, some were naming their dogs after him: 'Mugabe, Mugabe', they'd call out and think it was funny. Robert knew about that trend: there were always plenty of people in and around white households, the informal anthropologists of our society, to report those things to him.

Despite the war having been fought, the whites were never told the truth about its causes. They did not ask the right questions and nobody gave them the right answers. They had no interest in knowing. They were told it was a fight against Marxist communists and terrorists in order to safeguard Western Christian civilisation. That's what they believed. Nobody told them that their ancestors had grabbed the land and killed people in the process. Their psychological backwardness and lack of factual knowledge were a major part of the problems that gave rise to the war and that later arose to torment them again more recently over control of the land. But they never learnt. They thought all their rights and supremacy came with the colour of their skin.

Some whites even continued celebrating November 11th, the day they unilaterally declared their independence from Britain in 1965, well into the 80s, says Mukonori, his voice rising with indignation.

Mugabe kept telling them it was unacceptable. But they had to be told over and over again. Why? Why didn't they know this was unacceptable to the new black government? They didn't know because there's no humanity they recognise, no hurt, no disappointment outside white supremacy. If they'd said, 'Let's accept and regret the wrong we did in the past', it would have been a very different Zimbabwe. But they were too ignorant and they lacked appropriate leadership. Ian Smith, the symbol of their racist past, was still their leader. They had voted for him in the last election in 1985 before the minority representation they were guaranteed in Parliament under the Lancaster House constitution expired in 1987. Mugabe had seen then that white supremacy was still an issue, and he had wondered then about the wisdom of trying to accommodate whites.

Father Mukonori tells me that another nail in Zimbabwe's coffin was the Economic Structural Adjustment Programme (Esap), which was hammered into place by the World Bank and the International Monetary Fund (IMF) in 1991 but failed comprehensively in its objectives. Widely seen in retrospect as the worst policy move ever made by Zanu-PF's decision makers, it was the source of much bitterness to Mugabe, says Father Mukonori. Zimbabwe's president had always seen his primary mandate as bringing social justice to the poor in Zimbabwe, he explains. Although well aware that constraints had become necessary due to the economy having been mismanaged by his government, Mugabe also knew that he had spearheaded important investments in human development, particularly in education and health, which he felt should not be undermined at the behest of Western institutions favouring profit before people.

Although Mugabe's government failed to implement most of the Esap package, Father Mukonori talks as though its terms were observed.

Robert had to be forced to cooperate in Esap. He had looked closely at other economies where it had been implemented and at the problems it created, killing small-scale initiatives, weakening social development, and so forth. He believes most World Bank and IMF policies are designed to keep trade good for the West at the expense of the developing world: these institutions ignore how the West's artificial trade barriers impact on development elsewhere. When Zimbabweans' standards of living began to decline in the wake of Esap, Robert blamed the West.

Mugabe's finance minister Bernard Chidzero and I were bosom friends and it was he who told me that Robert always knew that Esap was not going to work. He had accepted Esap, saying he had little choice because it was imposed by northern hemisphere bigwigs who never questioned its wisdom or side effects and who would refuse to work with you – and make sure that nobody else worked with you either – if you didn't. Coupled with Zimbabwe's worst drought in 1992, it caused a lot of suffering and Mugabe believed it marked the beginning of Zimbabweans' dissatisfaction with Zanu-PF.

Among the biggest mistakes Robert Mugabe made is one which was understandable in the circumstances, according to Father Mukonori:

It concerns education. When Robert came to power, he had many well-educated ministers to talk to. In terms of experience of government and all that it implies though, he had nothing – zero. Only the whites had that. As a result, many of the existing structures were kept after independence; existing laws were simply left intact. Development money flowed in for conservative approaches to projects and people were generally comfortable with what they already knew. Some of us wondered about this but most were happy with the situation.

In education, however, we pursued existing, completely wrong policies with disastrous consequences. It was Mugabe's vision that every child should be not only educated but well educated, and he must certainly be commended for reopening the 65 per cent of the rural schools that had been closed during the war. But he should have found a more appropriate system of education instead of the old one that suited the Rhodesians' elitist needs. It should have been a system designed partly for self-employment but it wasn't. University students inevitably become job seekers. We needed to grow the economy at an ever-faster rate to meet the educated masses but we didn't. There wasn't the required technical economic push: there was no one with the experience to drive that. Mugabe needed another educational vision entirely, or at least a fuller vision. His own Western-oriented dream, which values education almost for its own sake and which led to him acquiring no less than seven degrees himself, was the dominant vision after independence. If there had been recognition of the need to change course, Mugabe would have done it. But there was no recognition. He educated all these people and they all rushed to the cities, where many became dissatisfied, frustrated. 'There's no growth,' they said. 'We want a new government. Mugabe must go.'

By 1999, it had become clear that a strong opposition had grown out of the country's disaffected urban population and formed behind trade unionist Morgan Tsvangirai, recalls Father Mukonori, who was at the time a member of the Constitutional Commission set up to explore the need for governmental reform. It became equally clear during the

Commission's deliberations that land was the priority issue, he says. 'I can tell you this was the case from my own experience. Everywhere we went canvassing the proposed constitution, from town to town and village to village, the cry was the same as it had been during the war and throughout our history: "The soil is ours. The land question was never resolved: we want it resolved. The former constitution was decided in London: we did not vote for it."'

According to Father Mukonori, it was this voluble demand for land in rural Zimbabwe, as well as threatened walkouts from war veterans in response to lobbying designed to play down the land issue within the Commission's report-back groups, that accounted for the draft constitution being amended by Mugabe to allow expropriation without consultation. The amendment, added by the president without consulting anyone after the draft had already been adopted by the Constitutional Commission, stated that Britain, as the former colonial power, was responsible for compensating farmers for land seized. If Britain defaulted, then 'the government of Zimbabwe has no obligation to pay compensation'.

When put to the people in February 2000, the proposed constitution was rejected. This was not only because educated urban voters didn't like it, according to Father Mukonori, but because a lot more whites came out to vote against its proposed executive presidency and land acquisition than had been the case in earlier elections. The fact that white farmers misused their feudal influence over their farm labourers, manipulating a sizeable vote against the constitutional proposals, incensed Mugabe. 'Their mobilising, actually coercing, their labour force on the farms to support the one position opposed to government has exposed them as not our friends, but enemies,' Mugabe told a national television audience on the occasion of Zimbabwe's 20th anniversary of independence from Britain. Addressing the white farmers directly, he went on: 'Our present state of mind is that you are now enemies because you really have behaved as enemies of Zimbabwe. We are full of anger.'

Father Mukonori explains that the rejection of the constitutional proposals was also due in part to Zanu-PF officialdom's half-hearted campaign for a constitution that envisaged a reduced Cabinet, fewer deputies and no provincial administrators or governors. A lot of people in comfortable positions in Mugabe's government stood to lose their jobs so they did not want the new constitution either.

Robert Mugabe appeared at first to be gracious in defeat. For the legislative election that followed a few months later in June 2000, however, he mobilised his resources with a vengeance, threw human rights to the wind and disregarded the rules of free and fair electioneering in order to win, albeit narrowly, at any cost. The MDC took 57 seats against Zanu-PF's 62. Knowing that some European countries, including Britain, had given financial and other forms of support to the MDC, Mugabe was furious when British premier Tony Blair told the House of Commons a few years later that his government was continuing to work with the MDC towards a change of regime in Zimbabwe.

Having witnessed white farmers giving cheques to Morgan Tsvangirai on television during the 2000 election campaign, Mugabe concluded that the opposition's attempts to unseat him would not have come as close to success without the support of the white farmers, as well as Britain and some Scandinavian countries. 'That television footage was shot by an American network and I never understood why they wanted it shown. It did serious damage to Tsvangirai. It did serious damage to the white farmers, who had previously portrayed themselves as representatives of farmers' unions pledged to being apolitical and supporting the government of the day,' says Father Mukonori.

> When Robert saw this footage, he was profoundly disillusioned. That's when he started to say, 'Maybe the reconciliation we attempted with whites was a mistake.' The white farmers had all the land he wanted and needed, yet he let them keep it. He had honoured Lancaster House, yet they did not even honour their own unions' undertakings to stay out of politics. Instead, they extended their hands to a new party that wanted to replace Mugabe. It was illogical on the part of those white farmers who got involved with the MDC, but you have to understand the arrogance of white Rhodesians, the logic of white supremacy. They wanted a party that would ensure they kept the land. They just wanted to keep the land; it was the key to their lifestyles. But they couldn't see that black people wanted it too.

Much of Father Mukonori's discourse is cast in racial terms. While there is no question about the racial injustices of the past and the need for reparation, he understands most of what has happened subsequently in Zimbabwe along the lines of grievance and something owed by white Rhodesians to black Zimbabweans. Taking back by any means what Zimbabweans are owed is portrayed as good. The reason Father Mukonori does not disagree with Robert Mugabe is because he has explained events to himself in a particularly narrow way. He has never confronted Mugabe because the two think the same way. They are smart men but their cleverness, it turns out, was not enough: a good heart, which you might expect from a priest, would have served Zimbabwe better.

It is the British, the whites, the World Bank who are responsible, never Mugabe. There is always a seed of truth in what Father Mukonori is saying. If it were entirely wrong, it would be less confusing. Listening to him justifying Mugabe, you find yourself thinking, 'Yes, he was abused. This was not right, those people were dishonest, they changed their minds.' But the basis of truth is used to prop up reactions that are neither honest nor justifiable. Right and wrong are so confused that the listener, particularly in Africa, cannot identify the moral line any longer. Mugabe has managed to stay at the helm for nearly 30 years, despite a dismal human rights record, because of this confusion. It would seem that Father Mukonori has given the confusion respectability. He has done little more with his powerful influence than entrench Mugabe's view that he can do no wrong.

There is not a hint of compassion or thoughtfulness anywhere in Father Mukonori's political language. He and Mugabe have established the unassailable view, the truth, and never revised it. While his observations on white supremacy are accurate, playwright Bertolt Brecht's vision of the old coming over the hill masquerading as the new seems never to have occurred to Father Mukonori. He does not appear to have engaged in any self-reflection. How is the land problem going to be resolved if it is no longer a black and white issue?

In not offering a moral position to the emotionally stunted Mugabe, Father Mukonori has had a negative influence on Zimbabwe's president. He would doubtless have been expelled from Mugabe's court if he had been critical, which would have severed the secular power he has come to enjoy alongside the veneration accorded him as a leading churchman. But in failing to make distinctions between right and wrong while in the president's favour, he has helped to create

Mugabe the monster.

'After almost losing the 2000 election,' Robert said several times, 'we were caught napping.' He thought it wasn't so much that the MDC had performed brilliantly but a combination of Zanu-PF's arrogance in failing to deliver and understand its vulnerability and the support given to the MDC by the whites, Britain and other countries.

I had seen him in March that year while I was chairing a land committee following some killings that had taken place around land invasions. I told him that Harare and Bulawayo were going to go to the opposition. I told him that urban people were dissatisfied with the ruling party, which had become inept and insensitive. I gave him all my reasons. He listened and then told me that his ministers had assured him that Zanu-PF would win. I said, 'They're not telling you the truth. If for no other reason, urban people will vote for change for its own sake.'

When I met him shortly after the election, he described how shocked he'd been at the results. He said I was the only one who had warned him, even though he had questioned his ministers closely. He said, 'I sat there looking at the results on television from 7pm until 7am the following morning – the whole night. I couldn't believe it.'

He was astonished that some of the Zanu-PF elite with expensive cars and staff to help them campaign were swept away by young professionals with no political experience whatsoever, some of whom were campaigning on foot because they had no money for vehicles and secretaries, recalls Father Mukonori. 'It was clearly a protest vote and Robert knew that. I can tell you he contemplated stepping aside at the time. He thought seriously about it. But the land issue still hadn't been dealt with and Mugabe would never leave office with land still unresolved. No, never.'

Mugabe's shock at the election result was one of several occasions when one could see that the people around him had briefed him convincingly but not honestly, says Father Mukonori.

It took him a long time, too long, to realise that. He believes in being honest himself but what has proved one of his biggest problems is that he has always assumed he was getting honesty in return. While the people he'd appointed to keep him informed were lying to him, he insisted on believing them. He told me more than once that he couldn't be a minister of every ministry: he had to believe in the ministers he had appointed. He has had the greatest difficulty accepting that his own people lie to him simply because they're afraid of telling the president what he doesn't want to hear.

It seems that Father Mukonori cannot see that he and Mugabe have twisted and distorted events in order to set themselves up as moral, truthful and correct. They have idealised a right and a wrong way of thinking when the truth, typically, is somewhere in the middle. His description of Mugabe's shock at the election result shows how cut off Mugabe was from the truth, not how much his colleagues had lied to him. Father Mukonori claims that Mugabe believes in being honest, when it is clear after his many years in office that the president does not have anything like an open mind to take in another view, consider it and perhaps modify his own opinion. There is no self-examination. Mugabe might argue and split hairs to outwit an opponent but never to reassess his own position. To say he believes in honesty is hypocrisy. When faced with evidence that his view is incorrect, Mugabe is not reflective but outraged. Even the churches came in for racist attack when some clerics condemned the land grab that Mugabe termed Zimbabwe's Third Chimurenga. 'The most insidious side of the resurgence of white power came by way of the pulpit and in the human form of church figures who do not hesitate to "render unto God" things that belonged to Caesar,' thundered Mugabe. 'Especially in suburban parishes and in rural Matabeleland, prayers became full-blooded politics and congregations became anti-Zanu-PF political communities united around hackneyed grievances to do with tensions we had before the Unity Accord,' he is quoted by the Catholic publication *Moto* as saying in 2006.

Mugabe has not created a new order in Zimbabwe. What he has done is perpetuate the corruption of colonialism. Still in a relationship of abuse with Zimbabweans, he cannot justify his plunder in terms of race or two wrongs making a right. Father Mukonori has stood shoulder to shoulder with the country's president rubber-stamping his corrupt position. With God on their side, they could do no wrong. Their 'respectable relationship' has been about smoothing things over and making Mugabe look good. It has never been about honesty. The difficulty is that theirs is not a conscious self-delusion. Like Mugabe, Father Mukonori would be hurt to hear how he self-justifies his position because he genuinely sees himself as the good guy. And he is indeed a generous man with the best of intentions.

According to the man the media refers to as the president's spiritual adviser, Robert Mugabe's 'intellectual rigour' comes from his formation by the Jesuits in a particular kind of discipline. 'As a boy, he learnt self-consciousness of everything he was doing,' explains Father Mukonori:

He was taught to defend his actions but always to take the blame for them. In many ways, he still lives by that discipline and behaves like a Jesuit. Jesuit training teaches total silence after night studies: you talk to yourself until the following morning after breakfast, which is what he does to this day. I've often said to him, 'Take time for yourself. Listen to the heart, listen to the head – reflect.' And he nods knowingly.

He often gets into his office without having had breakfast. I comment sometimes because I particularly enjoy the first meal of the day, and he'll say when a tray of tea and sandwiches finally arrives at 11am, 'This is my breakfast.' Once when I suggested it was brunch, he waved the subject away, saying, 'Whatever you want to call it, Fidelis.'

He does exercises very early every morning, not only to keep fit but because it helps him to reflect. Whenever possible, he eats African food with his fingers because it is simple and healthy, and he doesn't want to be concerned about extraneous things like meals. He isn't interested in his own needs, no. If there's something to be done at the office, he gets it done, quickly and efficiently.

People say many, many things about him, of course. Some say he's aloof, which is part of his Jesuit heritage. Others say he changed for the worse after his first wife died. They claim he was so overly excited to get a beautiful young flower when Sally was dying that he ended up marrying the wrong person.

Father Mukonori laughs at the thought, shaking his head.

He is not the type for such behaviour, such excitement. And there's a dichotomy in such an analysis, because he can't be aloof and passionate at the same time, can he? Wives are not the issue, no. That's an explanation provided by people who have no time to think intelligently; who look for simplistic answers. He is completely dedicated to Zimbabwe and always has been. The country has always come first.

Actually, Mugabe is aloof and passionate simultaneously, but about revenge rather than love. And while he may be dedicated to Zimbabwe, it is his control of the country that has always come first, not its best interests, as Father Mukonori implies.

Eleven

In the eyes of God's deputies

The support given to Robert Mugabe by key members of the Catholic clergy in Zimbabwe continued long after he had committed post-war human rights abuses in the 80s. Many priests gave him credence even after he had unleashed a vicious campaign of torture across the country in order to force Zimbabwe's increasingly disaffected citizens to vote for him in 2000. To find out why, I spoke to a number of Catholic clerics who have dealt personally with the freedom-fighter-turned-tyrant over the past 30 years.

Nothing frustrates Harare-based Catholic Church spokesman Oskar Wermter more than those who continue, in the face of overwhelming evidence of Mugabe's malevolence, to believe in the goodness of their president. 'His apologists may be dwindling in number at last,' he says, 'but you still hear them, including priests, saying in response to an outrage obviously committed by Mugabe, "Oh, but the president couldn't have known." I find it incredible that people still believe in him after all he has done to destroy their lives.'

Having long ago seen through Mugabe's self-serving rhetoric, Father Wermter says that almost every statement the Zimbabwean president makes is a distortion of the truth. As an example, he cites Mugabe's portrayal of recent state-sponsored violence as the Third Chimurenga or continuing war of independence. 'It is cynically misleading,' according to the German-born Jesuit.

One might just as well say that the Second Chimurenga (the bush war

145

against Ian Smith's Rhodesia) has never come to an end. It is routinely reported to us that people who somehow displease the party and the government are being beaten up. National service youths are assaulting business people 'for unauthorised price rises'. Trade unionists trying to stage a demonstration against the impoverishment of the workers were beaten up so badly that several had to seek treatment for broken bones in hospitals both in Zimbabwe and South Africa. Women with babies on their backs are being beaten up and put for days into filthy police cells for peacefully demonstrating against corruption and decay.

Father Wermter, who is one of Mugabe's most outspoken critics, has often pointed out that violence committed by Zanu-PF during the Second Chimurenga was not only directed against the white government and its supporters, but also against Mugabe's own supporters. 'Violence in the form of cruel beatings was common practice to maintain "party discipline" within the liberation movements,' he wrote in a recent edition of the Jesuit journal *Mukai Vukani*, meaning 'Rise', which he edits. 'The most loyal and ardent supporters of the freedom fighters lived in constant fear of being beaten up, even killed, by the Rhodesian security forces, but just as easily by the boys or *vakomana*.'

There was no arguing with the guerrillas in those days, he says. 'You just did as you were told. If you incurred their least displeasure, there was serious trouble ... independence in 1980 did not put a stop to political violence. It remained an option.' He gives as an example the continuous reports of female trainees in national service camps being sexually abused in 2007, just as women guerrillas were routinely violated by some of the leaders of the struggle, political rape being a common means by which Zanu-PF has always punished individuals, families or communities for disloyalty. 'What has changed?' Father Wermter asks. 'People out of step with the political line of the day are still being punished by sheer terror. And this is not just the overenthusiasm of some minor officials. It is being backed up by the highest in the land.'

Father Wermter quotes Robert Mugabe in a 2007 speech reminding opponents of the state that Zimbabwe employs armed men and women with permission to shoot dissenters. 'He said it in Shona. It was not part of his prepared speech. But he said it,' Father Wermter insists, adding that Mugabe's security minister Didymus Mutasa explicitly endorses bloodshed in defence of government policies. He notes that even priests have been threatened by Mugabe. 'When the church leaders start being political we regard them as political creatures – and we are vicious in that area,' the president told a crowd in response to the Catholic Bishops' highly critical pastoral letter, which was published in April 2007.

So why do some clerics continue to make excuses for Mugabe's behaviour?

Part of the explanation, according to Father Wermter, lies in Mugabe's public relations skill. Among the tools he employs to burnish his image is the Catholic Church itself, which used to be proud to cite Zimbabwe's president as the well-educated protégé of one of its earliest missions, Kutama.

> For some years now, we haven't been inviting him into our midst because of what he's become. Yet he sometimes turns up uninvited, as he did when Archbishop Pius Ncube, his arch-enemy in the Church, was consecrated in 1998. After the Mass, when Mugabe was given the opportunity to say a few words, he spotted Ncube's mother at the front of the congregation and asked her to come up and stand beside him. Ostensibly focusing on her religious life, he was in fact using the opportunity to tell stories about his own Catholic upbringing. It was brilliant public relations for him to present himself as an ordinary Catholic before a packed congregation of the entire hierarchy.
>
> He again used a requiem Mass in 2003 as a political platform, although on that occasion he appeared to find it more difficult to maintain a charming persona and he ended up attacking Archbishop Ncube. Some of the congregation got up and walked out. He lets it be known that he is still a practising Catholic but this hasn't been true for 30 years. I lived in the house behind the cathedral where Sally worshipped in the 80s after she converted to Catholicism. She came regularly every Sunday but he never came, even in those days.

Zimbabwe's million-strong Catholic community has faced one embarrassing inconsistency after another in respect of the president's relationship with the Church. The Catholic Commission for Justice and Peace (CCJP), which fearlessly exposed the Smith government's human rights abuses, tried hard to orchestrate condemnation of the horrendous acts of Mugabe's militia, the Fifth Brigade, in Matabeleland during the 80s, for example. Mugabe was so furious when the Commission prepared a devastating report on the mass murder, rape and torture committed in the president's name that he begged Archbishop Patrick Chakaipa to suppress it – which the senior priest did, much to the Church's shame. When the damning document was finally released years later, Mugabe lashed out at 'men in religious garb who have become stooges of imperialism'.

In 1996, Mugabe's insistence on his marriage to Grace being performed by Archbishop Chakaipa divided the country's Catholic community. Apart from his relationship with Grace being adulterous and their first two children having been born out of wedlock, it was unclear if Grace had ever been baptised. Father Wermter and others argued that by sanctioning the president's marriage in such circumstances the Church would be seen to be confused about its own morality. Yet under intense pressure from Mugabe, Archbishop Chakaipa wilted and agreed to officiate.

Mugabe appeared in these instances to have somehow forced Archbishop Chakaipa into submission, but this was not necessarily so. The president may well have succeeded in cajoling high-ranking Catholic clerics less through cynicism than a genuine belief in his own omnipotence. Convincing precisely because he entertains no self-doubt, Mugabe believes sincerely, like his late mother, that he is some sort of saviour sent to Zimbabwe by God – and he behaves accordingly. Many churchmen like Archbishop Chakaipa were never politically neutral, but unashamed allies of Mugabe and his party.

A Catholic insider, Swiss-born Sister Angelika Laub, who admits she supported Mugabe despite inklings of his cruelty, says she suspected early on in the liberation struggle that he endorsed violence behind his façade of respectability. Now living in South Africa, she was stationed at Berejena Mission not far from Beit Bridge during the bush war. She says she was so angered by the racism she witnessed all around her in Rhodesia that her support in those days was firmly with the guerrillas.

I used to ride my bicycle straight past the Rhodesian soldiers on a daily basis as I took medical supplies to wounded guerrillas hiding in the bush nearby. The Rhodesian security forces had started to camp inside our mission after they discovered that the comrades had been in the area since 1973. They had made it a liberated zone for Zanu already. So it was a very dangerous area. Every day before curfew, I would arrive back and the soldiers would ask, 'Where are they?' And I would point in the opposite direction. The Rhodesians eventually charged the head of our mission with treason and he was convicted and sent to prison at Chikurubi.

Once I heard a bullet flying so close to me that it missed me by millimetres during a shoot-out. The windows were open and the bullets just came flying in. Over the time I spent with the comrades, I learnt from them how intolerant Zanu's leadership was, even in those days, and how cruelly it dealt with dissent. Terrible things were done to their own forces if they were suspected of disloyalty, or even if they had a different opinion. Some of the comrades preferred to risk their lives in the field, living like animals, than go back to the camps in Mozambique.

These bad stories of cruelty didn't stop some of our schoolchildren, as young as 14, wanting to join the comrades. They would leave the mission late at night. But most were caught and brought back by the police. This was terribly humiliating for all of us. They had usually lost weight and been tortured and they were different people. So many of them were caught that the comrades told us to stop them going unless they had made arrangements. After that, there were a few teachers the children could discuss enlistment with, and the teachers would sometimes make arrangements with the comrades.

One day, she recalls, Robert Mugabe arrived to thank the priests and nuns at Berejena for their support. Not everyone there backed his party, but most did, says Sister Laub.

He had been expected a day earlier for a celebration arranged by the comrades but he never arrived. I don't know how he got there, not by car. Suddenly, he was standing there. Four of us sat down with him for a short time, about 10 minutes. He was wearing a grey suit, a white shirt and a tie. I found him a simple person in those days; nice and polite and humble. I didn't believe he was involved in the cruelty we had heard about, but I wondered. He had very penetrating eyes and I remember thinking, 'This is not a stupid guy.' He thanked us for what we had done for the freedom of the country. And then he disappeared.

Sister Laub's description of Mugabe's politeness, apparent decency and obvious victimisation at that time is one reason for his respectability in the midst of the violence committed by his own agents. Gratifyingly, in her case, Mugabe arrives at her remote and beleaguered mission station to thank the Catholic clergy there for supporting Zanu's war effort. Sister Laub has heard stories of cruelty and wonders about him, but she wants to believe in his goodness. She is struck not only by his intelligence but by his unearthly appearance and disappearance. He cannot move around in a car like an ordinary person but seems to arrive and vanish like a fugitive dodging death in an environment of threat and fear.

Mugabe has lived in similarly terrifying conditions ever since, she says, not only because of his paranoia but because there were real threats to his safety, initially from apartheid South Africa, from the earliest days of his presidency. The source of his pervasive and most evil idea – that anyone who is against him should be done in – is his own experience, Sister Laub points out. It is the way his opponents habitually attempted to deal with him. Caught up in violence for much of his adult life, he developed an eye-for-an-eye mindset.

It doesn't take much digging to discover that Mugabe's supporters and detractors within the Catholic clergy – a community in which you would expect to find broad consensus on good versus evil – are starkly divided. Their debate about Mugabe's position in Zimbabwe's moral history goes right back to the start of the liberation war when the country's Jesuits, for example, disapproved of colleagues such as Sister Laub actively assisting the guerrillas against the security forces. Today, it is the head of the Jesuits, Father Fidelis Mukonori, who supports Mugabe even in the full glare of his disgrace. Not surprisingly perhaps, those who defend their president as opposed to those who condemn Mugabe for his misrule and human rights abuses tend to be divided on racial lines: black priests and nuns versus whites, with the latter more often foreign-born clergy than former Rhodesians. There are notable exceptions, such as Catholic Archbishop Pius Ncube, Mugabe's fiercest critic, but he is from the opposition's stronghold of Matabeleland and possibly a Mugabe detractor for more complex reasons than pure morality.

A man who has long supported Robert Mugabe, and who helped him to escape from Rhodesia to Mozambique in 1975, is Father Emmanuel

Ribeiro. Another in the coterie of well-educated Catholic clergymen who helped Zimbabwe's president achieve power and retain it, he was Mugabe's priest during his 11 years' imprisonment. Nobody seems to know where I can contact Father Ribeiro when I start searching for him in 2006. People tell me he is in Britain, in Mozambique, even possibly deceased. Eventually he turns up in the archbishop's house behind the Catholic cathedral in Fourth Street, Harare, after a long stay in the USA.

Sitting barefoot in an art deco armchair beneath a tapestry of the Last Supper, Father Ribeiro looks deceptively jaunty in khaki trousers and red braces decorated with Christmas trees over a patterned black and white shirt. He tells me his father was Mozambican but reveals little else about himself or Robert Mugabe, despite the emotion welling in his eyes when he speaks of the liberation struggle. Others have told me that he used to smuggle messages to the outside world for the detainees but he does not elaborate. At one point he starts to say, 'I remember when I was young . . .' but then brushes the thought aside to return to abstractions.

He does provide a bit of insight into the puzzling divergence of opinion about Robert Mugabe's presidency within the Catholic Church, an institution dedicated to moral ubiquity if ever there was one. According to him, Africans deeply resent Westerners flaunting their hypocrisy on the continent almost as brazenly today as a century ago. 'I blame everybody for what has happened in Zimbabwe, not just Robert,' he says. His interminable list of the ways in which the World Bank, the British and American governments and the former rulers of Zimbabwe, among others, ensured the failure of newly independent Zimbabwe contains more truth than mythology, but also sounds like a catalogue of excuses.

Listening to Father Ribeiro's largely racist discourse, I finally distil a theme from what he is saying and the vehemence with which he is saying it. Africans all over the continent blame Westerners in general for their woes because the two are essentially at cross purposes. While independent Africa is still primarily concerned with eradicating racism, those lumped together into the 'Western' category are preoccupied with human rights and democracy on their own terms, not with racism. What particularly frustrates Father Ribeiro is the ease with which all parties to African oppression have discarded their responsibility for 'the built-in failure of African rule that existed in the wake of deliberately racist policies'. He believes the West's concern over democracy in the developing world is more a guise to make the world safe for Western trade than to ensure that everyone has a vote of equal value and the right to take part in politics.

I press Father Ribeiro to be specific about Robert Mugabe the man, or about the president's resentments, rather than his own. He refers repeatedly to the cruelty meted out to prisoners like Mugabe but refuses to provide examples. So much remains unsaid. His secrets seem deliberately withheld, although accounts from those who have worked with torture victims are often shrouded in the unspoken, so perhaps Father Ribeiro is respecting Mugabe's right to silence. One can only imagine the suffering of Mugabe the prisoner. Perhaps the abuse was so comprehensive that Father Ribeiro does not even remember specific incidents – just that they have all played a part in Mugabe's infinite rage. Or perhaps the violations were too traumatic to discuss.

Eventually, Father Ribeiro tells me that during the 11 years Mugabe spent in Rhodesian prisons he found fortitude through his concern for the prisoners around him.

When a person faces years and years in prison, he can be tempted to give up but Robert was never that type of man. You would see some detainees broken by the experience; some who would complete their sentences and not go back into politics. You could always see that other prisoners looked to Robert to solve their problems. He was very helpful towards the other prisoners and some of them like Edgar Tekere did unexpectedly well educationally because of him. Robert was not just sitting there but always busy – learning, teaching or organising. He was positive and practical, wanting life in prison to be interesting and fruitful. He used to tell the others that they could thank Ian Smith for giving them the opportunity to learn to survive in such a difficult situation because it would help them survive other difficult conditions later on.

Robert survived those years in a context not of his choosing partly through the strength of his spirituality. He got strength from the expectations of others too. But his real strength was study and helping others to learn. There is no doubt that he was a compassionate man with a real concern for others in prison. I saw that side of him often. But in my experience, given certain adverse circumstances and disappointments, that same caring person might be driven to react differently. That is what we've seen with Robert. At a certain point he stopped trying to please everybody.

No matter how many different ways I frame my questions, Father Ribeiro will not build this sketch of Mugabe's prison years into a more colourful picture. I am left feeling that although agreeing to see me repeatedly and flattered by my efforts to talk to him, he does not wish to talk to me. He will not indicate where or how or why he believes the president lost his way or 'stopped trying to please everybody', except in the most abstract terms.

It seems to me that Robert Mugabe might first have become disillusioned and cynical in prison on the occasion when he backed down from his own determination not to oust the incumbent leader of Zanu, Ndabaningi Sithole, under pressure from Edgar Tekere and other inmates – at some considerable cost to his own integrity. Although Father Ribeiro knew Mugabe well at that time, he will not shed any light on the matter.

He, like Mugabe, is a man who hides behind his intellect. I get the impression it pains him even to think of Mugabe as a failure. I have heard on the Catholic grapevine that Father Ribeiro was so distressed towards the end of his ministry as prison chaplain that he became ill, which is why he spent many years thereafter in the United States. According to a nun in Harare who knows him, the secondary trauma he suffered while working with prisoners and internalising their suffering led to a nervous breakdown. He and I end the last of three interviews talking about his favourite subject, music. Suddenly animated, he describes his personal triumph in writing the Shona words and score for the sung parts of Zimbabwe's Catholic Mass in 1962, when the church stopped using its Latin version.

Some in the Catholic community have stories to tell about the president's kindness. A nun at St Anne's Hospital, where Bona Mugabe stayed while she was ill and where she eventually died, remembers him bringing flowers not only for his mother but for the nurses as well. There is evidence from Father Ribeiro that Mugabe, in going to great lengths to help fellow detainees, had a good heart in the prison years. He risked his neck to thank Sister Laub for her support during the bush war. And he rang me to make sure my child was safe after I had left the toddler unattended at home in order to drive him to the station. Later, once ensconced at State House, he gave lessons to illiterate members of his household staff to help them pass exams.

Another member of the Catholic clergy, Brother Kazito Bute, who knew Robert Mugabe over many years, admits to a selective memory and says he prefers to recall only the good in him. 'The president has made mistakes, you could say, but his achievements are greater than his mistakes. We can discuss the achievements.' The former maths master at Kutama, where the president was born and educated, is 'nearly 100 years old' and first met Robert when he was a student teacher shortly before the future president left St Francis Xavier College in 1945. What Brother Bute recalls most vividly about those faraway days is Mugabe playing tennis:

> I stayed next to the courts so I often watched the students playing. Robert would hit that ball and hit it hard. He was keen and good. He often won and then he was happy. But when he was losing you would hear 'love this', 'advantage that', and then 'game, bang' and his racket went on the ground. You would know Robert was going to be hurt and angry. You would see his head fall and his shoulders drop down and he would leave the court without saying anything to anybody. He did not like to lose. But he often won, so overall it was all right at that time.

Although Brother Bute seldom saw Mugabe after he left Kutama, he was in regular contact with the former student's relatives living in the area. Once, during the bush war, he was in the chapel at Kutama when he heard some comrades arriving in a truck and talking outside a window close to where he was kneeling. One of them opened the chapel door and told the others he was going inside to pray but Brother Bute did not turn around so he never discovered if it was Mugabe or another old boy. 'It sounded like Robert,' he says.

After Mugabe became president, he built a house next door to the school and visited Kutama regularly. 'He was married here in the chapel to his second wife Grace. He often gives the school gifts. Recently, he gave our headmaster a car but he continues to ride his bicycle because there is no petrol for the car. When a member of Robert's family marries or dies or is baptised, he comes to Kutama, but quickly in and out. He gave money for the burial of James Chikerema and he spoke beautifully at the funeral, which some people were very much surprised to see because the two of them remained political opponents unto death.'

Teachers at Mugabe's alma mater, including the retired Brother Bute, admit that textbooks are not being replaced, classrooms are falling apart and blackouts prevent evening study because the country has been disastrously mismanaged by Mugabe. St Francis Xavier used to be Zimbabwe's top school, they note wistfully. But they are all grateful for the free eggs and chickens from Mugabe's adjoining estate. 'He looks after us,' says Brother Bute. 'He always looks after his own people.'

At Silveira House, a Catholic leadership training centre east of Harare, a prominent churchman is too busy to talk when I arrive for an interview with his retired predecessor, who is taking a nap. He agrees to discuss Robert Mugabe's ability to pull the wool over Catholic eyes with me at a later date. But while I am waiting for my delayed appointment, he dashes in, saying he has a magazine article which he believes might explain the president's behaviour. I return to the office with him to photocopy the *Newsweek* story, which is on narcissistic personality disorder.

Entitled 'Of Criminals and CEOs', the article is in the magazine's science section and contends that narcissistic personality disorder, known as NPD, afflicts some of society's most successful members. Bold, creative visionaries in the world of politics as well as in business are as likely to show the traits associated with the personality disorder – grandiosity, lack of empathy and exploitativeness – as criminals and psychiatric patients. The question of how to manage such super egos has become a hot-button issue in boardrooms across America, according to *Newsweek*. 'Narcissistic bosses may make bold leaders but they can also let aggression and selfishness fester in the workplace, to the point where cruelty and deception are condoned.' Those in the international community charged with persuading Mugabe to step down would do well to consider the Zimbabwe leader's personality disorder, whether it be NPD, paranoia or both, says the churchman, who plans to write a paper on the subject. His guess at a clinical diagnosis reflects widespread attempts to makes sense of the enigmatic Mugabe's behaviour, it being something of a relief to attach a label to the mystery of what makes the once-respected Mugabe tick.

This churchman, who worked tirelessly to dislodge Ian Smith's Rhodesia, used to meet the future president often in the years before he discovered that Robert Mugabe's Zimbabwe was just as hostile to ordinary people as Smith's regime had been. After Mugabe's release from prison in 1974, the Church gave him an office and telephone at Silveira House, where his sisters Sabina and Bridget were employed to work on development programmes for women. 'He was quietly spoken and articulate,' he recalls. 'There was no rancour.' What happened to him subsequently is a subject they ponder continually at Silveira House, he says, speculating that NPD might run in families. 'Even his sister Sabina, who we knew so well, is a different person today. We barely recognise her as the gentle woman we knew.'

After a while, I am taken to see Father John Dove, the founder of Silveira House. We first met 30 years earlier when he was running the centre in support of the liberation struggle. Then a large, energetic former British army officer, he would discreetly warn his staff of the presence of security police by saying, 'Today we are sailing close to the wind.' He would not hear a bad word against Robert Mugabe in those days.

Now an old man, Father Dove says he is happy to talk about the president as he knew him.

> But I'm told that he has changed. I understand the country is in a terrible mess now, which is surprising because he did such a good job early on. I don't get about much any more but we used to be ever so proud of Robert, you know. It was as if, coming from such humble beginnings, he represented the potential achievement of all Zimbabweans. And now, sadly, I'm told there are those who see him as representing the potential weakness of all Zimbabweans. If what I hear is correct about so many in the government, the police and the army being corrupt and callous, then Robert has a lot to explain before God.

So much pride was invested in Mugabe making good that priests like Father Dove struggle to this day to condemn him outright. Their blind faith became part of Mugabe's identity: indeed, a whole country believed, like his mother, that Robert Mugabe was going to be more brilliant and more successful than anyone else. How Mugabe coped with this intense pressure of expectation is anybody's guess, although it probably confirmed what he had believed since childhood – that he was the chosen one and could do no wrong. Had he had inklings of mortality, the responsibility may well have disturbed him in the way that clever students in universities all over the continent, whose educations have been sponsored by rural villagers with the scarcest of resources, often crack under the strain.

Like the parent who invests all his hopes in a child and cannot bear the disappointment when his offspring messes up, many in the Catholic Church who continued to support Mugabe might have feared, as Father Dove suggests, that the failing president, once their protégé, was a reflection of themselves. Africans all over the continent, for whom the historic injustice of racism is an ongoing blind spot, are equally reluctant to condemn Mugabe. Men like Father Ribeiro, Brother Bute and the multitudes throughout Africa, who continue to give Zimbabwe's president their mindless loyalty, refuse to confront their disillusionment, not only because they cannot contemplate siding with the white West against one of their own, but in case their criticism reveals something about themselves. The reason Germanic and British-born clergy can criticise the president freely is because they are at more of a distance. Being Europeans, they feel Mugabe is not, ultimately, one of them.

'The man I remember was considered and honest,' Father Dove continues.

> He used to sit right here in this room with me, discussing the country and the future. He cared deeply for his fellow Zimbabweans and he was well ahead of his time on women's issues too. He told me once, shortly after he came out of prison, that he was irritated by the slogan 'one man, one vote' and wanted it changed to 'one human, one vote'.
>
> I used to ask him if he had become embittered by his treatment in prison, where the warders would make him stand on one leg for long periods; that sort of humiliation. He laughed and said his strategy had been to concentrate on staying calm during such ordeals.

The satisfaction Mugabe got from his jailers' inability to make him angry was hard-won, but worthwhile, because they wanted him to misbehave so that they could punish him further, make an example of him and strip him of his dignity, explains Father Dove.

> That's what he told me. He talked about it quite unemotionally. Somebody

once told me that he first cultivated his little Hitler moustache to irritate an English warder who was especially mean to him. He always seemed to me to have come through that dreadful experience remarkably unscathed but perhaps he was seething underneath. It rather looks that way now, doesn't it?

Evidence that Mugabe was tortured in prison, mentally and physically, is cited by Father Dove and others as the reason for the terrifying anger he has shown towards his own people in recent years. Being prevented from attending his only child's funeral, for example, may well have broken his heart, cracking him into pieces so that, like Humpty Dumpty, he could not be put together again. He may have suffered fear of such intensity in prison that he cut himself off from his feelings as a survival strategy. Believing that nobody could thereafter reach him to hurt him or make him angry again might have left him irretrievably damaged. How is a vulnerable person supposed to find his way back to his humanity after cutting off his feelings for his own protection? Some former prisoners, notably Nelson Mandela, recover but not everyone can. Mandela was a secure man who remained a caring person. For Mugabe, emotionally fragile since childhood, conquering similar odds may have been unrealistic.

The sort of abuse Mugabe suffered at the hands of his enemies is of course embedded in the history of humanity. Apartheid and Nazism broke countless people. A few, like Mandela, emerged from the wreckage as heroes; others came out of the torment so damaged that the healing work can only be done by future generations. For Mugabe, the damage inflicted by his enemies was compounded, ironically, by his admirers in the Catholic Church giving him ample rope with which to hang himself.

Twelve

The man in the elegant suit

If it is true that we make our own reality, then Robert Mugabe's world was constructed from his delusions of omnipotence. In his world, he could do whatever he liked until the economy started to collapse, when money rather than moral limits became the reality. In this precarious environment, where Zimbabwe's president continued to strut his stuff in the audacious style that had become his hallmark, I visited some of the people who served him over the years.

One of the tailors who was chosen to dress Zimbabwe's elegantly clad president says Robert Mugabe is unfailingly polite and punctual. Khalil 'Solly' Parbhoo of Liberty Tailors, suit maker to the country's heads of state since the late 50s, was summoned to State House to measure and fit Mugabe several times. 'He was always there to meet me, shake my hand, offer me a cup of tea. "Sit down, sit down," he would say, as if I was there for a friendly visit rather than for business. If he was going to be late, a member of his staff would always phone ahead and say so. If he was running just a bit late for our appointment, even five minutes, he would immediately apologise when he walked in.'

Solly's tiny shop with its distinctive pressed metal ceilings and oak door is in a single-storey building erected during the 20s. It used to be in the smartest part of town but is now among Harare's most noticeably decaying business premises. Crying out for a coat of paint, the once-proud House of Liberty Tailors is surrounded by two derelict pawnbrokers and a coughing pavement watchmaker. Several hawkers offer bananas and peanuts to occasional passers-by in front of the shop. A few dusty travellers are slumped in the shade of its veranda.

Although nowadays there is little commercial activity in the city centre apart from a brief flurry at the end of the month, Solly's shop is crowded on a Tuesday morning. A couple talk in undertones to each other as they finger bolts of cloth. A portly man in a crisp pink shirt is being measured for a suit by Solly's son. He is talking so loudly about his farm that you cannot help listening. I assume from the ostentatious chatter featuring approving references to Zanu-PF that his farm is one of the formerly white-owned tracts handed out to party loyalists in the government's disastrous land grab.

Solly reels off an impressive list of the political leaders he has dressed in addition to Robert Mugabe. Included is Britain's last governor in Rhodesia, Lord Soames, and the toppled Ethiopian tyrant, Mengistu Haile Mariam, who has lived in Zimbabwe as Mugabe's guest since 1991 in the hope of evading international justice. 'It was Lady Soames who used to bring in her husband's mending, usually broken zips or trousers to be let out. She still sends me a Christmas card from London every year,' Solly explains breathlessly. 'I was asked to make a long-sleeved Chinese-style safari suit buttoned up to the neck for Mengistu just three weeks ago, but he doesn't call himself Mengistu any more. He doesn't live in town any more either.' Solly interrupts the loud farmer's conversation to ask his son what Mengistu calls himself now that he too lives on a farm. The younger tailor slings his tape measure around his neck irritably, shooting his father a meaningful glance. 'We don't talk about that,' he says in a quiet voice, as his boastful client eyes me thoughtfully.

We are standing beneath the Zimbabwean president's unsmiling portrait, which hangs above ancient calendars and posters of slinky women advertising cloth and zips. Changing the subject, I ask Solly quietly what State House looks like these days. He went there before Mugabe was in office to fit a suit for Ian Smith and says the elegant residence has not changed much.

It might even look a bit better, with some new things in it, I'm not sure. By the way, Ian Smith was not a stylish man like Robert Mugabe. He stuck to the conservative styles of the 50s; narrow jacket lapels and wide trousers with turn-ups. He didn't like change; he never wanted to try anything new. He was also very polite though. I did mainly alterations for him. And I do mainly alterations or mending for Mugabe now too. His staff bring in the jackets and trousers for him so I don't see him personally any more. His measurements haven't changed. The last time I saw him was at the funeral of one of his doctors some time ago but he remembered me and said hello. I went to talk to him in front of everybody.

Solly was given his nickname by a Jewish employer while he was still in his teens. He started his business with a single foot-cranked Singer sewing machine 50 years ago. His family arrived in Southern Rhodesia in 1903 after catching a boat from Bombay to Beira and walking all the way to what is now Zimbabwe.

This old street used to be known as tailors' row but now I'm the only one. Tailoring is a dying trade. Most of our Cabinet ministers are suited in ready-mades but not the president. His suits were always made in London or I think somewhere in Malaysia, now that he isn't welcome in Britain any more. He still dresses like an English gentleman; that's always been his style. He acts like an English gentleman too, a wonderful person when you're in his presence, although not when he's on the public platform. You can't believe he's the same person you see on the stage, shouting about this and that.

Solly laughs explosively, presumably at the dual image of the Savile Row gentleman and the crazed orator in gaudy African prints and a baseball cap.

I made him a jacket once which should have been double-breasted but he didn't like that at all. He knows what he wants. One of his aides used to come into the shop to choose a few swatches, which I would take to State House for his final selection. He goes for dark cloth, sometimes with a stripe or a check. He likes vents on the sides of his jackets.

Unexpectedly, the loud man in pink bellows, 'He needs a few vents to let out the hot air!' and doubles up at his joke. Parbhoo Junior is beginning to look very uncomfortable so I prepare to leave. As Solly follows me out of the shop, he confides, 'His Excellency told me he didn't want any publicity but that was a long time ago. I don't suppose it matters now.'

My next meeting is at the shop of another Harare tailor, Bhula Bhagat. Like the Parbhoos, he is of Asian descent and has been dressing Robert Mugabe since selling him a pair of shoes a few days before Christmas in 1960.

> Robert told me then that he was a teacher on his way back on holiday from Ghana, but I used to see him at political meetings after that. He always stood out because he was well-educated, quietly spoken and respectful. We became a bit friendly. The following year, I went to his wedding.
>
> I got to know him during a campaign called Citizens Against the Colour Bar, when we used to go defiantly into whites-only cinemas, swimming baths, that sort of place, where we were not allowed to go as non-whites. He was in hospital for some reason around that time and I went to visit him there, and took him some things. Then he was in prison for a long time and after that he went to Mozambique to start the war. So there was a long vacuum when I didn't see him at all.

We are sitting in Bhagat's office on the mezzanine floor of his shop Nagarji's. He starts to rummage in the drawers of his desk for some old photographs with which to endorse his own political credentials. There is a faded picture of him standing in a group of men at the detention centre Gonakudzingwa in south-eastern Rhodesia, where he had obtained a rare pass to visit detainees. One picture is of his late father, who used to talk politics with the young Mugabe whenever he came into the shop; another is of Mugabe and Leopold Takawira, a leading activist and mentor to Mugabe when he first entered the political arena, who died while they were in prison together.

Talking to Bhagat about the president's life and one of his best-known characteristics – his sartorial elegance – I get a sense of time passing but things not staying the same, and I wonder what it means in my search for insight into this enigmatic leader's tyranny. Among Bhula Bhagat's throwaway remarks is a single sentence that conceals all the most painful things that ever happened to Mugabe: *Then he was in prison for a long time and, after that, he went to Mozambique to start the war.* I realise that in more than two years of research, I have heard little about the losses incurred by Mugabe in the cataclysmic events of his life. So much is unacknowledged, no doubt by him as well as by those who knew him. If he were to have acknowledged and dealt with the pain of what it meant to spend 11 years in prison, for example, the pain of losing his mentor who died there, the sorrow of losing the small son he barely knew and was prevented from burying, and the double-dealings of the two-faced people who used to be his colleagues and then turned against him, the monster Mugabe may never have emerged. Instead, his boyhood pattern of dealing with emotions by denying and burying them prevailed in Mugabe's adult life so that his experiences of hurt and trauma, humiliation, betrayal and fear accumulated like a festering sore.

Mugabe comes out of prison, puts on his immaculate suit and carries on as though he is still the same person. But the man you meet in the beginning cannot be the one you see at the end. That is an illusion. Like the soldier who has been to war and witnessed too many inhuman acts, he returns with the emotional numbness known among war veterans as shell shock. Being unacknowledged and therefore untreated, it continues to negatively impact on him later. His tailors fit Mugabe into his suits, altering this and mending that, but never addressing of course the area that most needed repair – a traumatised psyche held together by an elegant veneer and an omnipotent view of himself.

All of us can remember moments right back to our schooldays when someone delivered an insult or a cruel quip that continues to hurt life-long. We can, if we choose, proceed as if the cruelty never took place, putting it in a compartment of the mind out of reach. That way we can survive as if it had never happened and believe, as long as we do not open it up, that we will be fine. But then ... it did happen. The pain and loss is buried and just awaiting stressful reminders that will trigger its emergence. Mugabe's life experiences in prison, the circumstances surrounding the loss of his son, what he saw as Britain's betrayal and the ingratitude of Zimbabwe's white community provided the triggers that re-evoked his earlier suffering. The monster that emerged was attempting to silence the pain.

Because of the difficulties in the family he grew up in, especially his mother's inability to cope with her situation and her resulting depression, Mugabe lacked the emotional support to build inner strength. He was ill-prepared to manage strife. His character weaknesses could have manifested in a cranky schoolmaster with pedantic tendencies, perhaps prone to sulking when things did not go his way or when others argued with him. Instead, he becomes the leader of a conspiratorial political party and then the premier of a nation with a deeply troubled history. Flung into circumstances that provoke his weaknesses, particularly the inadequacies of his emotional development, he lashes out and becomes increasingly resentful. The image of the world leader His Excellency President Robert Mugabe shaking hands with heads of state and helping to shape international politics in his immaculate suits, conceals the damaged person underneath.

'I remember my father and Robert once discussing how long it would be before apartheid was defeated in South Africa,' continues Bhagat. His father felt sure it would take much longer to topple the white south than Mugabe reckoned. They had a long and at times quite heated discussion on the subject, he recalls. 'The president proved to be right on that one,' muses Bhagat. 'He enjoyed a good discussion. I don't remember much else about him for many years after that. The next time I saw Robert was after he came out of prison, when he stared at my bald forehead and asked jokingly, "What happened to your hair?"'

After becoming premier, Mugabe sometimes swept into Nagarji's with his extensive entourage, sirens wailing, to purchase clothing. In recent years, the president's children have sometimes been brought to the shop by aides to buy school uniforms. The business is on the corner of Robert Mugabe Road and Leopold Takawira Street and calls itself 'the symbol of quality in fashion', although its shelves seem to be stocked mainly with garments from China. Bhagat says the president seldom comes to the city centre any more, due to his unpopularity in the urban areas of Zimbabwe.

Bhagat last saw Mugabe in person at Nagarji's more than a decade ago when the president's mother Bona was ill at St Anne's Hospital. All Bhagat remembers of that occasion is the presidential motorcade appearing suddenly in the street outside. The bodyguards alighted in a rush with Mugabe, who walked briskly into the showroom and made his way straight to the ladies' section. There he chose a couple of nightdresses to take to his ailing mother. 'I can't remember everything he bought; some other nice things for her. She died soon afterwards. Of course, by now the president was His Excellency and I couldn't call him Robert any more.'

Some years ago Bhagat remembers his delight on receiving a phone call from the president.

> He said he wanted to send his gardener in from State House with a note asking me to allow him to choose clothing for his family as a Christmas gift. It was completely unexpected. I picked up the phone to hear him saying, 'Mugabe here'. He asked me to invoice him, which I did, and he paid very promptly. The gardener selected various things for his wife, his children and himself. He had a wonderful time in the shop. It was a very generous gift from his employer.

So what made Robert Mugabe, apparently a good man in some respects, go off the rails and act against the best interests of the people who trusted him?

Bhagat shakes his head. 'Power,' he offers several times, shrugging helplessly. 'I just can't understand what happened to change him so much, really.' Surprisingly though, considering Bhagat is a man who prides himself on his own liberation record, he answers with patent indifference when I ask for his insight into the outrage called Operation Murambatsvina, a brutal campaign in which thousands of impoverished people were swept from their makeshift homes and shops in Harare and other Zimbabwean cities. 'That was actually a good thing,' he insists firmly. 'The inner city areas were blocked up by these illegal street dwellers. They weren't paying any rates and taxes. It is much better now. You can drive your car in and out very easily.'

Confused by his callousness but moving on swiftly, Zimbabwe not being a place where you linger to argue against the state's policies, I hear of another supplier to the president, albeit in the service of his health rather than his wardrobe. Dr Jan Smit[4] is an Afrikaner; a specialist at the Garden City Clinic in western Johannesburg. He says he treats his celebrity Zimbabwean patient on a regular basis and in exactly the same manner as all the others who consult him about their medical problems. If Mugabe arrives late for instance, as happened on one occasion, he is routinely informed that his consultation has been abbreviated accordingly.

---

[4] Not his real name.

Mugabe's appointments are nevertheless disruptive events as his bodyguards storm into the waiting room, frisking staff and patients and generally making a nuisance of themselves. Mugabe himself is meek and quiet. Because only Mugabe is admitted beyond the waiting room to be examined by the specialist, his bodyguards do not get the opportunity to search the doctor for weapons – which is just as well, seeing the doctor has a revolver strapped to his chest and concealed beneath his waistcoat. Having carried the gun for years on the grounds that he is frequently called out late at night in emergencies and needs protection in crime-ridden Johannesburg, Dr Smit relishes his secret status as the potential assassin of one of the world's most reviled politicians.

Another service provider to the president of Zimbabwe is Sue Chapman, the woman who grew and arranged the flowers on display at Robert and Grace Mugabe's lavish wedding in Kutama in 1996. A Trelawney farmer's wife in those days, she went to enormous expense to decorate the venue for the 12 000 guests who had been invited. Joaquim Chissano, the president of Mozambique, was the best man and world icon and then president of South Africa, Nelson Mandela, was eagerly awaited by everybody attending one of the most glamorous events in Zimbabwe's social history.

Enlisting the help of other farmers' wives, Sue Chapman had spent months planning the flower arrangements. 'I thought it was an honour at the time,' she recalls. 'We grew our own flowers for export and we supplied all of them for the wedding, a truckload. But I am still waiting to be paid. It was a wonderful occasion and the flowers looked beautiful but I couldn't believe it when nobody ever bothered to pay for them. I dealt with "Amazing" Grace, as we called her, so perhaps the oversight was hers rather than the president's, but it was terribly disappointing for me.'

Like the rest of the Zimbabwean president's wedding entourage, Sue Chapman couldn't help noticing that Nelson Mandela was the real star of the occasion. Many among the guests observed too how irritated Robert Mugabe was to be upstaged on his own wedding day by the more famous former freedom fighter who had replaced him as the darling of Africa.

Foremost among the continent's hospitality venues that used to enjoy making Robert Mugabe and his family feel at home is the famous

Victoria Falls Hotel. Zimbabwe's most glamorous tourism location remains almost as awesome as the natural wonder it celebrates, despite being in a country distinguished by a plunging economy. One of the few viable businesses left in the former British colony, it is still listed among the best hotels in the world. Ironically though, its elegant style and architecture boast of the very colonial past that is blamed by Robert Mugabe for the slide to ruin that lies beyond its pristine white-washed walls.

Over Christmas 2005, the sun beats down relentlessly and monkeys sitting on the hotel's long green roofs appear at times to be aiming their chewed mango pips straight at guests strolling on the soft lawns below. But this is a minor drawback. In a timeless institution like the Victoria Falls Hotel, a monument to better days for some, though possibly a ridiculous imperialist relic to others, tasteful solutions are found to all problems. The primates are discreetly lured away from the public areas by staff proffering peeled fruit with the pips removed.

There is nothing that foreign currency cannot buy, even amid stratospheric inflation in the world's fastest-declining peacetime economy. Tourism dollars remain plentiful at the Victoria Falls Hotel. Its renowned bars and restaurants feature the Gothic grace of the Livingstone Room, where guests no longer require a jacket and tie, and Jungle Junction's spectacular views of the famous bridge over the Zambezi, which is shrouded in spray from the world's longest fall of water at this time of year.

Old posters along the hotel's wide corridors shamelessly extol the bounty accruing to the British Empire from its African colonies during the 19th century. The English tradition of high tea has been an afternoon ritual on its shady verandas, kept cool and mosquito-free at sundown by fans discreetly whirring overhead, since the late Queen Mother came to visit with her husband George VI. They were accompanied by their shy daughters, princesses Elizabeth and Margaret, whose portraits hang everywhere.

Pretty paper umbrellas decorate the iced drinks we are served on silver trays at the poolside by waiters with straight backs and confident smiles. The wildlife is a perennial problem, whispers a very tall doorman in maroon tails and matching top hat as he summons a gardener to chase a baboon from the roof of a departing car. On the short walk from the hotel's perimeter wall to view the majestic falls, we are accompanied by a guard whose job is to spot lurking buffalo or elephant and re-route guests accordingly. He is followed at a discreet distance by a trail of skinny hawkers selling salad bowls carved in exotic woods, clay animals and beaded bangles. When there are no buyers, the traders try bartering: 'Your trainers for a rhino, missus; your cap for a bowl, or two bowls'; and finally, proffering a yellowing toothbrush, 'A squeeze of toothpaste for one soapstone crocodile?'

From the chapel down the corridor comes the sound of a Christmas choir. I am on my way to look at the presidential suite where Robert Mugabe has stayed with his family on several occasions. Decorated in pleasing shades of green and Wedgwood, it features a bed enclosed in gorgeous floral folds. With white mouldings on the ceiling and doors, fine brass detail even on the luggage rack, the air lavender-scented and prints of stylised monkeys and botanical drawings by famous painters hanging on the walls, it is a quintessentially English hideaway.

During breakfast, I talk to a couple of suited waiters ever so casually, posing questions as if I already know the answers because Zanu-PF is not a regime that takes kindly to political curiosity. Foreign journalists, banned from entering Zimbabwe, estimate that one in five locals works for the Central Intelligence Organisation (CIO), a ferocious network of spies, saboteurs and assassins. This cannot be true if Robert Mugabe is as unpopular as the same journalists claim. It would mean there were millions working for the CIO, which is highly unlikely, but one does have the uneasy feeling of being watched even in the blissful surrounds of the Victoria Falls – and not only by the monkeys.

I say nonchalantly to the staff hovering around at breakfast time: 'Your president was here in the hotel for the party conference last year.' One waiter looks faintly affronted but nods as the other smiles perfunctorily. The village called Victoria Falls is situated in Matabeleland, the ethnic headquarters of Robert Mugabe's traditional opponents. The Ndebele are a politically defeated but historically formidable group. There is no love lost among them for Mugabe and his supporters in Mashonaland. But they have become fearful, as anyone would in the circumstances of mass murder that prevailed in Matabeleland during the early 80s, when relatives and friends of the man pouring our coffee and the chef scrambling our eggs disappeared in a purge of thousands of victims that had been ordered to allay the suspicions of a leader with the power to do as he pleased.

After dinner that evening, when three members of staff in bow ties are expertly counting the mountains of local money proffered by one of the guests at our table, a well-built waiter sidles up. 'I am the silver service senior,' he explains quietly. 'I served the president – twice.' A bit startled, I suggest we talk after breakfast the next day. He tells me his name and bows.

In the morning, I do not see him or look for him. It is Christmas Day. Having reflected overnight on a disconcerting experience in Harare a month earlier, I have resolved not to discuss the president with total strangers. On the earlier occasion, after meeting a man who claimed to have a friend who cleaned the Mugabe children's bedrooms at State House, I incautiously arranged for the two of them to come to dinner at York Lodge where I was staying. I promised to pay for their taxis since fuel was scarce and transport a problem, but otherwise offered nothing more than a meal in return for the interview. What I wanted to verify were bits of gossip: that Mugabe's older son Robert Junior, a teenager, had taken to playing the drums, for example, which made his father angry in the evenings when he came home from what one can only imagine to be the intense stress of running Zimbabwe into the ground. I had been told too that relations between the president and his wife Grace, who is 30 years his junior, had become increasingly strained since his discovery of her infidelity in 2004.

My dinner guests were due to arrive at 7pm but failed to show up. Neither answered his mobile phone. By 9pm, I was nervously questioning my gullibility. Why would a man with a menial but prestigious job at stake at State House, and his signature almost certainly on an Official Secrets Act contract to boot, want to talk to a forbidden outsider like me for no reward or even a guarantee of anonymity? I could not eat my meal and sent the untouched dishes back to the kitchen so that the staff could go off duty. By 10pm, I was beginning to panic. What if one of my missing dinner guests had betrayed the other? Perhaps the man who had introduced me to 'Mugabe's bedroom boy', as the State House cleaner called himself, had been arrested and was being subjected to unspeakable forms of CIO interrogation even as I trembled in my room?

The night was deeply dark and still. Every now and then the security guard patrolling the lodge grounds received a call on his walkie-talkie, which crackled in the blackness. What if my absent dinner guests had failed to pitch because they had informed on me? I waited, peering towards the gate through barely parted curtains and praying that the voice talking to the guard was not coming from a hidden police car.

Despite my new-found caution at the Victoria Falls Hotel and the silver service senior's own misgivings after, as he later told me, having been beaten by the CIO on several occasions, he and I end up talking at length about Robert Mugabe because he simply refuses to let the matter rest.

'We failed to have our meeting yesterday,' he notes quietly, standing beside me at the breakfast table. Zimbabweans are well-spoken, dignified and forthright. His directness in the face of my opacity makes me feel foolish. Nevertheless, I suggest we meet later without specifying when, at which point he holds up his hands in a gesture of frustration and disappears into the kitchen. When he returns, he is carrying a coffee pot and a cup on a silver tray hoisted aloft at shoulder height. 'Come,' he commands politely. 'Let us go together. What is your room number?'

I follow him to my room, where he places the tray on the floor, sits uninvited at the desk and begins to tell his Mugabe stories. I want to laugh at the incongruous scene but he is looking very serious indeed so I scramble for my notebook. He remembers the president's visit to open the 1998 Zanu-PF conference. All the Mugabe family's food was prepared in the Stanley Kitchen, which is opposite the presidential suite on the ground floor. Only the residential staff was in attendance until he was summoned to serve two meals.

I was called in because it was beef stroganoff served straight on to the plate. The way they were doing it was wrong and the president knew it. He is fussy about presentation and so he asked the manager to bring a senior in. I was proud to serve His Excellency.

I remember it being quite a noisy family meal because Chatunga, the president's smallest child, was putting one of the silver covers that we place over the dishes to keep the food warm on the floor and sitting on it. The president was very patient with him. He was a nice father, the way he talked to his son. He explained several times that Chatunga was not supposed to sit on the silver cover. 'Sit on the chair,' he told him. 'This hotel has been the home of kings and queens and presidents from all over the world and they sit on the chairs, not on the food covers,' he told him.

Then he explained to his son that the British Empire was once the greatest kingdom in the world and the way they did things was the civilised way. The kid said he liked it better on the floor. The first lady ate and took no notice. The other children were laughing.

At the opening ceremony at the flagpole in front of the hotel, South African President Thabo Mbeki was sitting next to Mugabe on the platform. Yvonne Chaka Chaka was the singer performing that night, I remember. She asked Mbeki, her president, to dance. He got up to join her but he was too stiff to dance so he sat down. Then Mugabe, who is much older than Mbeki, got up and began to boogie. He was enjoying himself and it was enjoyable for us watching our president having fun. Yvonne was shouting, 'Get down, get down,' but he couldn't manage that.

Two years later in 2000, when the Blue Train began its Victoria Falls route from Johannesburg, the Zanu-PF conference was again held here because everyone wanted to market the destination. By then, Mugabe was a different person. Everybody noticed it. He was shouting instructions to everyone, including his family. His staff was telling us that he was not friendly any more; that he didn't trust anyone any more. There were no sweet words for him. We were told by his staff that he was very disturbed at the formation of the Movement for Democratic Change (MDC), which was campaigning against the government's constitutional reforms.

His family was not allowed to leave Room 25, which is the presidential suite, although we were told not to call it that while Mugabe was in residence. They could not even cross the passage into the Stanley Room, where there was a dining room for their exclusive use, or into the Bulawayo Room, where Mugabe's office was (situated). When he opened the conference, he addressed the delegates not from the veranda as expected but from inside the Bulawayo Room. The whole area was cordoned off and we were told not to go near it. All his food and supplies came from Harare, even the fresh fruit and vegetables – even the drinking water. Only his chefs and waiters from State House were allowed into the Stanley Kitchen.

He and the family ate in their suite. Members of his staff were scared of him and always worried they might be doing something wrong. I did not see him once or any of his family except for Chatunga, who ran away to the pool area. We were all alerted that he had disappeared and the presidential security was running all over looking for him. My friend and I found him at the pool. When we told him that he was not allowed out of Room 25 and the restricted area, he said we were wrong and told us he was part of the security staff. We laughed but that small boy was very frustrated, you could see. He did not want to stay in the room all the time with his sister and brother, who were just sleeping and watching TV all day, or with the mother shouting at him to be quiet because she was also wanting to sleep all day. There was nothing for them to do except wait for the president to come in.

Time was passing and nothing but the greenery stayed the same. Zimbabwe's cities had decayed and the president had let things slip. He used to be a diligent payer but no longer bothered to settle his debts. He used to go shopping but could no longer face the possibility of being confronted in the street. Withdrawing gradually, he did not meet people outside his official arena any more. His family could no longer lead remotely normal lives. The world was shrinking, reality receding like the hair on Bhagat's head, as Mugabe stayed well away from any evidence that he was not who he thought he was.

He started spending more time at home in the suburban mansion he had built for Grace, who is not well liked by Zimbabweans. Reputedly empty-headed and vain, she had her nails painted and repainted almost hourly while at Victoria Falls by a beautician on her personal staff, according to the silver service senior. Gossip about her abounds in Zimbabwe. She is said, for example, to have repeatedly asked guests attending a Geneva banquet for Africa's first ladies who they thought she most resembled among the Spice Girls. Mrs Kibaki, the first lady of Kenya, who was present, is alleged to have said afterwards that the two suggestions that sprang into her mind in response to Grace's question were Scary Spice and Old Spice.

Grace's predecessor Sally, who died in 1992 of kidney failure, was energetic politically and her husband's intellectual equal, whereas the current first lady is said to be preoccupied exclusively with herself. Mugabe apparently plucked his second wife out of the typing pool in his office on the strength of her youth and good looks, because he desperately wanted children. She bore him three, two of them before Sally died. One of Sally's colleagues in a charity she used to support told me on condition of anonymity that Mugabe's first wife had blessed the relationship with Grace because she believed a young family would give the ageing leader a new image as a virile man.

At a graveside ceremony held in 2006 on the anniversary of Sally's death, Mugabe was reported by *The Zimbabwean* to have wept openly as he laid a wreath at Heroes Acre cemetery in Harare. He was consoled by Sally's niece Patricia Bekele, who had led a delegation of relatives from Ghana to Zimbabwe for the occasion. In a halting eulogy, pausing often to dry his eyes, Mugabe recalled the night before his first wife's death. 'I visited her in hospital and she took my hand and told me that she loved me very much. I said, "I love you too",' he told mourners.

The president's second wife features as a character in a hit play called *Breakfast with Mugabe* written by Fraser Grace, which was first staged by the Royal Shakespeare Company in Stratford-Upon-Avon in 2005 and subsequently ran in London's West End. In it, a young British playwright who has never been to Zimbabwe explores the relationship between Mugabe, Grace and a Western-trained psychiatrist summoned to State House to treat Mugabe's delusions. The play is beautifully crafted; a technical masterpiece.

One London critic hailed it as 'a stage production which pins Zimbabwe's woes on a malevolent spirit that has haunted its president for years'. Explaining that Mugabe has long been portrayed as a power-crazed madman who has brought his country to its knees with a barbarous campaign against his own people, the *Independent on Sunday* says the work is based on a supposedly oft-repeated story that Mugabe spent time being treated by a psychiatrist for depression brought on by the spirit of leading political figure Josiah Tongogara, who died in a car accident shortly before the country's liberation.

The paper quotes the play's director Anthony Sher on Mugabe: 'He grips me. I can't stop watching him and he is more mesmeric the worse he behaves. In the play, Fraser has shown the complexities beneath the monster as well as the pain and suffering. If the play works, the audience should feel some compassion for him.' The playwright adds: 'The bottom line is that if he (Mugabe) came to see it, I hope he might recognise himself.'

The trouble is that the sad events the play traces, including Mugabe's abandonment by his father in childhood, the death of his first wife when he most needed her guidance, and the death of his son while Mugabe was incarcerated for more than a decade by Rhodesian authorities, are mentioned in passing and by the Mugabe character, who is portrayed as unstable. His suffering is therefore discounted even as it is presented to the audience. The focus of the play is Mugabe's alleged traditional African spiritual belief in the living dead as exemplified by a rumour that the president sets a place at his table for a deceased colleague. This highlights the most negatively stereotyped of any of the world's belief systems – African religion. Fraser Grace's psychiatrist is a white man, which posits whiteness as the norm. The patient Mugabe is typecast as an unpunctual African who does not, of course, keep his appointments.

Does the audience feel compassion for Mugabe? Certainly not. Would Mugabe recognise himself in the play? Not likely, if he is delusional. 'Nobody apart from him (Mugabe) and the original psychiatrist knows what took place,' the playwright points out. And neither of them will see *Breakfast with Mugabe*, the latter because he probably never existed. Aside from the improbability of a proud old man like Mugabe going on to the couch in the first place, there is the dominating, sophisticated stage character of his real-life airhead wife to ponder.

'But it's a play, it's speculation,' the playwright told a reporter shortly before one of Grace Mugabe's nieces came backstage to tell him that he had 'made her far too clever'. It is a play that is supposed to be about understanding but has none because it turns out to be about dramatic opportunism, albeit in the interests of entertainment based on hearsay.

So much of what we think we know about Robert Mugabe is in fact speculative. Among rumours that have persisted and been embellished over the years, for example, is the allegation that he has only one testicle or barely half a penis. The story varies but has been passed on for three decades, originally by policemen and prison officers and later by soldiers who sought to ridicule and humiliate Zimbabwe's nationalist leaders.

A doctor specialising in urology, who used to work at one of the University of Zimbabwe's teaching hospitals, sometimes assisted the surgeon Mugabe consulted on the sensitive matter of his genitalia. He told me it was completely untrue that the president had been castrated by the Rhodesian authorities. Confirming that a legitimate medical procedure was performed on Mugabe for a correctly diagnosed condition, he was bound by professional ethics not to disclose further details but conceded that Mugabe's condition was not sexually transmitted, as some of the rumours have persistently claimed.

However, a Zimbabwean journalist who is currently operating underground in the country told me, 'If you go to the rural areas where people still support Mugabe, they will quote the story that Smith's security forces lopped off his dick as evidence of how much Mugabe sacrificed for Zimbabwe. So it might as well be true.'

Another example of perception devoid of reality is the strange case of long-time Zimbabwe prisoner Kevin Woods, a disaffected white Rhodesian who became an agent for apartheid South Africa when Mugabe won the country's first free election in 1980. Woods was charged with, and subsequently admitted to, helping to orchestrate the Super-Zapu machinations that contributed to Mugabe's decision to kill thousands of Ndebele during the Gukurahundi massacres in the early 80s. In 2006, after Woods had been jailed in squalid conditions for a quarter of a century, Father Fidelis Mukonori persuaded Mugabe to release the self-confessed saboteur on humanitarian grounds. Woods set up home in South Africa where, as one of the key figures in the deliberate and tragic destabilisation of Zimbabwe in its most vulnerable early days, he became not a pariah but a hero in the media. Far from disappearing into obscurity, he was presented to the public as a brave survivor because white South African journalists simply assumed he must be a good guy if he had been imprisoned by Mugabe. Indeed, Woods published a book to celebrate his popularity among whites in post-apartheid South Africa. Such is the fear and loathing of Robert Mugabe that many people totally suspend their judgement on encountering his name. Just as he could do no wrong when it suited Western interests to portray him as the good guy in the years following Zimbabwe's independence, so he can do absolutely no right today.

One of the most peculiar stories I heard during my attempts to find out how Robert Mugabe went from shy schoolmaster to ruthless tyrant was from Dan Stannard, the CIO operative who served under Ian Smith as well as Mugabe, and who proved to be a reliable informant on a number of other occasions when I sought his assistance. According to Stannard, the officer in charge of Rusape, the police station nearest to the border point where Mugabe and Tekere crossed into Mozambique to crank up the war in 1975: 'I was made aware of the fact that Mugabe and Tekere would be exiting Rhodesia via Nyanga with the assistance of Chief Reyaki Tangwena, who was then living just inside Mozambique. But I was told that no attempts were to be made to stop this exfiltration. People at the highest level had pulled strings and had apparently come to some sort of arrangement by allowing Mugabe to exit Rhodesia.'

If this were true, one could speculate that it was Ian Smith who gave Mugabe his biggest break in politics. Dan Stannard says he never understood the logic behind the strange directive. 'They may have calculated that Mugabe's and Tekere's radicalism would somehow lead to their downfall, or they may have thought that the move would lead to war among the competing political factions in exile to the benefit of the Rhodesian government. Rightly or wrongly, this decision was to have a huge impact on the escalation of the war thereafter. Politicians!'

Thirteen

Two of a kind

Jonathan Moyo is invariably addressed as 'professor' despite his current commitment to politics rather than academia, which may indicate that the value of an elevated education remains as important in Zimbabwean politics today as it was when Robert Mugabe rose in the country's leadership ranks on the strength of his sophisticated image. But Moyo will need more than an impressive title to achieve the high office he craves, not least because he is from a minority group in a land obsessed by ethnicity. Although once powerful as the spin doctor in the presidency, he has been living in the political wilderness as an independent MP since falling foul of Mugabe a few years ago. A dauntingly ambitious man among a number of similarly unscrupulous politicians who await Mugabe's demise, he is nothing if not unpredictable; a chameleon ready to change his colours when opportunity beckons.

Moyo's critics at home, noting racial ambiguity in his background, used to refer to him scornfully as Mugabe's Goebbels, but they now eye him with even graver suspicion. He may be out of the limelight, they say, referring to Moyo's decision to stand as an independent candidate in the parliamentary elections in 2005, but he could return to centre stage at any moment.

An outspoken critic of the president prior to becoming Mugabe's chief propagandist during the years of Mugabe's disastrous land grab, Jonathan Moyo was born in Matabeleland and lived abroad for several years. He has a shady past by all accounts, his misdemeanours, including fraud, having been forgiven on his return to Zimbabwe in exchange for his blind loyalty to Mugabe – while it lasted. Moyo discounts the suggestion that things went horribly wrong in Zimbabwe between 2000 and 2005 when he was a key member of Mugabe's administration. He agrees, however, that this was the period when the country became visibly unstable. 'But 1999 did not mark the beginning of the disaster,' he insists.

Referring to my preamble about having had a personable, considerate Robert Mugabe to dinner at my home 30 years ago, Moyo says: 'Some analysts locate the date when things started to go wrong at 1975 – soon after you met Mugabe yourself – when he left Rhodesia to help wage war in Mozambique. His life after arriving in Mozambique, when he was imprisoned by Samora Machel, through his assumption of Zanu's leadership in 1977 and up to 1979, when he represented Zanu at Lancaster House, is the period that may have dramatically altered the man you met in the mid-70s. He may have become a very different person involved in a much more dangerous ball game during those five years.'

The prevailing view in academic literature is that Robert Mugabe changed during the Mozambique period, says Moyo.

He left Rhodesia just after the murder of Chitepo, who had been in charge of the liberation movement. It seems that he may have wanted to get into Chitepo's shoes. There are crucial questions to be answered about how Mugabe assumed the leadership of the movement. In assuming the leadership of an armed, violent organisation like Zanu outside the democratic process, knowing how much internal blood was being spilt inside the movement at the time, and knowing that he was not within a reasonable shot of elected high office, Mugabe would have had to ask himself how he could best obtain the position in the first place and then how he could keep it. Answers to those key questions would be the most fascinating in understanding the Mugabe we see in Zimbabwe today.

People have not dared to speak much about this very controversial five-year period that included the death of Josiah Tongogara, who was arrested in Zambia after the death of Chitepo at the same time as Mugabe was being detained in Mozambique. These events – including the way Mugabe's rival Tongogara was tormented in Zambian prisons after Chitepo's death – and how they affected Mugabe's leadership will remain uncharted territory until after Mugabe's death. Many people believe that had Tongogara lived, Mugabe would never have led Zimbabwe.

It is true that there is a sense during Mugabe's years in Mozambique of the stakes going up dramatically. Politics is no longer a game for him but a deadly survival course. People are being held in captivity, tortured and killed within their own ranks, leaving aside the deadly war being waged against the nationalist armies by the Rhodesian security forces. Mugabe's cynicism may indeed date back to his fraught years on the battlefront.

It is also true that hardly any witnesses have come forward to describe Mugabe's behaviour during that critical five-year period. One of the few former guerrillas who has dared to speak out is Wilfred Mhanda, who was the third in military command when Zanu and Zapu's guerrilla armies combined to form the Zimbabwe People's Army (Zipa) in 1976. 'It was my task to brief Mugabe on our military operations and I found him both attentive and receptive, a good listener,' says Mhanda. 'However, the guerrillas and refugees who met him did not find him an easy man to deal with, and soon formed the opinion that we would not go very far with him. He was secretive, stubborn and uncompromising, and the more I got to know him, the more I too began to fear for the future of the liberation struggle,' Mhanda told the BBC in January 2000. 'When Mugabe takes a dislike to someone, he becomes vindictive and never changes his mind.'

According to Mhanda, Robert Mugabe disbanded Zipa as soon as he felt secure as the leader of Zanu in 1976 because he feared that Joshua Nkomo might gain control of the united force. Shortly before leading a delegation to Geneva later the same year to attend an abortive settlement conference, Zipa regrouped and backed Mhanda in disowning 'the factions trying to lead us'. When Mugabe returned from Geneva, having forged an alliance with Josiah Tongogara, he persuaded the Mozambican president Samora Machel – who had by then decided to support Mugabe – to put down the Mhanda-led rebellion. Fifty of Zipa's top commanders were consequently arrested along with around 600 dissident guerrillas in Tongogara's camps. Some were shot. It was the first of Mugabe's purges, says Mhanda, and it marked the start of the Zimbabwean president's ruthless campaign to neutralise anyone he perceived as a threat.

Wilfred Mhanda's account of the events surrounding Mugabe's assumption of leadership in Mozambique is one of several versions of the moment when things went irrevocably wrong in Zimbabwean politics. What Jonathan Moyo believes after studying his country's history over the last three decades, however, is that the revolution lost its way in 1980 when Robert Mugabe became the first prime minister of independent Zimbabwe. 'He should never have become a politician in the first place, let alone prime minister, because he did not have any political values of his own.'

Moyo's observation of Mugabe's shallowness is not only true of Zimbabwe's president, and indeed of Moyo himself, but it applies to many in the political arena worldwide who are drawn to power rather than service. Mugabe's motivation seems to have been strongly driven by self-interest. Given his childhood belief that he was destined to be a leader, one can imagine him suddenly realising what was to be gained by becoming a politician rather than a schoolmaster.

You need to go right back to the very beginning of Mugabe's political career if you're looking for a nuanced view of what went wrong. You would expect to find a foundation for his politics in his disposition, his humanity and his general orientation in the early years. But you do not find a self-driven nationalist. Mugabe was never a leader by virtue of generational political consciousness and his reactions to the issues of the day, even though he was exposed to all of it as an educated person and, indeed, as one of the very few black Rhodesians who had attained university level.

On examining his biography, you do not find the kind of activism associated with nationalist leaders. He goes to Fort Hare University in South Africa where, by all accounts, he is merely preparing himself to be a teacher. Then he teaches peacefully at various places in Rhodesia. He goes to Ghana amid the high African nationalism of the times in Nkrumah's country, its headquarters, but he is not involved in politics there either. He works simply as a teacher-trainer. He meets his future wife, who is actually more politically inclined than he is.

Looking at the record, he comes home on holiday; a man bringing his future wife to meet his family and intending to return to Ghana as a teacher to teach. He wants to settle in Ghana, where he has a well-paid job, which he hasn't resigned from. And then the Rhodesian nationalist movement, which is going through turbulence including leadership deficiency, hears of him, this articulate man called Robert Mugabe. Word goes around that he trains teachers so he is more articulate than the teachers, who are the most respected people in the country at that time. And of all exciting places, he lives and works in Ghana, where Nkrumah is leading the way to African liberation. He has Fort Hare qualifications. His wife is impressive. So he is approached, persuaded to join the liberation movement, and he agrees to give it a try.

Nowhere in his record prior to becoming the leader of Zanu do you see Robert Mugabe driven by political passion or a vision of a better future for Zimbabweans. He has not left his well-paid job in Ghana to join the nationalist movement at home. No, not at all. He has simply taken leave to go on a visit to Rhodesia. Nowhere is there any logical progression from there to the Marxism he espouses so eloquently later on. The man who comes from Ghana in the early 60s is not a Marxist.

On the contrary, says Moyo, Robert Mugabe was a man who defined himself in the colonial paradigm. 'You go to school, if you can. But seeing you can't qualify for anything except teaching, that is what you do. So Mugabe takes up teaching, goes to university, gets a good job – and then he meets these others who are not defined by the colonially approved path but by the rocky road of nationalism.' He pauses to catch his breath, looking exasperated. 'They want him, not because he is committed to their cause but because he is educated, he sounds good, he speaks English well,' Moyo continues incredulously. 'He has a salary in Ghana, which in itself would have been impressive to those approaching him, none of whom would have had any money or any hope of attaining funds at a time when there was little philanthropy to support African nationalism. Mugabe looks very different to them, even superior. And that becomes the reason for him being chosen and given high office, which he did not seek, let alone earn.'

Moyo's description is of an ambivalent man. Mugabe hedges his bets, does not give up his job, and keeps his opinions to himself. For some reason this image brings to mind an anecdote I heard from an American banker, Veejay Mehta, who sat next to Mugabe on a long-distance flight many years ago. What was most memorable about him, says Mehta, was his humour, his piercing eyes and his soft handshake. 'It was like the hand of a child; it felt as if there were no muscles in it.'

Who Robert Mugabe was in his deepest self then – or now – remains unknown. Cast in the role the party wanted him to play, little about him was authentic. It was only in helping fellow nationalists to pass exams while in prison and in his relationship with his Cabinet colleague Denis Norman, when he got involved in community development, that you saw Mugabe's own interest igniting. Otherwise, he was a cardboard cut-out in a dark suit, saying all the right things.

Almost everybody who knows Robert Mugabe has commented on his coldness. What happened to his heart? Did he lose his capacity for caring or did he fail to develop it? Moyo believes the answers to these core questions may lie in Mugabe's childhood, if not in the Mozambique period, but too little is known about him all those years ago for a penetrating analysis, he says. 'You have on the record one version of Robert Mugabe, the person born of a problematic father who left the family to start another one elsewhere. He let the small boy Robert down badly in terms of his wife, Robert's mother Bona, who thereafter leaned on her son too much, perhaps. We can construct a picture of him at that time: the introverted person with a disturbed upbringing, who loses a brother much brighter, by his own admission, than himself, and who then becomes committed to taking care of his beloved mother. He is a troubled person but he cares deeply about his family. This explains the sincere posture he still has when he meets you early in 1975; the posture of a sensitive, caring person.

'However, at around the same time, Robert Mugabe has been dragged into politics. He starts to develop a political model for himself in a completely artificial way. Having accepted a career that was not his chosen one, he becomes a shrewd and calculating politician who must develop a philosophy and a style as he hits the ground running,' Moyo argues.

Now you have two versions of Robert Mugabe. There is the troubled guy who struggled as a child – a person who is still there, even today. While working with him, I saw evidence that he became troubled when not being seen as reasonable, especially when he was compared in the media to Hitler – you could see that it bothered him. Alongside that sensitive guy is this other Robert Mugabe, a cold man who develops a disposition based on a calculation of consequences and opportunities. He does not exude natural political instincts, but works things out as he goes along:

what is the thing to do in this or that situation? After a nice dinner at your house with an important political contact, he calculates, 'I had better look reasonable and thank the hostess.'

Over the years I have talked to a number of journalists who knew Mugabe in the late 70s in Dar es Salaam and found him reasonable – not profound – but always reasonable and articulate. He can express himself well, that is his great strength. He tells everyone he wants to see a mixed economy in Rhodesia, racial harmony, all the right things.

A reluctant politician initially, Mugabe appears on the political stage as a puppet of other people's passions. He is put there specifically to express Zanu's ideas. At first, as Edgar Tekere notes, Mugabe fluffs his lines but he studies the moves and is soon good in the role. The party teaches him how to act like a Zanu politician and then he really gets the hang of it. As he starts to push the boundaries, he discovers that he can get away with more and more. Quite when he realises that he has absolutely all the power and has become untouchable is hard to determine, but he never looks back. Eventually, Zanu finds it has completely lost control of Mugabe: he has morphed from a puppet to a monster of the ruling party's creation.

Having entered politics through the persuasion of others rather than his own conviction, and having taken over as leader of an armed movement with a brutal internal history, Robert Mugabe rides to power in Zimbabwe on the crest of that ruthless organisation's bloody successes. Worst of all, Zimbabwe inherits Rhodesia's repressive mechanisms, which offend against every conceivable human right and freedom – and Mugabe adopts them wholesale. 'He proceeds to rule under Ian Smith's state of emergency for the first 10 years, a deeply corrupting process. As the prime minister, you see him vigorously arguing every six months in Parliament for the extension of these draconian laws. Where was the freedom of Zimbabwe during those years?' demands Moyo, throwing his hands in the air for emphasis.

The state of emergency shaped Mugabe's political approach for the first decade. No one was held accountable for militaristic actions and reactions during that time. It is the darkest period in Zimbabwe's history. Gukurahundi, a shocking misuse of the country's military apparatus, is hanging over Robert Mugabe's head, partly explaining his desire – or his need – to continue in office until he dies. The state of emergency enabled Gukurahundi and then covered it all up. There never was a democratic situation or a desire to reintroduce civilian norms. Those are the founding politics of Zimbabwe.

Slowly, Mugabe's fragile sense of self became as insurmountable a barrier to democratic progress as the ongoing state of emergency. Disillusionment appears to have been his fatal weakness, triggering bouts of revenge that knew no bounds. During Gukurahundi, having decided after some provocation to silence his traditional opponents in Matabeleland, Mugabe was rejected by the white minority, who voted for Ian Smith's candidates in the parliamentary polls of 1985. He was hurt but also furious. A more ruthless part of him started to take hold. The all-or-nothing man began to emerge. By the time his own people voted against him in the referendum and parliamentary election of 2000, Mugabe's anger was unstoppable.

Unable to come to terms with his own ordinariness and grieve the loss of his thwarted visions, Mugabe was emotionally incapable of dealing with defeat. His response to disillusionment was not reflection but rage, at which point destructiveness set in. He no longer cared who he hurt because his aim was to hurt, his motto being: If you hurt me, I'll hurt you back.

What happened in Zimbabwean politics from 1990 onwards was a reaction to Mugabe's first decade in office, according to Moyo.

What changed over the last eight years was that Mugabe almost lost his grip on power in 1999. He was almost toppled from within his own ranks and it was this threat that seemed to reveal a new and even more vengeful Mugabe. That internal power struggle took place around the constitutional referendum at a time when Mugabe was vulnerable because of the economic collapse two years earlier, the half-hearted attempt through the World Bank's Economic Structural Adjustment Programme to correct that collapse, the ill-judged military adventures in the Democratic Republic of Congo and, most importantly, the demands for compensation from the war veterans.

Mugabe did not want constitutional reform because he thought it was a move to unseat him, explains Moyo. But he had to embrace it because so many forces had begun to converge on the issue.

He wanted it to fail so he put a number of spanners in the works, the biggest of which was clause 57 on the land issue. Without consulting his own Constitutional Commission, he inserted the clause allowing land expropriation without consultation, in the belief that it would help secure the rural vote. Clause 57 held Britain, the former colonial power, responsible for land seized by the state. As Mugabe had calculated, the clause spurred white farmers and those encouraging them, including the British, to believe that they now had Mugabe backed into a corner. As a result, the farmers became more daring and arrogant. They started openly supporting rejection of the constitution via their support for the MDC. They fell right into Mugabe's trap. It was his strategy for political survival, and it worked. It kept him in office. He clung on to the land issue and, in fact, enhanced it as a new issue, which is typical of him.

Jonathan Moyo is balding, tall, superior and disturbingly affable to the journalists he abhorred so publicly while serving as Mugabe's information minister. I am disconcerted to find myself liking him, despite the way he persecuted my friends and colleagues. Wearing a dark suit and highly polished shoes on both the occasions we meet on the veranda of the suburban house in Harare where he lives and works, Moyo strikes me as not dissimilar in character to Mugabe. Known as a canny operator, he basks in the effect of his articulate analysis. Mugabe is said to have greatly respected his cleverness. 'I'm told that even now he says, "That young man Moyo should still be in government but he failed to take my advice,"' Moyo tells me. 'When he was angry with me and came to my constituency, Tsholotsho, to address a rally, he accused me of plotting to overthrow him and said, "That young man is very clever but not wise."'

Mugabe valued his information chief as a cunning strategist, according to Moyo, who conveniently happened to have surfaced in Zimbabwe at a time when the president's popularity within Zanu-PF was waning. In Moyo's estimation, the fact that he was in the Cabinet on merit rather than by kind favour of the president meant there was always an uneasy relationship between him and Mugabe.

Everyone else was there in an intricate network of patronage. If you don't have a protector, you don't survive for long in Zanu-PF. You either pander to the president and one or two of his deputies or you're out. My colleagues involved in the Tsholotsho affair – a so-called plot against Mugabe – who remained in government had to go with their wives, together and separately, to kneel in front of Mugabe. That's how they had to apologise to him. The same humiliation was expected of me but I refused. If I had agreed, I would have remained in his Cabinet: he asked me to stay. Now, when I see him in Parliament, he looks at me in a pitying way as if to say: 'You should have listened; you had your chance.' He tells everyone that I am clever but not wise.

Laughing languidly as he returns the president's insult, Moyo describes Mugabe as 'an old man, definitely not a wise old man'. He explains:

If you look at Mugabe's entire political career, what is always missing is the essence of the person. He is a shrewd politician, a great survivor, but very, very ruthless. There is nothing to commend him except his eloquence with words. He is mean-spirited even towards his own people. He is not moved by the plight of Zimbabweans, by people suffering and dying. He's immune to such calls on his feelings; he doesn't respond to pity.

Moyo cites Operation Murambatsvina, the forced removal of thousands of impoverished city dwellers from their makeshift homes and businesses during the bitter winter of 2005, as an example of the president's callousness.

But you can especially see it in Mugabe's indifference to the tragedy of Gukurahundi, the campaign of mass murder in Matabeleland during the 80s. It was terribly brutal. Perence Shiri, commander of the Fifth Brigade, the Korean-trained troops who carried out that massacre, reported directly to Mugabe. This same man Shiri is the head of the air force in Zimbabwe today – a killer. The very fact that he has been honoured all the way to the top of the air force shows what a spiteful man Mugabe is. How could he have been so callous to the community as to keep such a brutal man in such a prominent position? The Fifth Brigade bayoneted pregnant women, saying, 'Let's kill these dissidents before they are born'; they buried people alive and threw them into disused mine shafts; they forced some to do demeaning things to each other in public sex acts. People associated with such brutality ought not to have been rewarded. They should never have been allowed to hold public office, yet there are many prominent people in the security structures of Zimbabwe who were involved in that brutality. Regardless of Mugabe's own role and motivation at the time, it shows how contemptuous he is of Zimbabweans. (Among those killed by the Fifth Brigade was Moyo's father.)

Part of Mugabe's ability to remain in office despite his growing unpopularity is something Moyo attributes to an informal belief developed within the nationalist movement in exile 30 years ago, but still upheld by some of the ruling party's chief power brokers. When a Mugabe loyalist like Didymus Mutasa compares the presidency with a monarchy and states that Mugabe will remain in office until he dies, he is reflecting what Moyo terms 'a Maputo understanding' that none among the founding leaders should be subjected to the indignity of dying out of office. 'It's a deeply held belief,' explains Moyo, 'even among some of the older military leaders.'

Much as the divine right of kings was unquestioned in centuries past, the president of Zimbabwe believes implicitly that he has an absolute right to rule, says Moyo.

I discovered how genuinely Mugabe believes this – that he is there because the people want him there, and the reason they want him there is because he's exceptional and the only one for the job – when we were discussing problematic issues arising from his quarrel with me over my decision to stand as an independent in Tsholotsho. I was talking to him in the presence of the minister of justice. Mugabe was reprimanding the two of us for taking an active interest in succession politics in the context of a party congress. It was a supposedly friendly discussion late in 2004. Mugabe asked us in an agitated way, 'Why were you canvassing for Mnangagwa?'[5] He was clearly implying that our intention had been to promote ourselves. 'Why did you do that?' he demanded.

We told him that the constitution called for an election and we were electioneering quite properly in order to show the leadership strengths we admired and the programmes we supported. Mugabe rejected our

---

[5] Emmerson Mnangagwa, a Mugabe loyalist, was, for many years, expected to succeed the president.

arguments, all based on the most elementary democratic principles. 'No,' he declared, 'that's where you're wrong. You don't have to canvass. You've watched me and you've never seen me canvassing in 40 years.' When I asked him what he did to get into office and stay there, he replied, 'People always came to me. They wanted me without me doing anything to promote myself.'

To Mugabe, he is president not because he wants to be but because he's been told to be there. The experience in the 60s when he was asked to join the nationalists and then the experience in 1977 when he was asked to speak for Zanu were not only formative but enduring. He sees himself as the chosen one and he will go with that belief to the grave.

It is interesting to note how Mugabe has turned in his mind the fact that he had found himself in politics rather than choosing to be there. He saw it as a virtue confirming his special-ness, whereas he was there in the first place for quite different reasons – because he looked the part and had a respectable veneer in an organisation full of thugs. Being exactly the right actor, he got the part without even having to audition. And he was so well cast! To Mugabe though, his selection proved that he was no ordinary person. Contemptuous of Moyo's canvassing, he revealed his sense of being above the political fray. Much of his loftiness is due, of course, to the prophecy of greatness his mother supposedly received from God via Father O'Hea while he was a child.

During his decades at the helm, Robert Mugabe has been guided as much by his own suspicions, which he is quick to investigate, as his intelligence, says Moyo.

He thrives on confrontation. He threatened me outright, for example, saying all sorts of things might happen to me and my family in the event that I left the party to stand as an independent and he was no longer protecting me. His way of trying to keep me on board was by threat rather than persuasion. Only if you show ultra and extra personal loyalty to Mugabe and he trusts you not to go against him, come rain, come shine, will he take time with you at a personal level. He does not know the names of many of the wives of his ministers; he does not want to know those in his Cabinet as men and women, but only as functionaries and potential foes.

In other words, Mugabe does not let people matter to him. You either do what he wants or he will get rid of you. People are readily interchangeable in his world.

Moyo searches for an example of Mugabe's suspicious nature. Lounging on a white brocade sofa opposite the identical one on which I am perched, he apologises for his cracked voice, saying that he has been struggling unsuccessfully to shake off a cold. His mobile phone rings beside him and, switching it off, he looks suddenly animated as an anecdote presents itself. 'You see this phone?' he says, lifting the Blackberry:

> I like the facility it offers to work wherever I am. People in Cabinet and Mugabe's security used to think it was a spying device – can you believe it? I started using it in official meetings because it never took long for discussions to degenerate into absolute rubbish. I couldn't maintain my sanity listening so I used to receive and send emails. It became a widely held idea about me that I was spying, but I was shocked to discover that even Mugabe believed such nonsense. He said publicly once, 'Jonathan did not participate in meetings. He'd be very quiet but always taking notes and we used to wonder who he was writing for.' If you're the kind they don't trust because you don't expose yourself more than necessary, you're in trouble.

Moyo describes the atmosphere in Mugabe's Cabinet from 2000 onwards. An instant silence would descend as soon as the president arrived, invariably a little late, for Cabinet meetings. When he walked in, the ministers greeting and talking to each other noisily would stop abruptly and sit still. They were terrified of Mugabe, he says. 'He became isolated from his colleagues and lost touch with the day-to-day running of the country after 2000. You often saw him snoozing in Cabinet meetings, even when the country was in turmoil.'

The only time Mugabe encouraged ministers to chat to him was on overseas trips:

> I dreaded travelling with him and being asked 'to keep the president company'. It meant having to sit beside him on long flights, talking about nothing; opening up to him. What this really meant was political gossiping, although he would say very little, giving away absolutely

nothing. He might ask you questions though. Keeping him company involved telling tales on colleagues – that was the intention. I did not want to talk about other people or be asked about others so my approach was to discuss topical matters, the news of the day. Once, when we'd just pulled Zimbabwe out of the Commonwealth, I had to sit with him on a long flight and had to search my brains for things to say to him. I always tried to keep our conversations abstract because if he asked you a leading question and you didn't answer satisfactorily, that could be enough to raise his suspicions.

Most of Mugabe's suspicions were based on the ethnic tensions that have plagued Zimbabwe for centuries. As an Ndebele living abroad in the 80s, recalls Moyo, he watched the murder of thousands of his own people with total disbelief. Mugabe's overreaction then was on a scale never seen before, he says.

> Gukurahundi was a conflict between two power-hungry leaders from different ethnic backgrounds, basically. Both Mugabe and Nkomo wanted to hide some of their arms during the period following the implementation of the Lancaster House deal, in case the Rhodesians reneged on the ceasefire. These weapons were held back by agreement between the two groups, but when a conspiracy was uncovered involving 113 of Nkomo's men in an organisation known as Super-Zapu, which was a creation of South African intelligence, Mugabe overreacted. There was no real threat; Mugabe and the others involved have no way of justifying Gukurahundi.

Mugabe could have dealt with it differently, explains Moyo, but Gukurahundi came at a time when South Africa was dedicated to destabilising Zimbabwe under its new black leader, and he panicked.

> South African intelligence saw Nkomo's soldiers in Zipra (Zimbabwe People's Revolutionary Army) as a much more disciplined outfit than Zanu's army Zanla. They calculated that Zipra, being closer to the anti-apartheid African National Congress (ANC) than the forces loyal to Mugabe, should be kept out of the power stakes. The apartheid regime thought that would freeze the ANC out of Zimbabwe and prevent guerrilla incursions across a border they had not had to defend until Mugabe came to power. South African intelligence made a bad situation worse, infiltrating false reports

into Zimbabwe security structures and so on. The fire was already there and South Africa decided to pour petrol on it. Their intention was to blunt Zipra in order to shut the door on the ANC, but the consequences proved devastating.

Indeed, the tragic effects of apartheid South Africa's machinations in Matabeleland continue to this day as they are said to account more than any other factor for Mugabe's determination to cling to power rather than face legal retribution for Gukurahundi.

Although Jonathan Moyo saw Mugabe every week in Cabinet for five years, as well as in one-on-one meetings to discuss media strategy during the cataclysmic period between 2000 and 2005 when election results were in dispute and the state's farm invasions had hit international headlines, he says he knew little about the man:

> Mugabe reveals nothing about himself; that's one of his hallmarks. I can tell you that he no longer works as hard as he is reputed to have done in the 80s. I know he takes care of his health, following his doctors' advice to rest and so on. Having a young wife and family means, I think, that he makes himself increasingly unavailable for business in order to spend time with them instead. He has developed a laissez-faire approach to his job, not supervising his Cabinet as closely as he used to do when he was prime minister.

In Moyo's opinion, Robert Mugabe has deliberately fostered a cold leadership style over the years. 'He thinks that to be presidential he needs to be disdainful and aloof. That's his nature anyway, but it's also a way to cover his weaknesses. He feels he should be seen as a mysterious figure, an enigma. Mugabe is always trying to behave like a medieval king.'

Fourteen

Yesterday's heroes

Robert Mugabe believed he was born to rule and behaved accordingly. Once the king, always the king, he reckoned. In his idealised view, his loyal subjects would worship the ground he trod forever. In reality, the great majority of Zimbabwe's people supported him enthusiastically for 20 years. It was only when his policies began to impoverish the country that they turned against him. Characteristically, Mugabe never forgave them. Growing ever more vengeful, he ripped down their shelters, destroyed their livelihoods and snatched the food from their mouths. Those in his court who remained loyal to him were richly rewarded with money, property and power. In death, they were buried amid extravagant fanfare at Heroes Acre, the monument to Zimbabwe's liberation struggle on a hill outside Harare.

During one of my research trips, a colleague and I drive to the administrative building of the so-called heroes' cemetery. A glowering soldier hoists his AK-47 assault rifle and begins to record our vehicle number in a book while speaking into his walkie-talkie. My fellow scribe from a London newspaper and I have been warned repeatedly by local journalists that we venture at our peril into this ruling party stronghold in a country where foreign journalists are, for all practical purposes, illegal. For a moment, it feels foolhardy of us to have come.

Inside, the reception is warmer. Would we like a tour of the new Heroes Acre museum as well as the tombs, asks a bright-eyed young woman. She takes our money and leads us past a couple of amateurish drawings of female freedom fighters, including one of vice president

Joice Mujuru. In a courtyard behind the reception area, the only other exhibit in the museum is the wreck of a blue Volkswagen. It was the car in which one-time Zanu leader Herbert Chitepo was blown to bits early in March 1975, she explains, looking devastated. He had just turned the key in the ignition when a bomb exploded, killing him instantly. The sole of his right shoe is still stuck to the accelerator pedal, she points out, and we examine this morbid detail. She does not volunteer any of the disputed motives for Chitepo's assassination, such as ethnic rivalry between the warring Karanga and Manyika factions, the bungled military strategies that left 10 guerrillas dead for every Rhodesian soldier killed during the bush war, or the hopes of those who were desperate for a negotiated settlement at the time.

So who did it?

'Agents of the Smith regime,' she states, sucking in her breath. Although dangerous in this terrorised state to raise the subject of Chitepo's death, it has remained such a burning issue that even kids take the risk, according to Dr Terence Ranger, an authority on Rhodesia/Zimbabwe and a retired professor at Oxford University. 'Last time I spoke to secondary schoolchildren in Zimbabwe, the headmaster announced that they could ask any questions about history,' Ranger says. 'A dozen hands shot up. They all wanted to know who killed Chitepo.'

Chitepo was assassinated during the darkest period of Zimbabwean liberation politics, when Zanu militants were thought to be intent on toppling him. Some claim his murder was arranged by Rhodesian leader Ian Smith, Zambian president Kenneth Kaunda and South African premier John Vorster, who saw Chitepo as an obstacle on their way to installing moderate leaders in Rhodesia. Others, including Chitepo's widow Victoria, dismiss such claims. After 16 years of silence, during which time she served in Mugabe's Cabinet, Ms Chitepo announced in 2001 that her husband's assassination had been an internal Zanu job and demanded that his killers be brought to justice. Her plea followed the suicides of two of her children as well as statements by Kaunda that Chitepo's Zanu opponents, not Rhodesian agents, were responsible for the killing.

Some believe Mugabe was behind Chitepo's murder. There is said to be a legend in parts of Mashonaland, where many people believe in the power of ancestor spirits to restore justice, that a white bird flew into Mugabe's face during the ceremony surrounding the removal of Chitepo's remains from Lusaka for reburial at Heroes Acre. In some Manicaland villages, songs that call on Chitepo to rise from his grave and lead Zimbabwe have been sung for decades.

We walk solemnly behind the Heroes Acre guide up the hill on the 65-acre site towards the Tomb of the Unknown Soldier, a towering gold-painted statue. When asked whose vision gave rise to Heroes Acre, an extravagant memorial in polished black granite, her response is triumphant. 'The people of Zimbabwe,' she declares, adding that it was designed in the shape of an AK-47 by Zimbabwean and North Korean artists and architects who reported directly to the president.

Halfway up the slope, four unoccupied graves have been prepared alongside that of the president's deceased first wife Sally, who lies in pride of place among rows of identical tombs further back. Fresh red roses have been left in her memory. They were brought by the president a few hours earlier, explains the guide, pointing to similar flowers on another grave nearby, which is the final resting place of Mugabe's rival, Joshua Nkomo.

History records that Nkomo died a broken man, having been tormented by the brutality of Gukurahundi into a bogus unity pact with Mugabe. The guide's version though is that Nkomo's relationship with Mugabe was based on brotherly compromise and democracy. She says proudly, 'Every year on the day before our independence celebrations, the president comes here to honour the former first lady and the late leader of the opposition with a floral tribute.' Typically, Mugabe has refashioned history to ensure that it is his idealised version rather than the cruel truth about his dealings with Nkomo that lingers on at Heroes Acre.

Who will be buried beside Sally? 'Everyone asks that,' she replies, shrugging irritably. Left to speculate, we guess that Robert Mugabe will go into the tomb next to Sally's at the centre of the row of VIPs. The remaining empty graves next to his might be for Solomon Mujuru, aka Rex Nhongo; his wife and current deputy to Mugabe, Joice Mujuru, whose nom de guerre was Teurai Ropa, meaning 'Spill Blood'; and another long-time associate and possible successor to the presidency, Emmerson Mnangagwa. They are the three most prominent Zimbabwean rulers among those who led the country to independence in 1980 and remain in power.

Constantly jostling for ascendance, the Mujuru couple and Mnangagwa have risen and fallen in Mugabe's estimation and therefore in proximity to the presidency. He has been playing one off against the other for decades, as is his wont. All power must remain in the hands of those unconditionally loyal to him, which is one of the reasons so few challenges to his supremacy have occurred within Zanu-PF. The succession struggle in the dying days of Mugabe's presidency will never be resolved by him in the interests of party solidarity, because apart from believing he has the absolute right to rule until death, he thrives on the tension of disputes and conspiracies among enemies.

The most powerful of those hoping to succeed Mugabe is Solomon Mujuru. After wielding his influence from the shadows for the past 30 years, the publicity-shy former army chief may choose 2008 to pop up in public as a presidential candidate. Or he could opt to back his wife for the job by summoning his considerable clout in Zanu-PF, where real power resides, in her favour while settling for the post of first man.

Ms Mujuru, who is in her fifties, has wisely denied any presidential ambitions, having managed to avoid the president's suspicions until 2007, when both she and her husband were accused by Mugabe of treachery. The former guerrilla commander reportedly overstepped the mark by meeting the US and UK ambassadors in Harare in the wake of widely condemned attacks on the opposition MDC in March 2007. Mr Mujuru was also said to have met MDC leader Morgan Tsvangirai on a number of occasions, possibly to discuss a government of national unity for the post-Mugabe era. The Mujurus, each with an alternative name, behave as one, interchangeably, like a conjuring act where you never know who is who.

Mugabe, who has always portrayed himself as still fighting the colonial struggle against white oppression, was believed to have been referring to the Mujurus when he said after his recent fallout with the prominent couple that there had been 'an insidious dimension where ambitious leaders have been cutting deals with the British and Americans ... The whole succession debate has given imperialism hope for re-entry. Since when have the British, the Americans, been friends of Zanu-PF?'

This was a severe put-down for the Mujurus, who come from the same Zezuru branch of Zimbabwe's majority Shona people as Mugabe and have supported the president for more than three decades. As the guerrilla hero Rex Nhongo, Mujuru was second in command to the late and much lamented Josiah Tongogara when the latter met his untimely death on the eve of independence. Today, retired from public life in favour of his business career, Mujuru still has many friends in the military and intelligence establishments. However, he lacks confidence in himself, speaks with a pronounced stammer and is acutely aware of his and his wife's educational limitations. Some say he is the only man in the country who dares to talk back to Mugabe, even occasionally shouting at him. But a long-time member of the Cabinet, who requested anonymity, laughs at this interpretation of Mujuru's relationship with the president, and points out that Mujuru might appear to be raising his voice but he is in reality merely responding edgily to the effect of the long silences that Mugabe often uses to rattle his colleagues.

One insider who got to know Solomon Mujuru in the early days of Mugabe's presidency is the country's longest-serving intelligence agent, Dan Stannard, who worked for Ian Smith before being appointed liaison officer between the guerrillas and Rhodesian Special Branch after the Lancaster House agreement was signed in 1979. He joined Zimbabwe's CIO at independence and was decorated for saving the president's life. Stannard remembers army supremo Solomon Mujuru drinking Dumbarton whisky and Coca-Cola in the army officers' mess in Harare while trying to ascertain why his nickname among the Rhodesian security forces had been 'Missed' during the war. 'He asked me why and I told him that we had missed him here and missed him there,' recalls Stannard. Mujuru laughed uproariously, confirming that he had often been hiding just metres away from security forces as they scoured the bush. Mujuru's reputation for courage derives from anecdotes like this one, but less honourably, he is also known as an epic womaniser and hard drinker. Once, when Morgan Tsvangirai, the leader of the MDC, went to meet him at home late at night as arranged, Mujuru was too drunk to speak, according to an opposition activist.

Stannard recalls an occasion when he was invited to Mujuru's home for discussions one Sunday morning. 'He served me with Scotch and tripe and onions. The only problem was that there was green grass sticking out from the stomach lining on my plate. I had to excuse myself very quickly.'

Stannard's story reminds me of my meeting with Joice Mujuru way back in 1980, soon after she returned from the bush war. Still known as 'Spill Blood' in those days, she had agreed to an interview with the *Guardian* newspaper in London. But when a photographer and I turned up at her Harare address at the appointed hour, there was no answer to our repeated knocking. We waited outside the door for a couple of hours before she opened it, looking dishevelled and irritated. Inside, the place was a shambles following what appeared to have been a wild party the night before. Chewed mealie cobs were strewn all over the floor and furniture: I had to sweep a pile of them aside to sit on the sofa. She could barely string a sentence together that day.

I went to great – some would say ludicrous – lengths to talk to Solomon Mujuru in March 2007. Although he answered his cellphone each time I made around 50 calls, he kept telling me to ring back in 20 minutes, at lunchtime, tomorrow morning. After three days of doing virtually nothing but dialling his number or waiting to dial it, I had to fly home empty-handed. It seemed odd behaviour from someone who had agreed on the phone before I left South Africa to see me once I was in Harare, although people say he despises journalists almost as much as politicians.

Some say Mujuru, not wishing to enter mainstream politics through the front door, is sponsoring the only internationally respected of the possible successors to the presidency, the untainted, personable and pragmatic Dr Simba Makoni, who is the holder of a PhD in chemistry. Makoni, in his fifties, was the executive director of SADC's precursor, the sluggish Southern African Development Coordination Conference, before becoming Mugabe's finance minister. Mugabe's dislike of Makoni dates back to a ritualistic discussion about the heroism of the guerrillas during the bush war. Far from applauding as required, Makoni told Mugabe that his own father had been murdered by Zanu's guerrillas so he could not view them with the pride the president had expressed. Mugabe barely acknowledged Makoni after that.

Any threat to Mugabe from inside Zanu-PF will come from the Mujurus, both of whom are conspicuously corrupt. Solomon Mujuru owns so many farms in Shamva that the area is known locally as Rexville. Alleged to have links to the plunder of the DRC's diamonds, he is said to have gathered most of his vast wealth from defence contracts.

Joice Mujuru, who claims to have shot down a Rhodesian helicopter with the machine gun of a dying comrade, blocked the bid to set up Zimbabwe's first cellphone network long enough for a rival company part-owned by her husband to be established. She was also one of the biggest beneficiaries of a scheme set up to pay compensation to those injured during the liberation war. The huge sum of public money paid out to war veterans, including Ms Mujuru, was a major cause of Zimbabwe's initial economic plunge in 1997. Her attempts to educate herself in recent years have won respect among Zimbabwe's middle-class voters, who nevertheless see the Mujurus as a boorish, greedy couple, although one professional in Harare conceded that 'she at least has a human heart'.

The Mugabe/Mujuru fallout in 2007 will have given impetus to the ambitions of Emmerson Mnangagwa, albeit secretly. He knows only too well how dangerous it is to reveal presidential aspirations, having been demoted from several prominent posts after campaigning too enthusiastically in 2005 for the vice presidency, which Mugabe eventually bestowed on Joice Mujuru. Mnangagwa and the Mujurus have been business as well as political rivals for more than a decade after Mnangagwa blocked the Mujurus' bid to take over the country's huge Zimasco chrome smelting operation.

Born into the largest Shona group, Mnangagwa at 65 is clearly hoping to succeed Robert Mugabe as the anointed leader of the Karanga, who believe that their turn to govern is long overdue. Having been Mugabe's personal assistant for more than 30 years, Mnangagwa is known as 'the son of God' because of their close ties. For a long time he was the secretary of finance for Zanu-PF, which meant that he and Mugabe were the sole signatories to party funds. He was seen as 'the architect of the commercial activities of Zanu-PF' according to a UN report in 2001. This related largely to the operations of the Zimbabwean army and businessmen in the DRC where troops intervened in the civil war on the side of the DRC government and were accused of using the conflict to loot some of its rich resources of diamonds, gold and other minerals.

Emmerson Mnangagwa is an unpopular politician who has been defeated twice in his home constituency. Propped up by Mugabe on both occasions, he is often described as a cruel man. The opposition candidate who defeated him in Kwe Kwe Central after a bitter campaign in 2000 narrowly escaped death when Zanu-PF youths who had abducted him and doused him with petrol were unable to light a match.

Mnangagwa's fearsome reputation dates back to Gukurahundi. As the national security minister in the 80s, he was in charge of the special units, incorporated into the CIO, which worked closely with selected North Korean-trained soldiers to suppress Zapu. Thousands of innocent civilians – mainly ethnic Ndebele who supported Nkomo – were killed before Zapu and Zanu merged to form Zanu-PF. Among countless atrocities, villagers were forced at gunpoint to dance on the freshly dug graves of their relatives and chant pro-Mugabe slogans.

Mnangagwa enjoys the support of many of the war veterans who led the campaign of violence against the white farmers and the opposition MDC from 2000 onwards. They remember him as one of the men who, following military training in China and Egypt, directed the 1970s fight for independence. He married Josiah Tongogara's sister but is known and allegedly admired among the former guerrillas partly for his numerous and sometimes publicly embarrassing extra-marital affairs.

Having joined the struggle in his early teens, Mnangagwa was arrested and tortured for blowing up a train near Fort Victoria, now Masvingo, in 1965. White officers hung him upside down by leg irons from butcher's hooks that ran along a track on the ceiling, and then batted his suspended body back and forth from one end of the room to the other. The severity of the torture left him unconscious for days and partially deaf forever. As he claimed to be younger than 21 at the time, although he was in fact 23, he was not executed but instead sentenced to 10 years in prison. Much later, when he was about to take up the post of security minister in Mugabe's first Cabinet, Mnangagwa asked Dan Stannard to summon CIO Detective Inspector Paddy Gardiner from Fort Victoria. 'He wanted to thank the officer for the well-investigated case against him when he tried to blow up the train,' recalls Stannard. 'He asked Gardiner to remain in the organisation ... and he stayed.'

It is not clear whether Mnangagwa actually blew up the train or merely attempted to do so. The punishment was brutal either way. It nearly killed him as a young man. He survived it, but what did it do to him? He might be the one to lead Zimbabwe into the post-Mugabe era, but what sort of a man is he? The fact that he became friendly with his torturer is presented as a virtue: it is normalised as a way of relating. Yet it is far from normal. So many in Zanu-PF's hierarchy have lived with similar, appalling violence woven into everyday life as if it were normal. The bush war, or Second Chimurenga, has never really ended in Zimbabwe because it is internalised in the country's leaders.

Another possible successor to Mugabe, though no struggle hero and too young to be considered for a front row tomb at Heroes Acre, is Gideon Gono, the president's banker and Zimbabwe's de facto prime minister. He has a direct line to Mugabe as well as to his wife Grace, on whom he is said to rely for insight into the president's moods, fears and suspicions. Mugabe relies in turn on the fabulously wealthy Gono, the head of the Reserve Bank, to find money for the state in the most dire of economic circumstances. Gono's resultant unconventional fiscal policies have made him many enemies among the rich elite, who accuse him of targeting their businesses to settle scores. Like the other presidential contenders, he has cultivated important friendships in the military and security establishments. Gono is the mastermind of the widely condemned crackdown on urban settlements, Operation Murambatsvina, albeit partly in an attempt to crush the foreign currency black market. A day before its launch in May 2005, he spoke of 'the need to cleanse the individual rot on the streets of the nation and the need to destroy the shadow forces in the economy'.

One of the ringside graves at Heroes Acre might be for Didymus Mutasa, described by some as Mugabe's Rottweiler. He executed Operation Murambatsvina alongside Gono. His status in the president's court soared after cracks began to appear in the security forces during 2006 and he took brutal remedial action on Mugabe's behalf. As lands and security minister, Mutasa is a close confidant to the president. Having been charged with infiltrating the divided MDC and scuppering its prospects of unity, Mutasa's most urgent task is to get a grip on a security establishment weakened not only by desertions but collusion with the opposition in the sale of grenades and tear gas from state supplies.

Mutasa has sacrificed his soul to get close to Mugabe. Once a quietly spoken, caring individual, he was educated by Anglican priests and became a living legend among white liberals in the 70s. Not only had he helped to make the famous activists' refuge known as Cold Comfort Farm into a first-class agricultural training centre and crucial early retreat for nationalists on the long journey from colonial oppression to majority rule, but he was also hailed by the farm's visionary, Guy Clutton-Brock, as 'a sensitive leader ... with a profound belief in his fellow man, regardless of race, colour or creed'.

How Mutasa became the feared politician who, having played a key role in Mugabe's disastrous land invasions, vowed to drive all remaining white Zimbabweans from the country, is a matter of considerable speculation among those who knew him 30 years ago. He may have an undisclosed past, according to a former intelligence agent, who says Rhodesia's Special Branch long suspected Mutasa of having links with British intelligence but could never prove it. Some say that as parliamentary speaker in the years following independence, Mutasa once criticised Mugabe to his face over unconstitutional practices. Shaken by the extent of the president's coldness to him afterwards, Mutasa is said to have gone on an increasingly reckless campaign to prove himself worthy of Mugabe's respect by endorsing sentiments that would have been anathema to him before. By 2002 he had become sufficiently brutalised to say of the Aids crisis decimating Zimbabwe's 12 million population at a time of severe drought: 'We would be better off with only six million people, with our own (ruling party) people who supported the liberation struggle. We don't want all these extra people.'

Mutasa's earlier hero, Welsh-born Guy Clutton-Brock, is the only white person to have been buried at Herocs Acrc. Expelled from Rhodesia in 1971 for helping the nationalists' cause, he died in Britain in 1995. Mugabe and Mutasa attended his memorial service at the Church of St Martin's in the Field in London, after which they were given his ashes to take back to Harare. At the time, Mutasa commented that he hoped to be buried next to his mentor at Heroes Acre but much has changed in the interim. Whether the saintly Clutton-Brock would have chosen to remain at Heroes Acre alongside the discredited Zanu-PF politicians he once admired is doubtful.

A frequent visitor to Heroes Acre is Evelyn Tongogara, the widow of the guerrilla commander whose death is often blamed on Mugabe. She told me in the living room of her home in Herbert Chitepo Avenue, Harare, that she recently found knobkerries (clubs) and spears on her husband's grave. This warlike gesture seems to amuse rather than distress her three decades after Josiah's death. The circumstances of his death have been the source of so much dispute and debate over the years that she says she no longer ponders the matter. She clearly loathes Robert Mugabe, accusing him of making endless laudatory references to her late husband but never bothering to visit the dead hero's family. She stops short, however, of blaming Mugabe for her husband's death.

There is unlikely ever to be conclusive closure on the deaths of either of Zimbabwe's lost leaders, Herbert Chitepo and Josiah Tongogara, who lie in adjacent graves beneath elaborate headstones at Heroes Acre. Ms Tongogara, a well-educated businesswoman, says that although Mugabe has never come to see her in person, he has sent several delegations of his closes aides to negotiate a truce with members of her family. 'It is not for us to forgive,' she believes. 'It is between the two of them, Josiah and Robert.'

The supernatural notion of the angry dead awaiting a day of reckoning with the guilty living is said to haunt Mugabe. There are persistent rumours that his household staff is instructed to set a place for Tongogara whenever Mugabe eats a meal. Evelyn Tongogara says she has heard from several sources that a pair of trousers and a shirt purportedly worn by her late husband are laid out on an empty chair at the president's table. It is not a subject anyone discusses publicly.

In the opinion of Dan Stannard, 'Tongo, as we called him, died in a motor vehicle accident while travelling around Mozambique telling his guerrillas of the outcome of the Lancaster House talks. Emmerson Mnangagwa was Tongo's brother-in-law and he told me emphatically that Tongo died from injuries received in the accident. I actually spoke to the driver, who had joined CIO, and a witness who survived the crash. Both of them confirmed that he died as a result of injuries sustained in that road accident. Tongo would have made an excellent army commander and he supported Mugabe totally. The timing of his death on the eve of independence was unfortunate and sceptics just wouldn't believe that it was a mere accident. His body was kept in a mortuary in Beira after being tidied up in preparation for later burial at Heroes Acre once the cemetery had been established.'

One man whose name will not be on the Heroes Acre burial list is Morgan Tsvangirai, despite his brave contribution to the democratic cause in his country. Mugabe's shock on being defeated in the referendum of 2000 and his subsequent narrow and fraudulent victory against the MDC at the polls two years later left the president overtly hostile to any form of power-sharing. 'No matter what force you have,' he told his opponents in 2001, 'this is my territory and that which is mine I cling to unto death.'

On our way back to the city centre, my journalist colleague and I drive past the president's office in Samora Machel Avenue. The clock on a tower above the place where Robert Mugabe toils was earlier stuck at five minutes to midnight but is now ticking onwards. Unsure of the route to our next appointment, we pull up alongside the pavement to ask directions from a passer-by. Suddenly, my colleague sees an AK-47-wielding soldier running up behind us, shouting. The man we have been talking to on the pavement flees as the soldier bellows, 'Get out! Get out!' He searches my handbag feverishly, demanding that the driver open the boot. We explain repeatedly that we were merely seeking directions from a pedestrian. After prodding at packets and an empty backpack in the boot of the car, he calms down, explaining that the camera atop Mugabe's office will have recorded us driving slowly past and then pulling up. If he as the guard on duty has no explanation for such suspicious behaviour, he will be in deep trouble.

The next day is April 18, the anniversary of Zimbabwe's independence. We drive back along the roads that lead to Heroes Acre, this time to attend the annual celebrations at Harare's National Stadium, which is opposite Zanu-PF's cemetery. It is stiflingly hot for the time of year and we are nervous, having been assured by local journalists how conspicuous we will be as the only white faces in a massive black crowd.

At the turnstiles into the stadium, a Zimbabwean in the queue behind us comments in loud English with contemptuous overtones, 'Repentant whites.' Although we attract a lot of stares as we enter, the numerous policemen we pass, perspiring in their thick winter uniforms, pay us little attention. The stadium is packed, not to listen to the president, we have been told, but because the annual needle match between the country's top football teams is traditionally played after Mugabe's speech.

Fifty thousand people are in their seats when Mugabe appears on the field, two hours after his scheduled arrival. Joined by his elegantly dressed wife and their three children, Mugabe looks serene in a crisp grey suit covered in medals and draped in a green sash. The crowd greets him uproariously. He may have impoverished his country but he is still the Big Man, the independence hero, the African leader who brought down the white elite and returned the land to his people.

He watches a parade of the country's air force, army and police, and overhead, a precision formation of Chinese-made Zimbabwe Air Force fighter jets. Then, in the same strong, steady voice that inspired his people and indeed much of the world when he took office in 1980, he lectures the cheering spectators for an hour. Breaking into Shona from time to time, he disparages countrymen who have gone to seek a better life in England, where many have found jobs as low-paid private nurses. They are 'the BBC', he tells the crowd, which seems to delight in this oft-repeated witticism: the BBC, England's national broadcaster, stands for 'British Bum Cleaners' in Mugabe-speak.

Shaking his fist, Mugabe declares in Shona, 'Anyone who dares go against the security and stability of our country will be inviting the full wrath of the law to descend mercilessly on him or on those who follow him.' The parts of his speech delivered in the vernacular provoke either laughter from the crowd or complete silence. Mugabe has made a habit over the years of delivering his crudest jokes and threats in Shona. On the 26th anniversary of his presidency, there are noticeably more silences than laughter.

There was a time when Robert Mugabe's paranoid projection of hatred successfully mobilised fear in an urban crowd this size, but no longer. You can hear that some still offer him unconditional support, though. Their continuing loyalty even in the face of their country's ruin is partly due to the crowd being artificially swelled by bussed-in rural supporters, some of whom continue to back him blithely. This is because Zimbabwe has a history of passive subjugation to powerful authority. The politics of deference, obedience and loyalty continue to challenge democracy of the purest Western kind, with democratic values taking hold only gradually and within the grain of the prevailing political culture.

Mugabe's skill over the years in focusing Zimbabweans on an array of enemies – the British, the white farmer, the parliamentary opposition – is deliberately designed to mobilise hatred in his followers in such a way that apparently disconnected adversaries appear to form a single category against whom the masses can rage and rally. After briefly calling for unity and brotherhood at independence, Mugabe has relentlessly inflamed frustrated, angry Zimbabweans with the power of his rhetoric, sometimes using their resultant aggressive energy to attack his chosen enemies.

Such group paranoia has been a feature of a number of the world's worst dictatorships. The unifying malevolence in Hitler's paranoid world view was a cluster of enemies but predominantly the Jew, fear of whom gave focus to Hitler's hatred as well as the nation's grievances. Paranoid leaders like Hitler and Mugabe need enemies and indeed nurture them. Asked in the early days of the Nationalist Socialist Movement about destroying the Jew, Hitler responded: 'No ... We should then have to invent him. It is essential to have a tangible enemy, not merely an abstract one.'

The individual who inspires the politics of paranoia is often caught up in a primitive psychological defence that guards against depression, emptiness or meaninglessness. While Mugabe's mother treated him with the adoration (albeit conditional adoration) he had been led to believe was his due, a feature of his childhood was rejection as well as humiliation. Later, having admired and aspired to all things British, he felt that the English had spurned and betrayed him. Deeply hurt and choking back a child's anger in his immaculately suited adult body, Mugabe was particularly vulnerable to rejection. These hurtful experiences may have been consolidated when his humanity was threatened by imprisonment or torture because the basic building blocks for surviving such extremes of emotional stress were shaky. Rage is a way of feeling strong in the face of impotence. Denying his own negative feelings, he projected them on to others and proceeded to punish them in the individuals and groups who became his implacable enemies.

When this tendency occurs in leaders like Mugabe and Hitler, it expresses itself in the idealisation of an in-group and the demonisation of out-groups. Ironically, the enemies from which such people most passionately distinguish themselves are those to which they are most closely bound. Hitler believed his paternal grandfather was Jewish, while there are indications that Mugabe considers himself more English than African.

It is never reassuring to a paranoid leader to hear that there are no enemies plotting to destroy him. In fact, such a statement will often provoke intense anger because it threatens important psychological props. The paranoid holds tenaciously to his comforting, sense-making delusion that he is surrounded by enemies, when what he may really be under attack from are his own internal demons.

Fifteen

As it was in the beginning

After numerous discussions with people who knew Robert Mugabe personally, I end up with a humanised picture of how the considerate man who phoned me to enquire about the well-being of my child 30 years earlier became Zimbabwe's monster president. While his determination to hang on to power regardless of the consequences certainly dominated his motives from 2000 onwards, there were other factors that helped drive his destruction.

The man you see at the end of Robert Mugabe's life seems a far cry from the shy little boy who read books while other kids were having fun. He hoped in those days to compensate for his father's abandonment of the family by fulfilling his depressed mother's self-serving dream of her son's leadership destiny. In his middle years, having reluctantly undertaken a tortuous journey to become the first black premier of Zimbabwe, Mugabe basked in the greatness to which he and his mother had aspired, but the lonely boy with long-buried grievances was crouching behind the scenes, even then. Although his first wife, Sally, enhanced his self-esteem and freed a more emotional side of him, she was politically ambitious and saw Robert partly as the means to self-fulfilment. Her devotion to his every whim only added to his inflated fantasies of himself.

Unable to tolerate criticism since his childhood, Mugabe sets himself up in a world where everything runs according to his dictates. Inevitably though, others come forward to challenge him and the idealised world he has built for himself starts to fall apart. Once the omnipotence he has claimed as his God-given right is threatened, his rage seeks revenge. Always socially isolated and theoretical in his thinking, he is left in his old age with a grudge version of reality constructed in his own mind and based on a catalogue of the ways in which he has been used and abused throughout his life.

My search for an explanation of how and why freedom fighter Robert Mugabe became the tyrant known contemptuously around the world as Mad Bob has produced multiple perspectives from characters with patently different agendas. Woven together and analysed psychologically, however, they give a complex internal and external view of a man who has played a tragic role in African history. Few of those interviewed blame anyone but Robert Mugabe for the destruction of the once-prosperous nation of Zimbabwe. They identify a variety of turning points in his descent from the soft-spoken statesman, who unexpectedly proffered the hand of friendship to the country's frightened minority in 1980, to the despot whose ruthlessness had become unstoppable 20 years later.

Former Rhodesian spy master Mac McGuiness believes that Mugabe resorted to brutality very early in his premiership because he panicked in the face of destabilisation of the newly independent country through major acts of sabotage and assassination attempts on his life by apartheid South Africa. But for the South African-sponsored havoc and Britain's broken promises in respect of land redistribution, McGuiness believes that the current Zimbabwean crisis might not have occurred. On the other hand, the co-founder with Mugabe of Zimbabwe's ruling party, Edgar Tekere, says dictatorial tendencies became apparent in Mugabe soon after independence because, having initially been politically naive and willing to consider the opinions of others, the new premier became 'spoilt' by the obsequiousness of those around him to the point where his word was law and dissent was intolerable.

What Edgar Tekere did not say in so many words, but implied throughout two interviews, is that Zanu-PF was always a thoroughly unscrupulous organisation intent – like many political groups every-where – on using its leader to achieve its own ends. His scornful comments on Mugabe's naivety during his early years in politics, added to the crucial exploitation of Mugabe's declining popularity by Zanu upstart Chenjerai 'Hitler' Hunzvi during the land grab, give the impression that had it not been Robert Mugabe who destroyed

Zimbabwe, it would probably have been someone else from Zanu-PF.

The British foreign secretary who brokered Zimbabwe's independence, Lord Carrington, believes that Mugabe found himself in domestic difficulty due to mismanagement of the economy and then found a cause behind which to cover up his failures and rally his supporters – namely the reclamation of land from white farmers. 'He acted the way he acted because if he acted in any other way he would lose power,' says Carrington. Former Rhodesian prime minister Ian Smith agrees with Carrington in the same unequivocal terms. By contrast, Lady Soames, the widow of the British governor who handed the former colony to Mugabe, experienced a warm side of the Zimbabwean leader during his first decade in power and struggles to comprehend how he changed, unless his utopian ideas concealed his darker nature all along. Britain's overseas development minister in Tony Blair's Labour government, Clare Short, believes that when things started to go wrong in Zimbabwe Mugabe longed to relive his glory days, so he used Britain as a scapegoat.

The farmer who became one of Mugabe's most trusted ministers, Denis Norman, says Zimbabwe's premier was deeply hurt and angry when, despite all his efforts to reassure them, white Zimbabweans voted racially against him and in favour of Ian Smith in 1985. He also blames Britain for destabilising Mugabe by withholding the funding required to accomplish land redistribution. According to Norman, the land grab which ruined Zimbabwe's economy began spontaneously and was claimed by the president as his own initiative only once Mugabe realised he had lost control. In addition, Norman argues that Mugabe's acute jealousy of Nelson Mandela's rise to fame at a time when Mugabe's own star was on the wane significantly embittered the Zimbabwean leader. Father Fidelis Mukonori, Mugabe's long-time confidant, blames white supremacist attitudes, Britain's failure to honour its responsibility for land redistribution, and Zimbabwe's unreformed educational system – which accelerated unemployment by favouring university graduation over more practical types of training – for the decline in Mugabe's popularity. Mugabe on the other hand, attributed his decline in popularity to the failings of others.

Other priests who once hero-worshipped Mugabe as the Catholic Church's protégé cite the cruelty and violence that permeated Rhodesia during the war years, and which continued after Mugabe became premier, as a fatal fault line in the new country and Mugabe's misuse of power. Those among the Catholic clergy who knew him during and immediately after the years he spent in Rhodesian prisons say Mugabe's suffering at the hands of torturers may have had devastating psychological consequences in his later years. However, Jonathan Moyo, the president's spin doctor during the Zimbabwean government's disastrous land grab and escalating repression around 2000, points out that the abusive emergency powers prevailing in wartime Rhodesia were retained by Mugabe for 11 years after independence. In Moyo's opinion, the fact that Mugabe entered politics reluctantly and for the wrong reasons meant that he lacked genuine political convictions and behaved expediently from his earliest years in office.

One of the difficulties in finding the precise moment in 30 years of history when the liberator became the oppressor is the fact that Zimbabwe's president has never had any friends. Very few people got close enough to him to discover what made him tick. Among the people I interviewed though were some who had observed the enigmatic leader throughout his life, such as the historian Lawrence Vambe, who was at school with Mugabe. Vambe insists that there was not one decisive moment when Robert turned toxic, but two. 'The first was when the whites took sides against him after he offered the hand of reconciliation in 1980,' says Vambe. 'The second was the death of Sally. Something closed down in him. He returned to being a lonely, isolated little boy in an old man's body. I no longer recognise the man I once knew and greatly admired, who has disgraced the name of Zimbabwe.'

Vambe contends, however, that part of Mugabe's campaign of rage and revenge was not as self-interested as many believe, but was rather designed to expose Western double standards. 'It is tragic that the world looked the other way when Mugabe's Fifth Brigade killed thousands of black men, women and children in Matabeleland, but went wild with anger when white-owned farms were invaded by Robert's hooligans, leading to the death of a handful of farmers. This was British and white man's hypocrisy at its worst.'

After what he saw as the British reneging on pledges made at Lancaster House in respect of land redistribution in Zimbabwe, Mugabe decided he would be the one to expose their duplicity once and for all, according to Vambe. 'He was always settling scores. That was his nature, even as a child, unfortunately. He wanted love and affection from his siblings and later from his people, and he firmly believes he has given them what they most wanted: the return of the land taken by the whites in the 1890s. He doesn't care that he destroyed the economy in the process. He thinks that was just the sacrifice that had to be paid – but by others, not by him, of course.'

Mugabe's younger brother Donato, who died in May 2007, gave me an important insight into Robert's own view of his worst economic blunder – the seizure of white-owned farms – as an aside when I was leaving his Kutama house after interviewing him in 2006: 'One thing I found out is that he didn't want the white man to fight. He wanted to pay for the land but he didn't have any money,' the barefoot Donato told me in a self-conscious roar while his wife was out of earshot. 'Then some of his friends said, "We are going to chase every white man off (the land)." They didn't help themselves by chasing the farmers away – even the whites didn't help themselves by fighting with Mugabe. Robert himself told me that. But I don't know why he didn't stop it. I asked him why but he could not tell me. I used to think Robert was the one who knows everything and can do anything, but now I see that even he is confused.'

Much of Mugabe's confusion goes back to his childhood. Although he became his mother's favourite, Bona's conditional adoration combined with his siblings' scorn left Robert with a worry deep down that his mother's view of him was not based on a truth about himself. Perhaps he feared that somebody would find out that he was not really God's chosen one, but an ordinary little boy with defects as well as attributes. Being expected to be only half a person – the good half – he had to deny the other half of himself that didn't fit the idealised picture. The denied half, Robert's shameful secret, would almost certainly have been linked to his skin colour in racist Rhodesia, where he was likely to have suffered insults related to his blackness, including being called a 'kaffir' – the dreaded word that retains such power to shock and hurt that even I was left feeling disturbed long after Father Mukonori, while walking me to the door at the end of our first interview, gave me a message to deliver to Clare Short on my next research trip to London: 'Tell her you've got some kaffirs behind you,' he suggested with a twisted smile.

Exactly when the young Mugabe – whose black Africanness had at some point joined the despised and denied part of himself – came to see the idea of Englishness as elevated and offering the perfect cover is unclear. Reference to blackness as bad is invariably related to whiteness as Godliness, and the early missionaries at Kutama are said to have been generally hostile to African culture. At any rate, somewhere in his years at a school under European tutelage in a country under British rule, Mugabe seems to have grasped Englishness as an antidote to his self-loathing. Provided he could mimic it, as well as becoming extremely well educated, no one would discover the disdained part of him: once he was English and clever, the kaffir would be hidden under a veneer.

The difficulty for Mugabe is that once he has subconsciously denied his Africanness because it is associated with despised aspects of himself, he has to manage complex contradictions in his own world view. What does it mean to be an English person? What does it mean to be an African person, and a Marxist person? They are at odds with each other. He becomes increasingly at odds with himself because he cannot say, 'I am not an Englishman and I do not agree with the way the British operate, so I'm going to stand by what is African, which I do believe in.' Instead, he begins to reveal his contradictions as if he were at war with himself. He admires Sally for sitting on the ground and eating with her fingers in the style of Zimbabwean rural women. He denigrates Britain at every opportunity, yet teaches his own children to admire the table manners of the English aristocracy. The warring parts of himself have not been integrated into a single coherent identity. He cannot pull off the pretence of being both an Englishman and an African because the one despises the other.

His Marxism is also borrowed as part of a fragmented identity. Cobbled together with his Englishness, it is meant to form a universally impressive image – underneath which, however, is the real person he is ashamed to be. The part of Mugabe on the side of the deprived little boy is a Marxist wanting to build community projects with Denis Norman. So he starts to set up far-reaching education, agriculture and health initiatives. Then along comes the tyrannical English king inside him, declaring, 'Surely you're not going to waste your time on this snotty-nosed black child?' There is doubt and denial hovering in Mugabe's mind, which begins to undermine what he is trying to build.

Interestingly, Mugabe's classmate Lawrence Vambe recalls one of Robert's most vivid childhood memories, dating back to a visit made by British governor Cecil Rodwell to Kutama in 1933: Father O'Hea, lobbying for money to build a hospital at the time, never forgot or forgave Rodwell for remarking, 'Why do you worry about a hospital? After all, there are too many natives in the country already.' Mugabe, then a nine-year-old who idolised Father O'Hea, also deeply resented the comment.

As the years pass, it becomes an increasingly tormenting task for Mugabe to reconcile the contradictions. The angry child unable to deal with keenly felt injustices becomes the adult who resents Britain's role in his country's history. But then, having idealised Englishness and the importance of kings and queens and grandeur, it is the despised, deprived and desperate little boy who is punished by Mugabe during Operation Murambatsvina, which means in Shona 'clean up the filth' and involved thousands of poor black people living on the margins of Zimbabwean society being literally swept out of sight.

Apart from his hidden self-loathing, Mugabe suffers from the conflicting loyalties of clashing cultural values. He hails from a collective social system characterised by the expectation that people will not oppose those above them in the hierarchy, ie, authoritarianism. The Africans around him observe group rather than individual loyalty; collective rather than individual responsibility. Mugabe, meanwhile, is trying to live a life loyal to the English mode but finds it impossible to be true to himself because he is an African. The Englishman in him likes the semblance of justice presented by court judgments, parliamentary amendments and constitutional agreements because it proves that he is not a barbarian. But while he insists on doing things the 'proper' British way, he also does them his own way. Although governed to some extent by his Englishness, he simultaneously undermines the democratic values he purports to uphold. The contradictions pile up.

When Mugabe sidelines Edgar Tekere because he is a murderer, powerful party colleagues turn against him. When he re-arrests white air force personnel after their court acquittal because he firmly believes them to be saboteurs at a time when he is the target of sustained sabotage, he is condemned in the international media. His own relatives expect a free lunch; then they proceed to raid the larder. White Zimbabweans accept his generosity but give nothing in return. The British betray his trust. The contradictions seem irreconcilable.

Whether Mugabe rebelled – and 'stopped trying to please every-

body', in the words of his prison priest Father Emmanuel Ribeiro –
because he felt he had nothing left to lose after a lifetime spent playing
a game as the 'good native', or because he was in a rage about being
misunderstood, or simply because he was in danger of losing power,
the continent he half-despised, Africa, stood by him.

Africa's indulgent view of Robert Mugabe, added to his distorted
internal landscape, proved a lethal combination. The mythological
status accorded Mugabe as a liberation hero during his early years in
power, on top of Bona's fantasies about his messianic destiny, steadily
consigned the country to the decrees of a president with profound
delusions about himself.

Coming as he did from a deeply religious background where
God's endorsement was required for every move, Mugabe's growing
megalomania and immunity from accountability might well owe more
to prominent Catholic Father Mukonori's indulgence than the good
Jesuit realises. On the other hand, it is possible that Mugabe simply used
Father Mukonori to achieve his own ends. There is, after all, a strong
strategic aspect to Mugabe, experienced by most of my interviewees
as the distant, cold man they saw playing his cards close to his chest,
and epitomised during his childhood in the image of Robert the bird-
catcher laying traps for doves at the riverside.

It is quite possible that Mugabe's grievances simply accumulated
to the point where, unable to bear the humiliation of being rejected
by his own people or believing he had been made to look a fool by the
British, he decided to strike back at all those he reckoned had betrayed
him, regardless of the consequences. Among the people I talked to
were several who firmly believed that Mugabe had waited lifelong for
his chance to avenge colonialism.

One of the most pressing questions posed by Mugabe's tyranny
is how it endured for so long. The answer seems to lie in African
loyalty. While opposition politicians, notably Morgan Tsvangirai
of the MDC, tried to stop him, Africa did not. Time and again the
continent's collective leadership undermined the Western-funded MDC
and endorsed Mugabe. Even South Africa, which bore the brunt of
the refugee crisis created by Mugabe's catastrophic policies, failed to
condemn the one-time liberator.

Part of the explanation is in the liberation politics that continue
to dominate the discourse of the region. Robert Mugabe's name,

regardless of his failures in office, will always be writ large in the annals of the continent's struggles against oppression. Another reason is that the failed state of Zimbabwe, having given former oppressors the opportunity to gloat over African incompetence, is a deeply humiliating experience for those on the continent who resort to denial rather than facing the facts. Mugabe is also the most senior leader in a culture that reveres its elders. In addition, African leaders with their own experience of Western domination refrain from criticising Mugabe because they are determined to retain continental solidarity for fear of losing their hard-won collective influence.

The warm reception Mugabe has continued to receive throughout Africa, as well as in much of the developing world, is redolent of respect for the big man who boldly says the things that other African leaders would like to be saying in defiance of Western hypocrisy. Much of what Mugabe has publicly denounced as the victimisation of an African head of state by Western bullies is true. The British government did indeed dodge its moral, if not legal, responsibility for land redistribution in Zimbabwe: the former colonial power did attempt to topple Mugabe by stealth in an era when regime change was fashionable. It is one of the grim ironies of Robert Mugabe's rule and misrule that he – an entirely inappropriate messenger – has accurately exposed the hypocrisy of Western powers, earning opprobrium abroad but kudos in Africa as a result. Indeed, Mugabe seems to epitomise Western double standards in the eyes of many Africans. It was, after all, Queen Elizabeth herself who awarded him an honorary knighthood following his Gukurahundi campaign. Only after the murders of a handful of white farmers during Mugabe's land grab was the British prime minister asked in the House of Commons to consider stripping him of the title.

There is no doubt that Mugabe has conducted a brilliantly success-ful propaganda campaign. By alleging that Western sanctions – com-prising merely a visa ban and an asset freeze on 140 of his named officials – were responsible for ruining Zimbabwe's economy, and by claiming that neo-colonialist machinations had made the catastrophic land grab inevitable, he secured Africa's acquiescence to his vengeful destruction. Mugabe is, astonishingly, treated as a hero in most Third World countries because he has successfully peddled the lie that he is still being bullied by those bent on oppressing the weak.

Africa's indulgence of behaviour that should not be tolerated seems to be based on a form of 'parental' collusion: 'My child has suffered so he can do anything he likes.' Mugabe is one example of this syndrome; South Africa's unacknowledged crime crisis is another. It appears that Africa acts as if it is in agreement with the delinquency because its leaders feel that the wayward child has had a hard time and therefore deserves understanding or possibly compensation. Believing that the delinquent has been led into wickedness by others, ie denial, Africa is so blinded by the overarching historic injustices of colonialism and racism that it would rather indulge Mugabe's tyranny than risk collusion with the old enemy by condemning him. In the process, though, the continent supports further injustice, albeit of a different hue.

Undoubtedly, the often-expressed Western view that time lapse is irrelevant in Africa's white supremacist past, colonialism being a relic of history, does not take into account the continent-wide post-traumatic stress embodied in men like Mugabe. All over Africa, every attempt to discount the suffering and exploitation of colonialism and white racist rule is received as a fresh insult, whether Westerners deem it reasonable or not. The extent to which past injustice in Zimbabwe is brushed aside by the British and former white Rhodesians is quite clearly provocative and Mugabe, in taking on those dismissive attitudes, is voicing objections that the rest of the continent's leadership tiptoes around but wholeheartedly endorses.

Whatever else we know about imperialism, repressive rule and war, we might do well to remain aware that these gigantic assaults leave people bewildered with grief, hatred and revenge. Few countries in the world have managed to come of age with dignity and honour in such circumstances. Recovery takes time; perhaps generations. Although nearly a generation on from Zimbabwe's independence might seem long enough for those with an interest in forgetting, it is apparently not long enough for Africans who remember. Perhaps we ought to rely on psychologists, rather than politicians, to tell us how long such an impact should last.

Equally, it might turn out to be the practice of positive discrimination, specifically designed to atone for the exploitation of the past, that has most damagingly aided and abetted Mugabe's tyranny. The belief that it is sometimes right not to judge individuals on their merits is widespread in Africa, and wide open to abuse. As long as journalists and historians continue to sift through the collaborators and causes of

Zimbabwe's tragedy, affirmative action in the overall African context is likely to remain suspect. As former United Nations secretary general Kofi Annan said at the fifth annual Nelson Mandela Lecture in Johannesburg in July 2007, it is high time African leaders stopped shielding each other from criticism when guilty of bad governance and human rights abuses. Anan called the practice 'a pernicious, self-destructive form of racism that unites citizens to rise up and expel tyrannical rulers who are white, but to excuse tyrannical rulers who are black'.

Human history is littered with attempts to right wrongs with wrongs. Robert Mugabe's downfall was primarily his determination to extract revenge for the rejections he had suffered in his life, beginning with his father's desertion of the struggling family when he was a 10-year-old. In the decades following his deprived childhood, the isolation of Mugabe's youth was relieved only by Sally, whom he trusted completely. She was the only person who knew what he had experienced in the years when he disappeared into prison in Rhodesia and into custody in Mozambique. She made him feel less alone. Her untimely death was fate at its cruellest, not only for her husband, but for the country that subsequently fell apart. Ultimately though, it was Robert Mugabe's own choices that destroyed Zimbabwe. Too weak to tolerate rejection, too angry to resist revenge, he succumbed to his power lust as well as to retribution rather than serving Zimbabwe in the best interests of the people who once idolised him.

Sixteen

The good, the bad, and the reality

In hoping to stir deeper thought and feeling about the tragedy of life, the writer's task is to look at a subject from every possible angle. Although many people who had known Zimbabwe's president had shared with me their impressions of him and his motives, still missing at the end of 2007 after more than two years of research was Mugabe on Mugabe.

It had been more than 18 months since Father Fidelis Mukonori had agreed to help me in my difficult quest to interview Robert Mugabe. I had telephoned the priest countless times from Johannesburg when he decided at long last, albeit on the eve of my final copy deadline, that I should come to Harare and wait there for an opportunity to see Zimbabwe's freedom-fighter-turned-tyrant. Mukonori told me he had already given copies of my published books by way of a testimonial to the president, who had apparently indicated his willingness to talk to me. However, since Mugabe's last interview with the Western media had been granted three years earlier, I considered my chances of meeting the feared leader slim but worth pursuing.

I arrived in Harare on 20 November 2007, the day Ian Smith died in South Africa, to hear the Zimbabwean government declare the country's former premier an unrepentant racist who would be neither mourned nor missed. After two punishingly uneventful weeks of constant calls and visits to Father Mukonori's office at the Society of Jesus headquarters opposite Harare's moribund university in Mount Pleasant, I received a startling midnight visit from the priest. We sat together on the veranda of my room at York Lodge in the moonlight, there being no electricity in the city, as usual. 'Tomorrow,' he announced with a grin, describing how he had gone earlier that Friday evening, dutifully, to a Christmas concert at Hartmann House – the Jesuit school attended by the president's younger son – only to find himself seated beside Mugabe in a roomful of parents.

Mukonori gave me a comical rendition of the school choir, wide-eyed and open-mouthed, singing carols, while 12-year-old Chatunga greeted his infamous dad self-consciously. 'As all this was going on,' he explained, 'His Excellency and I were talking in whispers about the author who had been waiting to see him for two weeks. So after a while he agreed, "Okay, Fidelis, tomorrow it is."'

The following day Father Mukonori rang to tell me the meeting would not, after all, take place on Saturday but possibly on Sunday instead. That evening, he called again to say he was coming to talk to me. 'High-ups' had visited him to discuss my proposed interview, he said on arrival at York Lodge. On Sunday, he phoned again, revealing the name of one of the officials who had been in touch with him: George Charamba, permanent secretary for information in the office of the president and Cabinet, and the man charged with keeping journalists out of Zimbabwe. Feeling nervous at being propelled into the official domain, I asked Father Mukonori if he thought I was at risk. Wouldn't Charamba's nose be out of joint now that he knew I had gone over his head and behind his back in seeking to talk to Mugabe? Mukonori thought not.

Shortly after lunch the following Monday, when Father Mukonori had left Zimbabwe on a week's church business in Kenya, I was summoned to George Charamba's office on the first floor of the presidency in Munhumutapa Building, opposite the high court. Security proved surprisingly casual. The pleasant woman sitting beneath a stern portrait of Robert Mugabe did not look inside my bags at the tape recorder and camera I was carrying, or notice that the married surname in my identity document did not match the one she was checking with Charamba's assistant. I wandered up the stairs unescorted. There, alongside a large photograph of Mugabe and Fidel Castro, near the entrance to the Information section, was a massive banner bellowing 'Mugabe is right'.

A tall, smartly dressed man with strong features and a commanding manner, George Charamba ushered me into his office, where two suited men proffered their hands. I sat as directed on a red sofa. Six more identically clad men then walked into the room, shook my hand and arranged themselves on straight-backed chairs around me. No one sat beside me, though I moved up to the corner of the sofa to make space. It was pointedly to be an interrogation of sorts. I did not recognise the names of any of the officials around me, though they did not look unduly hostile. So I let down my guard and smiled when Charamba began the screening by saying, 'Normally, we inform the president about journalists in the country. On this occasion, he informed us.'

Later, he referred again to my unorthodox route to the presidency. 'You decided to come through the back door,' he said with a whiff of resentment.

Only because the front door was closed.

'Why didn't you talk to any members of the government?' he asked, after I had listed some of my interviewees.

Because I was too scared.

Charamba fired questions at me for over an hour. The others took notes, although one of them slept peacefully throughout the proceedings. They wanted me to describe not only the book I was writing on Robert Mugabe but my own history and political beliefs. It was clear that Charamba had checked some of the information supplied to me by my interviewees – and relayed to him by Father Mukonori – with the president because he interrupted a few times to correct me, saying, 'No, HE (meaning His Excellency), says it was not like that but like this.' At one point, when I said I believed South African presidential candidate Jacob Zuma would cost the country international credibility if elected to office because of the fraud charges pending against him and the poor judgement he had shown over rape allegations, Charamba lost his composure and started shouting at me.

When he asked what I thought of Zimbabwe and I replied, 'It's a tragedy,' I expected him to raise his voice again. His snarled comment, 'So you've written a Eurocentric book,' to which I responded, 'Of course, I can only be who I am,' seemed certain to incur his displeasure. Instead, he wound up the proceedings with the assurance that I would meet HE the following day. 'Be ready to come immediately,' he said.

Three weeks followed, however, with barely a word from Charamba's office. Mugabe was busy meeting various heads of state, flying to neighbouring Mozambique to attend a post-independence ritual, travelling to a summit in Portugal amid strenuous protests, delivering his annual state of the nation address, and organising the forthcoming election via his politburo and a party congress.

Finally, my patience paid off. On 21 December, when I was about to return empty-handed to Johannesburg for Christmas, the long-silent telephone in my room at York Lodge rang at 9.30 in the morning. It was Charamba's office telling me to be at State House in half an hour. I dressed, grabbed the car keys and was on the road in less than 10 minutes.

Once inside the grounds of the imposing colonial mansion, I was escorted by one security agent after another past rows of police cars, armed soldiers and Mugabe's ever-ready motorcade towards the two stuffed lions that guard the visitors' entrance, and finally into Mugabe's domain. There, I waited in the elegant reception room amid displays of English porcelain, occasionally chatting to George Charamba, for three hours. He told me the interview had taken a long time to organise because HE viewed it as an opportunity to clarify some issues for the historical record and wanted to give it his full attention. When Father Mukonori came out of the foregoing meeting with Mugabe on Hartmann House matters, he sat beside me and explained that HE was clearly looking forward to the interview with me since he had sidled up to the priest a few minutes earlier to ask, 'Is our friend here?'

Fifteen minutes before we were called into the president's private office, all the attendants and officials in the reception area suddenly leapt to their feet and stood to attention. Charamba hissed at me to do the same. I turned to where their eyes were focused behind me and there, just inside a doorway, was Robert Mugabe. He was wearing a dark suit and white shirt, with a patterned tie and matching red silk handkerchief tucked into his top pocket. His gaze was obviously on me, the sole non-staff person present. Perhaps he felt a little threatened at the prospect of being interviewed by a journalist, albeit one who did not want to show him up as much as try to understand him. He might have intended to get the measure of me in that quick preview, despite having had me vetted to make sure I wasn't going to be hostile.

On entering the president's office, my handbag having been searched by the plain-clothed security agent accompanying us, I was inexplicably startled to see Mugabe sitting bolt upright in a tall, mustard-coloured chair behind his vast desk. He seemed oddly vulnerable, but frightening too. Perhaps it was his stillness combined with his forbidding public image, his smallness amid the pomp, my accumulated fear and adrenalin rush, plus the sheer joy of finally conquering a supposedly impossible mission that gave me such an intense sense of excitement, tempered by apprehension, that I felt like walking forwards and backwards simultaneously.

I sat as directed in a chair opposite the president of Zimbabwe, flanked by George Charamba and Father Mukonori, with another information official on the priest's right. At the back of the simply decorated room was a tall, khaki-clad, policeman wearing a lot of medals, standing beside a plain-clothed security agent who was glued to his radio earpiece.

I greeted Mugabe. He nodded, watching me closely. The tension in the room was suffocating. My strained voice sounded unfamiliar as I asked if I could record the interview. He nodded, waving his hand airily. Then he apologised for the time I had spent waiting to meet him. As I reached out to put my tape recorder on the desk in front of him, Charamba told me to describe my book to the president before proceeding with the questions.

I started by relating some of the flattering or supportive things people I had interviewed had said about Mugabe to let him know that I was not merely on a witch-hunt. Then I asked if he recalled joining my friend Dr Ahrn Palley for dinner at my house in 1975. He said he remembered meeting Ahrn for a discussion during the brief period between his release from prison and his departure for the guerrilla camps in Mozambique, but admitted that he only vaguely recalled the venue. When I described his banned face appearing on the front cover of the white-owned magazine I edited in 1978, at a time when he was waging war against Rhodesia, he looked pleased but baffled. Father Mukonori confirmed having seen it and the accompanying article I had written entitled 'Rebel Without a Pause'. Mugabe warmed visibly towards me: I had struggle credentials; I had once admired him. When I told him I had first seen him in person after he came out of prison at the end of 1974 to a welcoming rally at Silveira House, where I was one of only three white people in the black crowd, he slapped the desk and said, 'That, I remember.'

I told Mugabe to his face that he was not going to like everything

I wrote about him, and then quickly reeled off a list of the people I had talked to for the book, giving a brief summary of what each had said. It took about 20 minutes of the two-and-a-half hour interview. He interrupted to mention his weekly meetings with British governor Lord Soames, in the room we were sitting in, during the brief transition from Rhodesia to Zimbabwe in 1980. 'We had pledged that, win or lose (the Lancaster House-brokered elections), we would have an alliance with Zapu,' he reminded me.

His mocking account of Soames' disbelief on hearing Mugabe's admission that he did not know anything about governing a country brought laughter from those beside me. 'I have two areas of specialisation: One, teaching. I've been a teacher and a good teacher, very professional,' Mugabe said he had told Soames. 'Two, I have been a guerrilla leader. So help me form a government. "Really?" asked Soames. I said, "Really." "Reeeeally? You mean it?" continued Soames. "Yes, really,"' Mugabe admitted.

When the obsequious laughter had subsided, I asked Zimbabwe's president if he found it difficult to talk about himself.

'Yes.'

Why?

Because talking about oneself is praising oneself. I don't like to talk about myself at all. I'd rather other people talk about me ... Self-praise is not recommended, is it? Better others talk about you, about your shortcomings, your points of strength and so on. It's better that way. You can talk about yourself in terms of factual experiences you've had. I have no objection to that. That I can do ... But evaluation of that, you should leave to others.

Is it perhaps that you shy away from emotions?

'Perhaps, yes. I was a very shy person, a shy boy, as I grew up and, and, and, and – yes, I still have a bit of it, inevitably.'

Interestingly, when Mugabe told me he didn't want to boast, it did not initially occur to him that I was asking about self-reflection. His first idea was that there were only good things to discuss. He did not instinctively consider good as well as bad because there is a division within himself – known to psychologists as 'splitting' – where anything negative is externalised and only good qualities belong to him. It is a common enough affliction: most of us want to be right and see ourselves as good. In Mugabe's case though, it has become extreme because nobody challenges him. And it is extremely serious because he is in charge of a country.

I continued: Your brother Donato told me your books were your only friends as a child.

> That's what my mother also used to say. I always had a book tucked here (gestures under his arm) when I was a young boy. Yes, I liked reading, reading, reading every little book I found. Yes, I preferred to keep to myself than playing with others. I didn't want too many friends, one or two only – the chosen ones. I lived in my mind a lot. I liked talking to myself, reciting little poems and so on; reading things aloud to myself.

Mugabe went on to describe the Catholic mission Kutama, where he grew up.

> In those days, the Catholics were living saints, or at least the church thought it could make them living saints. We lived in Christian villages. We were born there. And no heathens – as they were called – were allowed in. Our grannies were heathens outside. We were not allowed to go out … You could go out on a mission to see your granny but you had to be back by 5pm.
>
> Father O'Hea was very radical. He asked why people should be encamped in this way. No, we must live with everybody else. How do we convert those who are heathens if we just concentrate on these ones? So go and live with the others (he said). He was a very highly educated man with a string of degrees.

Was he a father figure to you?

> Yes, yes. And every Thursday he used to carry us on the lorry; drive to the river, to a pool, where he taught us how to swim. Some youngsters used to sit on him (gestures to his chest) as he did backstroke. He was a nice Irishman, yes. Only an Irishman could do that; an Englishman couldn't.

He described the devotion Father O'Hea, who was a medical doctor, had for his students' education in every respect, including human anatomy. 'We could recite all the parts of the body; the skeletal system, the circulatory system.'

Mugabe's own father abandoned the family after his eldest son Michael died at 15 in 1934. 'That was a terrible blow. It was poisoning, and Father O'Hea was very sad. He thought this boy was a genius. He was very bright, very bright intellectually. And also very athletic, which I wasn't. It was a sad loss.'

> In those days, we used to be given some poisonous stuff to spray on grass to kill locusts. Michael possibly went into an auntie's room and fetched a gourd that had held poison and used it to drink water. That's what the person who was with him said he did. When he came home, having run there from seven miles away because the poison was working and he was very athletic, he was flat (on the floor) and my grandfather said, 'What's wrong with you?' And Michael said, 'My tummy, my tummy, my tummy.'

Mugabe described Michael's death as if he were his 10-year-old self watching a trauma so disturbing that he still recalled it as if it had happened yesterday:

> Ah, why not take him to hospital? 'No, we cannot take him to hospital. His father is not here, his mother is not here. If we take him to hospital, they'll take him to Salisbury and there, we understand, they cut people open. We will be blamed by the father. I am the grandfather, not the custodian, and I haven't got the permission to do it.'
>
> By the third day, my mother came. Then she went to Father O'Hea in the evening. Father O'Hea came and he applied an enema. I still remember the dish where pieces from Michael's intestines were lying. And Father O'Hea shook his head and said to my mother, 'Come, walk with me.' He was trying to convey to her that things are bad and perhaps he might survive with the will of God, but it was serious. My mother came back and within minutes Michael passed away. My father left only after he had passed away. Father O'Hea said if he had been sent to hospital early enough he would have been saved.

Mugabe speculated that his own life would have been easier had Michael not died because his elder brother would have assumed the family responsibilities that fell instead on his own young shoulders. 'He would have finished his teacher training in 1939 and he would have

... looked after us in the absence of my father. But my mother used to say, "if Michael were alive, you would (still) have been what you are". I don't know; circumstances decided it.'

Did your mother want you to be a priest?

'No. But because I was quiet, prayerful, she thought perhaps I might end up becoming a priest. It didn't turn out that way.'

Would you recommend politics as a career to any of your three children?

'No, I don't recommend anything, even to my relatives. I left it to them to make their choices. Those who chose politics, well and good: it was their own choosing. But I don't want anyone to say later, "We were pushed into this thing."' He paused, sighing as he looked down at his hands on his lap. 'It's painful, politics, yeah – it's not a profession to which people must invite themselves, really. They must be invited by others.'

Mugabe's voice dropped to a virtual whisper when referring to the pain of politics. It was a poignant moment, coming straight after his unexpected but convincingly democratic attitude towards his relatives' career choices, though before his omnipotent belief that only he – or did he mean God? – could appoint people to positions of power in Zimbabwe.

Throughout the interview, Mugabe's tone was barely audible when he talked about himself, or when I approached his personal concerns. It was as if he tried to hide away. He cleared his throat often, perhaps another sign of his discomfort with the unfamiliarly personal questions. Yet he did not reject any of them, despite my having invited him to do so. He seemed at times apprehensive rather than defensive, and often more frank than manipulative, which offered insight into the contradictions that make the man.

Though substantially truthful, he was often contradictory. But he did not see the contradictions because, like the seemingly respectable married man who makes his living as a drug lord, Mugabe holds parallel positions and talks about the one as if the other does not exist. The two are not coordinated in his divided self. As surely as the exposure of the respected but corrupt family man will leave his wife gasping, 'My husband is not that sort of man. It just doesn't make sense', Mugabe's apologists have been slow to grasp what he is capable of when his humiliated, bitter and vengeful side holds sway. While he was indeed the enlightened leader who wanted to develop the country, improve the plight of the poor and secure freedom by resisting colonial power, the once-admirable leader is also the person doing the terrible things that can't be mentioned because there cannot be a dark side to the character of the president of Zimbabwe. He gives you the benefit of his goodness as long as you are on his side, but if you cross him, he retracts all the charitable qualities as if they never existed.

Looking back, I asked Mugabe, would you rather have remained a teacher?

No. You see, there came a time when I went to Fort Hare. I joined the Youth League of the South African ANC and we used to go to meetings of the Youth League at Fort Hare. And I made up my mind in those days of Gandhi and passive resistance that I would teach for a while but only to get some funds to enable me to go to Britain and study law so that I could become independent financially and fight for the country. That's what I made up my mind to do. I had already taught for eight years.

In which ways do you feel most misunderstood as a man?

I don't know whether one is misunderstood. I think the people around me understand me very well. But it's the world outside that doesn't seem to understand. You know, they don't appreciate what our real calling was as leaders – they think we were just in politics to enhance our status. They don't realise that for us it was a real calling. We saw people suffer. We could not accept that our country was in the hands of a colonial power through settlers here. No ... We had to really commit and say, this is it, and it's a question of life or death. Those who take to politics after and didn't fight the struggle of life or death, they go into politics because either they think politics is a source of wealth or it's a source of greater enhancement of one's status. But not so for those who took to politics in our time, when you had to give a total commitment. You couldn't have roughed it the way we did, walking long distances into the bush and undergoing all that hardship, if your heart wasn't there. That sense of sacrifice had to be there: you had to sacrifice yourself.

People around Mugabe express understanding and appreciation of his sacrifices. If they don't, they're outsiders and denigrated. This has enabled him to create the personal reality 'bubble' in which he is a selfless and successful leader.

How do you feel about the 11 years you spent in Rhodesian prisons?

'Well, well, well, well,' he laughed uncomfortably, the repetition of words providing a cover for his feelings.

They were formative years, yes, yes, but it's a chunk of one's life that comes off you. It's not a happy experience. But you realise that people like Mandela were there for 27 years and you only did 11 years. You see, it's 11 years and then you have the reward, independence. Your people are free, your country is calm. Then the 11 years don't become a burden to remember. They become the price you had to pay for the reward you got.

The experience of the chunk of his life spent in prison was cut off, cauterised, as if it never happened. He had apparently tried to live around it. I assumed when planning the interview questions that the death of his first child while he was in prison would come up in his answer, but it didn't. However, his voice virtually disappeared. More than anywhere else in the interview, he was clearly seeking refuge from the memory of his prison years.

I asked: When you came out of prison, were you the same person who went in?

Mugabe paused to reflect. 'No, you came back with the sense that you had been punished for nothing, and that you must fight for that for which you have been punished – which has not come. We were released in 1974 but Smith was still stubborn and we needed to intensify our fighting.'

He did not believe he was the same after his prison years, clearly. Something had been taken from him. Something was due back to him for the unfair punishment. Thoughts of revenge sprang to mind.

How would you describe yourself in a few words?

I feel I am just an ordinary person. I feel within me there is a charitable disposition towards others, just as I find charitable positions towards me from others. And I don't make enemies, no. Others may make me an enemy of theirs but I make no enemies. Even those who might do things against me, I don't make them enemies at all. No.

If Mugabe ever feels ordinary, which is doubtful, he is more accurately an ordinary person in an extraordinary mess. But if he were to admit that, where would it leave him? It would negate his whole life. From his perspective, he does not make enemies – it's not me, it's 'them', he insists. He is in denial. When something is too much to bear, he makes it non-existent, an unconscious coping mechanism to protect him from the real world.

So you're not a vengeful person?

'No.'

Are you a forgiving person?

'Yes, I think so. Otherwise, I would have slaughtered lots of people, including Ian Smith. I always used to joke with Smith that he had borrowed hair (meaning Smith's scalp) which rightly belonged to us, but he could continue to wear it ...' He mused almost wistfully about Zimbabwe's white population's attitude towards his government. 'When it came to the land issue, there was no compromise on that one. But it was actually the British who spoilt things for the whites.'

In fact, it was the unforgiving part of Mugabe that allowed the land grab and spoilt things not only for the whites but for all those affected by the damaging policy. In his view, though, it was the white farmers who made him their enemy by supporting the MDC. He probably really believes that he is forgiving, otherwise why did he let Ian Smith stay on in Zimbabwe? He pushes his anger back, masking it with self-deception. His unresolved rage towards white Rhodesians as representatives of British colonisers was endorsed when Britain and the farmers supported the MDC, which is why Mugabe condoned the resultant violence. If he had given full expression to his resentment of whites, he could have done to them what another African dictator, Idi Amin, did to the Asians in Uganda. So while certainly not forgiving, he has been more controlled than people acknowledge.

Mugabe did not recall holding Ian Smith's hand in the deliberate way the former Rhodesian premier had remembered it in my interview with him in 2005. This may have been because hand-holding between men is a natural, unremarkable African custom, or possibly because Mugabe was sensitive – following recent politically damaging charges of appeasement made against him by his former ally Edgar Tekere – to the interpretation such a friendly gesture could be given by his enemies within the liberation-obsessed ruling party. But he quickly grasped my metaphorical use of the gesture. 'He did not respond,' he said of his first encounter with Smith. 'He accepted the effect of it (reconciliation), but he did not reciprocate.

'The Lancaster House constitution allowed for Smith to lead his group of 20 white uncontested seats in Parliament. At the beginning, when I got some whites in my government, Smith came to me and said, "But why go behind my back and take these without discussing it with me? These are my people."'

Mugabe said his response was to remind Smith of the harm he had done to the country while in office. 'But we are reconciled now. Don't you feel proud that I had to reach for these individuals within your party and include them as ministers in my government? That alone should give you a sense of pride and should exonerate us for it.'

Explaining that Zanu-PF had invited one of Ian Smith's former Cabinet colleagues, David Smith, to join the new government because they had got to know him well after he had given them 'a lot of information about what was taking place on the side of the internal settlement delegation' at Lancaster House, Mugabe described the crisis on the land issue that held up the eventual historical London agreement to the brink of collapse. 'In principle, we never could accept that the people should be taxed to enable them to get the land – which in the first place was taken – back. So the British had the responsibility. Lord Carrington said yes, but he said there were limited funds which had to be adequate. We had an impasse for about a week. We wanted that question resolved.'

Mugabe cleared his throat, throwing his head back in recall, his eyes narrowing until only the whites were visible, disconcertingly. He said:

Then the Americans, being anxious about the success of the conference, decided to intervene. It was the Carter administration at the time. The American ambassador approached the secretary general of the Commonwealth to say the Americans wanted to assist ... However, the American public would not want to hear that the funds had been given for the purposes of compensating British nationals in (our) country. The American taxpayer would view the funds as coming out of their pockets and going into the pockets of British farmers. 'But we will give the funds to the land reform programme in general. What you do with them is entirely your own business.' And that money was generously given (in the early years of Mugabe's administration) without strings attached.

Whereas the British funds from the start were very difficult to get. They wanted us to have half the equivalent amount of what we had demanded at the conference table, which was not what we had agreed. We started querying this. Then they decided to give the funds in the same way as the Americans were doing. But the Americans' generosity ended when Carter was defeated by Reagan. He said we were communists who had sided with the Russians and so few times with the United States and, on that basis, America could not continue to deal with Zimbabwe.

After Reagan came Bush senior, who said he wanted to improve relations. But he didn't go back as far as we wanted. He restored health aid but not the big amount for land. And so the problem started.

On the British side, Mrs Thatcher decided to stop funds after they'd given about £42 million, which we said was peanuts. At the time, we'd settled about 57 000 families only. We wanted them to continue and they said no. Then they said, 'Okay', reluctantly, and added another three or four million – that was it.

John Major followed Thatcher as Conservative Party leader and prime minister in 1990, he and Mugabe becoming 'friends', according to Mugabe.

We hosted the Commonwealth here in 1991. We talked about land and he committed to review the matter. He sent a six-man team (from London) and did some very good work ... recommending that the fund be reinstated. He asked us to send a team to London to help restore it in June 1996. They made their own input and the package (offered by the British) was a very good one. We looked forward to it being implemented here. But, alas, Major was defeated by Labour.

In came New Labour. I spoke to Blair in Edinburgh. We spoke at quite some length, after we had been sending messages which were not being responded to. He said he had a team in his office which was looking at the matter. Two years went by – no response – and we wondered what had happened.

Mugabe's voice had sunk so low that it was barely audible. Perhaps because he was remembering his rejection by the British, he looked away, his head slumping forward as he withdrew inward at the thought of his humiliation. 'We asked for some response and it came by way of

Clare Short's letter, which we still have,' he explained.

Here, Mugabe's memory was faulty. Clare Short's letter came a few days, not two years, after his meeting with Blair at the Commonwealth summit in October 1997. Those sitting alongside me were laughing uproariously at the mention of the contentious letter. 'And we said, "Ah, that's the end of the story",' Mugabe continued.

> They don't want our problems. They say it doesn't come under the poverty relief programme they are running. They're saying their policies don't derive from the Conservative Party, and this (funding for land re-distribution in Zimbabwe) was a decision of the Conservative Party. No colonial responsibilities any more. It was once a British colony, and Britain had long ceased to have colonial responsibility towards it.

His voice became eerily thin:

> That was quite a damning response. It was a very ignorant response. It showed ignorance on the part of New Labour. If you take the Conservatives – (they are) much more mature. They realise there is something called succeeding and honouring both assets and liabilities. It's part of international law in so far as it relates to governments ... This was the undertaking of the previous government so why can't it be your undertaking too? There was a whole package which Blair had on his desk, left by Major, agreed to between the Conservatives and ourselves. What was going to happen to it?

Mugabe was speaking in a menacingly low tone. I leaned forward in my seat to hear what he was saying. 'They were going to tear it up,' he growled bitterly. 'And we read then that it was a government without norms and principles at all, and they didn't deserve our respect.'

> The stance we took was: they can refuse their money but the land is ours anyway. So keep your money and we'll keep our land. So that became it. Then our people became disenchanted and the war veterans started moving on to farms and taking them. We said we would not arrest them, but we would not at the same time regard them as legal acts. They were political acts and we would as government later examine each situation and determine whether we would want a particular farm for resettlement

purposes. Our instructions (to the war veterans) were to take the farms but don't use anything and don't commit acts of violence. People said they should be arrested, they are trespassers, but we said no, we wouldn't arrest them. So from that moment on, we started moving on to farms and removing the war veterans where we felt they needed to be removed, and legalising the process. So that then became the point of departure between us and the Labour government.

People criticised us for not having taken action against the war veterans. And at the end it was the war veterans plus the youth and others who now felt that the people had to act in order for the land to come their way. They criticised us for having allowed this form of occupation to become legal. In fact, we didn't regard it as legal but we didn't disallow it because we were taking action against the British government, who had torn up what was a legal agreement made at Lancaster House. They had reneged on it, so why look at just our own act?

By now following the political line, Mugabe's voice became strong and confident as he described how he sat on the fence when the war veterans invaded Zimbabwe's predominantly white-owned farms. He appears to have condoned the abuse that accompanied the land grab without actually endorsing it directly, although I remember him remarking that white farmers were 'the enemy' on the day Martin Olds was murdered on his farm in April 2000. Perhaps the land grab was his way of acting out his own pent-up rage by proxy. Although stating his own reservations to me as if they were true, his response at the time clearly included the idea that the war veterans could do whatever they liked and he would turn a blind eye.

He went on to explain the dilemma of Zimbabwe's white farmers in not wanting to back his government by holding Britain to account for land compensation because such backing would, in effect, have endorsed the facility by which their land was taken from them. They wanted to keep the land by any means whatsoever, he told me. In fact, the farmers objected to Britain having a special responsibility for compensating them because it amounted to a denial of their Zimbabwean citizenship.

Mugabe's step-by-step explanation of his government's disastrous land grab was obviously the information he intended me to convey – and doubtless part of the explanation for his having agreed to speak to me when so many other interview requests from foreign journalists had been turned down over the years. While I was aware that he was hoping I would go some way towards proving, as he believes, that he was not the guilty party – 'they' were – my impression was that he was telling the truth about the actual events (although there has never been any evidence that any war veterans were removed from farms by his government).

Contrary to the account Mugabe gave of events leading up to the land grab, the prevailing pro-British belief in the West is that the Labour government under Blair was entitled to stop funding land reform in Zimbabwe on the grounds that money already given by the British taxpayer had been misused by Mugabe's government. The point that Mugabe was eager to get across was that John Major's Conservative administration had agreed, despite earlier charges of irregular use of the funds, to resuscitate Britain's Lancaster House land reform undertaking, and that Blair's refusal to honour the previous British government's promise had been unethical – a version of events that accords with my own research.

In my opinion, Mugabe was not so much trying to use me to rewrite history as taking advantage of what he believed might be a fair hearing from a Western-orientated writer with an involvement, albeit peripheral, in the politics of Rhodesia and Zimbabwe. There was never any attempt by George Charamba or Father Mukonori to see what I had written in *Dinner With Mugabe* before the interview with the president, nor to overtly influence what I was planning to write. In any case, Mugabe's account of events leading up to his land grab in no way justifies his actions and their catastrophic consequences, but it does apportion some of the blame to Britain and, to a minor extent, America. All the parties involved in the redistribution of land in Zimbabwe should have tried a lot harder to ensure a successful outcome.

I did not pursue with Mugabe, perhaps mistakenly, the assertion by Clare Short, the former British minister in charge of international development between 1997 and 2003, that the UN-sponsored land conference of 1998 had offered him the opportunity to recover his financial position in respect of land redistribution. In her view, he failed to take advantage of the Western donations that were available then for land reform, although Short made it clear (see Chapter 8) that only Britain among the nations attending the UN's conference was prepared to give money, albeit of unknown value, for the purchase of land in Zimbabwe.

My main purpose in obtaining the interview with Robert Mugabe – the duration of which was not revealed to me when it began – was not to dwell on the land issue, crucial though it has proved in Zimbabwe's recent history, but to continue with my exploration of the man.

Why do so many people fear you?

'Perhaps because I'm quiet, I keep to myself, and also because I believe in what I say,' he replied. 'We do this, we do that. We are being principled.'

Does that mean you don't compromise?

'No, we compromise a lot. But with principles, no. You don't sacrifice principles – you don't, you don't, you don't sacrifice principles.'

Mugabe's description of why people fear him shows that he partly understands the person he is – quiet, solitary, shy. But what people really fear about him is his instability. There are hidden, irrational responses in him that can neither be seen nor predicted. Although he claims to believe in what he says, meaning there are no contradictions, this is far from true. But he is unaware of the contradictions within himself. He can insist that he never sacrifices his principles because the way he sees it, he did not set out to murder, and the torture people suffered was of their own doing. While he may not be mad in a clinical sense, his is a mad way of being in the world; a cut-off, deluded way. We are all capable of functioning similarly to some extent, cutting off friends or family when we feel they have crossed an unacceptable line – it's a necessary coping strategy. But most of us remain able to negotiate the middle ground, at least some of the time.

When I asked Mugabe if he had ever been deeply in love, he replied, 'That's why I got married twice, isn't it?' Although citing two trips up the aisle did not adequately answer the question, the image of Grace armed with a frying pan flitted across my mind and I decided it was too unfair a question to pursue with a married man, even a monstrous one, when he may well have loved one wife more than the other.

What does it mean to love somebody? I asked him.

'Ah, well, that is to be natural, isn't it? You love somebody and you want to marry someone because you are desirous of having a partner in life. Having children gives your love real application, if you have a heart. The heart must exude itself by showing love to your children; other children as well, and to people as whole.' His voice had become tender as he moved from a purely sexual interpretation of the question to glimmers of intimacy, loyalty and sharing.

Returning to politics, I asked Mugabe what particularly soured his relationship with Britain. Was it Clare Short's letter?

'No, it was the attitude. That letter merely expressed the attitude of the British government. Her letter was a symptom of it.'

What would you say to someone like Lady Soames, a British establishment figure who was really very fond of you?

'A loving, loving woman. I was very sad she lost her husband,' he replied. 'They had become great friends. She remains a great friend at heart.'

But you don't see her any more?

No, the British attitude at the moment doesn't allow friendship. We've had every member of the Royal Family (to stay) at State House – every one of them. The Queen used to talk of the 40s when she was still a girl and came here in 1947, when she stayed in one of the buildings here at State House. When we had the Commonwealth meeting here in 1991, we had the Queen staying. And she loved it. We prepared a lot of things for her (to do) ... And now, to this day, we treasure those moments, and we have nothing against the Royal Family. If anything, we still have our love for the Royal Family, as I was telling Prince Charles when we met in Rome at the funeral of the Pope. I sat next to him. No, we haven't lost our love for them. But you know, the Blair government made even the Prince and the Queen say something against Zimbabwe. That's terrible! It's sad.

Mugabe seemed on the brink of tears as he remembered the Royal Family. But he did not take on board what it meant to lose a good friend like Lady Soames, or that she might have had her own independent view.

His voice became firm and resentful as he bemoaned Britain's dishonesty in world affairs:

This is what I don't understand about European politics. They can use lies in order to achieve a given purpose and get the public to believe that they are telling the truth, only for the public to discover later that they didn't tell the truth. And then the politicians have a way of justifying their actions. We don't want politics of that nature. You've got to be open and truthful. That's where we find the politics of Bush and Blair, you know, to be absolutely terrible, unacceptable. Where are their moral norms, their virtues of honesty and truthfulness, if they don't apply in what you tell people, what you believe, what you do?

We are told that Saddam Hussein had weapons of mass destruction. And they know in their minds that they are telling lies. They invade Iraq and get the international community to actually believe they are telling the truth. At the end of the day, they say no, now they have found that, no, he did not have weapons of mass destruction, which they had known before. In the meantime, they have caused lots of people to suffer and blood to flow. And they continue to kill people, the war continues, even after they have discovered (that there are no WMDs).

Mugabe is incapable of admitting that, just as Bush and Blair tell lies, so does he. In his internal politics, he disavows his own duplicitous and deceitful side, projecting these aspects of himself on to Bush and Blair.

Some people say the land acquisition process in Zimbabwe was a spontaneous movement and that you were not in control of it. What would you say to that?

We were in control of it. There was a moment when Chief Svosve started with his people moving on to land, and we sent vice president Muzenda to go and talk to him nicely. And this is how we were doing it. When the war veterans started, we could have appealed to them – had Britain not reneged on the issue. But when Britain reneged and we had this action by the war veterans and those who supported people moving on to the land, I said, 'Yes, now we have the weapon to respond to Britain's action in reneging. Fine, we are taking our land.' Now it will affect the farmers in a way that we would not have wanted, but let that be.

We had hoped that the British would take notice of it and that they would say, 'Let's meet and discuss this.' Indeed, seven years ago when we had the first European Union/African summit in Cairo, Britain's foreign secretary Robin Cook approached (Nigerian president) Obasanjo, requesting him to approach us so that a meeting could take place between him and our delegation. Obasanjo came to me and said, 'I'm bringing you this message from Robin Cook, and he tells me that they have the money for the land but he wants discussions.' I said, 'No, we have never refused discussion. Okay.'

So we met Robin Cook. He was quite a gentleman. And he said, 'Yes, we have the money. Send some people to London and we will resume it, but let's stop this business of calling each other names in the press and so on.' I said, 'Fine.' So we once again sent a team to London en route for discussions with Robin Cook, only to find that Clare Short and others were angry that he had arranged for this visit, and they told him that there was no money. He had his own team and he thought he had the authority of Blair. Our people came back. They did not meet anyone apart from Robin Cook.

He must have been very embarrassed?

'Yes, so he said. It was so sad.'

In fact, Mugabe's recollection of these events is false. Robin Cook met the Zimbabwean delegation in London for eight hours of talks on 27 April 2000. Cook said that Britain would give £36 million for land reform over two years – if the land invasions were halted. The Zimbabweans refused to stop the occupations, hence the meeting failed. Afterwards, Cook said, 'We cannot have future talks at ministerial level unless the farm occupations have ended.'

What struck me about Mugabe's references to Zimbabwe's white farmers was how keen he was to present them as representatives of Britain. They were easier to dismiss once he saw the farmers as part of 'them' rather than 'us'. They did not belong; they were British settlers in Zimbabwe and pawns in Mugabe's revenge game. Rather as a manipulative, vengeful parent might do in a vexed divorce settlement process, he was saying, 'I'll hurt the kid if the bad parent doesn't pay maintenance.' He was hoping Britain would step in and say, 'No, no, you can't treat our child like that! Here's some more maintenance.' However, many of the white farmers were their own worst enemies in the sense that they underpinned Mugabe's 'them' and 'us' view through their shocking racism. They could never portray themselves as Africans, trying instead to elevate themselves to superior, denigrating, British-type overlords.

When I asked Mugabe for his vision of Zimbabwe's land now that it was no longer a black and white issue, he replied that it must be utilised properly and listed, unconvincingly, the ways its current neglect and abuse would be corrected.

But realistically, sir, I said, many people would say that this country as it is going at the moment is light years away from restructuring agriculture to anything like the position it occupied in the economy previously.

My comment was a challenge so I had been careful to frame it politely and in the third person rather than directly from me. Mugabe reacted angrily. His eyes flashed and his voice rose. 'Light years?' he repeated indignantly. 'We don't even have to go two years. Look at what we will do next year, and you'll be surprised. We now have,' he faltered, then began again, 'You don't know,' he continued, searching for a response to my outrageous dissent. 'You have not travelled into the hinterland, have you?'

I admitted that I had not. He must have known that I had done nothing during the previous five weeks other than sit beside the phone waiting for an invitation from him. He pounced. 'How could you miss the amount of farming that the people are doing?' he demanded triumphantly. 'It's on an even larger scale than was being done before. There is greater commitment today. Even in the early days, the commercial farmers were not the greatest producers of maize. The seed maize, yes. But cotton also: it was always the peasants' crop. And they need our input. We are bringing quite a lot of inputs into it – irrigation schemes and so on. Now, with the equipment we have brought into the country, you can expect within two years to see that we will be exporting lots of things.'

Mugabe's hostile reaction gave me a foretaste of his response to criticism. There was little doubt that had I opposed him openly, he would not have tolerated it. So I returned to pussyfooting around him. My goal was to comprehend rather than to confront him, and I wanted to keep the interview going as long as possible to this end. Presumably, Mugabe's anxiety when I challenged what he said was to counter the humiliation he would have felt if I revealed the mess he has made in Zimbabwe – especially in front of all those in the room with us.

If Mugabe were to take sober stock of what his reward for the years he spent in prison and the harsh times he endured in guerrilla camps has added up to, he would be devastated. That is why he has such a strong drive to keep talking up the reward as it collapses around him.

He would be left staring into an abyss otherwise. The things he believed about himself and what he thought his sacrifices would achieve have come to nothing. To admit at the end of a largely well-intentioned life that what he set out to do has completely failed would be unbearable for him.

Interestingly, the president kept slipping down in his chair. His legs and arms were all over the place. You wanted to get up and go over to him, put your hands under his armpits and sit him up straight. His body language seemed to reflect his lack of grounding and integration. The emotional foundation to support all the work he had done on his intellect was not there.

What is your vision for Africa? I asked him.

What would I want Africa to be? Completely free, first of all. We are not free – far from it. Africa is dependent on donors. The majority of our countries are funded in the main by donors. Their budgets are sustained by the same countries that yesterday were their colonial masters. So we are not yet really free in the true sense of the word. We have got to translate our political freedom into economic freedom. And as long as we remain producers of primary products with no capacity to industrialise, so shall we remain subservient ... We appeal all the time to Europe to assist us, and assist us in developing ourselves so that we can become equal economically with them. And Europe is talking down to us. The first subjects they raise are not subjects that have to do with economic assistance. Good governance, human rights, the rule of law – that's what they put first. Let us discuss this first (they say). But the people want economic cooperation and all they want to talk about are human rights and so on.

What do they get out of this unequal relationship?

'They derive inequality and subservience in a perpetual way.'

Are you saying they deliberately perpetuate it?

'Oh yes, yes, of course it's deliberate.' He went on at length about how European governments give aid only to enable Africa to continue producing the primary products required by their own factories. 'The British buy our tea ... blend it and call it English tea,' he laughed. 'They don't even acknowledge its origin – never. Earl Grey – who was he? And Lipton – who was he? Where can you grow tea in Wales or Scotland? You can't even grow it in their greenhouses, can you? So there it is. We in Africa have no capital, you see. That is (the situation) we in Zimbabwe would want to get out of. Fortunately for us, we've had some industry started here, and fortunately we have raw materials that we can use – minerals and from agriculture – and get capital for ourselves to improve our industries.'

Here, Mugabe was defying the universal laws of economics. No country is forced to sell its tea in Europe or anywhere else. His main grievance seemed to be the fact that the British didn't acknowledge the source of the tea. He was intent on rubbishing existing trade practices when he did not have a viable alternative. His alternative, seizing the land that once produced the tea, was not about building but about destroying.

Is there a sense that you have of being prepared to sacrifice the welfare of Zimbabwe in order to prove your points?

Yes, we have already sacrificed our welfare and we have singled out a Zimbabwe which is going in a completely different direction from other countries. That's because of the empowerment of our people. We have refused economic colonialism or imperialism in the sense that we don't want our economic sectors dominated by foreigners ... You can't preach it to others unless you are doing it. We must demonstrate that we can do it in Zimbabwe and get our economy to transform. At the moment, we get no development aid at all.

But your economy shows it, I pointed out.

Mugabe sat up straight, his eyes flashing. 'Our economy shows it but it's far better, a hundred times better, than the average African economy. Outside South Africa, what country is (as good as) Zimbabwe?'

Is that true – even now?

'Even now,' he stated. 'What is lacking now are goods on the shelves. That's all. But the infrastructure is there. We have our mines, you see. We have our enterprises.'

Incredibly, Mugabe was saying dismissively that all Zimbabwe lacked was goods for sale. Everything was fine except that they didn't have food on the shelves. He was revealing that he was utterly out of touch with reality. Later, when I told Father Mukonori that Mugabe was deluded about the economy, he explained it as the fault of the officials who were not telling the president the truth. A more accurate explanation is that Mugabe's people are too scared to confront him or tell him the truth. Like the fable about the emperor's clothes, there are things that are not allowed to be said because someone is holding a delusional position. Mugabe could never say, 'Okay, our ideals are not achievable so we will establish – not in repudiation but in a creative way – something more modest that will be neither Britain nor America but will work well enough for us.' For that reason, he could never move on.

There are a lot of people who would disagree with you, sir.

'Why?' His eyes were on fire, glinting menacingly, so I retreated, mumbling about the economy possibly improving some time in the distant future. He seized the upper hand. 'Why disagree when they are not in the know?' he demanded. 'They don't know what we are doing. And they don't know what we are pumping into the system, you see.'

Mugabe's manner did not allow for any contradictory ideas. Whenever I was on tricky territory, I backed off in the interests of keeping the interview going. Had I stood my ground, there might have been an entirely different outcome. He silenced me whenever I drew attention to uncomfortable realities. He could not admit that he was in trouble and had made a complete mess of Zimbabwe. So he idealised the mess as if he really believed it was going to be wonderful two years hence.

Have you changed over the past 30 years?

'Yes, physically I have. I've grown old and bald. But the ideas and principles remain. I haven't changed at all.'

Do you worry about repercussions in the international justice system in respect of Gukurahundi (the campaign of beatings, arson and mass murder deliberately targeted at the civilian population and conducted by Mugabe's personal militia)?

Mugabe waved his hands dismissively and sighed in exasperation.

It's just political. It's just politics that people try to gain out of it. Gukurahundi – as it happened – what was it? You had a party with a guerrilla force that wanted to reverse democracy in this country. And action was taken. And, yes, there might have been excesses, on both sides. True, it's not the fact that there was Gukurahundi which is wrong. It's the fact that there have been excesses that have caused some people to suffer. But we'd have to start with the excesses of Ian Smith – and the colonialists, the British, who were still in charge – because lots of people disappeared; lots of people died.

But Gukurahundi happened during your time, I told him. Would you like to place on the record your regret about it?

No, there is no regret about the fact that we had to defend the country. But the excess, where it happened, yes. Any death that should not have occurred is a cause for regret, and wherever people have suffered. But the figures don't make sense because they don't represent the truth.

When I told him the estimates of deaths during Gukurahundi ranged between 8 000 and 30 000, he replied icily, 'Who are those people; who are they? We want to know.'

I had been expecting Mugabe to object to the question on Gukurahundi but it was my scepticism that bothered him. The question itself did not disconcert him because he simply justified his actions. He clearly feels Gukurahundi was legitimate on the grounds that he was aggrieved. He was settling a problem with a terrorist group, though he regretted the excesses. He sat on the fence, condoning the terrible violence without actually saying as much. Like the husband who beats his wife mercilessly and then says he did it because she provoked him, Mugabe takes no responsibility for his loss of control or what Gukurahundi says about him.

Do you have any regrets, sir?

'Of what?'

Anything.

'It would depend on what you have in mind.'

Politically?

No, no regrets. You go into a fight. It's a fight against colonialism. You make sacrifices. And naturally, when people die you regret the deaths of the people. And that's why we have created Heroes Acre in order to remember those whose deaths should not have occurred. Yes, we are sorry that there are those who have died, but other regrets, I don't know. We might have regrets where we've had a policy that we've had to revise. Or failures in our programmes because some people have not implemented them faithfully and honestly. Yes, you regret those failures. Failures in government are regretted, especially when they are because of corruption or inefficiency, incompetence or neglect. Sure, we regret.

How would you like to be remembered?

Just as the son of a peasant family who, alongside others, felt he had a responsibility to fight for his country. And did so to the best of his ability. And was grateful for the honour given him to lead a country and be remembered as one who was most grateful for the honour that the people gave him in leading them to victory over British imperialism. Yes, for that I want to be remembered.

He is more likely to be remembered as a leader who was out of touch with reality. The simple, traditional home he grew up in, where a grandfather would fail to take a dying child to hospital for fear of what the doctors might do, was inadequate for a bright child craving stimulation. So the bored boy in deprived circumstances created his own internal realm, as such children are prone to do. It was a parallel world where he could imagine that there was no injustice, where the prince rescued the princess, and little boys weren't left with nothing to eat. In his fantasy world of books and ideas, idealised goodness was valued above all else and he did not have to grapple with the daunting realities of everyday life.

He learned to distort reality; making it what he wanted it to be. He thought everybody would hold hands and achieve heaven on earth. But when someone wrote a letter saying they didn't want to do that, reality impinged: it was not going to be the way it was meant to be in the books. He was shocked and disillusioned.

He had thought his ideals would be achieved through suffering; that his sacrifices would be rewarded. His people would be free and laughing, their bellies full as they waved flags in the streets of Harare. But he had not taken into account the inescapable fact that freedom is an internal as well as an external matter; that people are sometimes limited by internalised experiences that can trap and hold as surely as a cell. The doors of the external prison might have swung open, but the internal cell remained locked and barred. He dedicated his life to his country without knowing what it was he could and couldn't achieve.

Limitations were never recognised by the freedom fighter who thought he could achieve everything – and still does. To be an ordinary person, he would have had to face not being the saviour he wishes he were. If he could have accepted his ordinariness, he might have adjusted his sights and had a more humble though realistic vision. But he was perhaps too deeply ashamed of his incapacities – despite a rare moment of candour when he admitted them to Lord Soames – and needed to see himself as invincible.

As an ordinary man, he could have listened rather than believed he had all the answers; made mistakes and learned from them, forgiven shortcomings in others and been forgiven; made friends and been a friend; asked for help – all the things that mere mortals do. But he believed he was special, different, born for greatness.

In the end, Robert Mugabe is a disillusioned man surviving on omnipotence and distortion as he approaches the end of his life. He will be remembered by most as a tyrant; by some as a sad figure who suffered and sacrificed. His ruined country, Zimbabwe, is truly the tragedy because it need not have suffered its devastating fate.

Selected bibliography

Astrow, A. *Zimbabwe: A Revolution That Lost Its Way*. London: Zed Press, 1983.

Auret, D. *Reaching for Justice: The Catholic Commission for Justice and Peace, 1972-1992*. Gweru: Mambo Press, 1992.

Bhebe, N and Ranger, T (eds). *Society in Zimbabwe's Liberation War*. London: Currey, 1995.

Blair, D. *Degrees in Violence: Robert Mugabe and the Struggle for Power in Zimbabwe*. London and New York: Continuum, 2002.

Bond, P and Masimba M. *Zimbabwe's Plunge: Exhausted Nationalism, Neoliberalism and the Search for Social Justice*. Pietermaritzburg: University of Natal Press, 2002.

Catholic Commission for Justice and Peace, Legal Resources Foundation. *Breaking the Silence, Building True Peace: A Report on the Disturbances in Matabeleland and the Midlands, 1980 to 1988*. Harare: CCJP/LRF, 1997.

Chan, S. *Robert Mugabe: A Life of Power and Violence*. Ann Arbor: University of Michigan Press, 2003.

Charlton, M. *The Last Colony in Africa: Diplomacy and the Independence of Rhodesia*. Oxford: Blackwell, 1990.

Flower, K. *Serving Secretly: An Intelligence Chief on Record, Rhodesia into Zimbabwe, 1964-1981*. London: Murray, 1987.

Godwin, P and Hancock, I. *Rhodesians Never Die: The Impact of War and Political Change on White Rhodesia, c.1970-1980*. London: Oxford University Press, 1993.

Herbst, J. *State Politics in Zimbabwe*. Berkeley: University of California Press, 1990.

Linden, I. *The Catholic Church and the Struggle for Zimbabwe*. London: Longman, 1980.

Makumbe, J and Campagnon, D. *Behind the Smokescreen: The Politics of Zimbabwe's 1995 General Elections*. Harare: University of Zimbabwe, 2000.

Mandaza, I and Sachikonye, L (eds). *The One-Party State and Democracy: The Zimbabwe Debate*. Harare: Sapes Trust, 1991.

Martin, D and Johnson, P. *The Struggle for Zimbabwe*. London: Faber, 1981.

McLaughlin, J. *On the Frontline: Catholic Missions in Zimbabwe's Liberation War*. Harare: Baobab Books, 1996.

Meredith, M. *Robert Mugabe: Power, Plunder and Tyranny in Zimbabwe*. Johannesburg: Jonathan Ball Publishers, 2002.

Moyo, J. *Voting for Democracy: A Study of Electoral Politics in Zimbabwe*. Harare: University of Zimbabwe, 1992.

Mutasa, D. *Black Behind Bars: Rhodesia, 1959-1974*. Harare: Longman, 1983.

Nkomo, J. *The Story of My Life*. London: Methuen, 1984.

Nyagumbo, M. *With the People*. Salisbury: Graham Publishing, 1980.

Shamuyarira, N. *Crisis in Rhodesia*. London: Deutsch, 1965.

Sithole, M. *Zimbabwe: Struggles Within the Struggle, 1957-1980*. Harare: Rujeko, 1999.

Smith, D and Simpson, C. *Mugabe*. London: Sphere, 1981.

Smith, I. *The Great Betrayal*. London: Blake, 1997.

Tekere, E. *A Lifetime of Struggle*. Harare: Sapes Books, 2007.

Vambe, L. *From Rhodesia to Zimbabwe*. London: Heinemann, 1976.

Index